MY MOTHER'S FRIEND

SALLY JAMESON BOND

My Mother's Friend by Sally Jameson Bond

Published by Sally Jameson Bond
www.sallyjamesonbond.com

Cover design by miblart.com

Paperback ISBN: 979-8-88759-046-2
eBook ISBN: 979-8-88759-047-9

A portion of the proceeds from the sale of this book will benefit the National D-Day Memorial in Bedford, Virginia and the Camp Algona POW Museum in Algona, Iowa.

For my mom, Phee Johnson
(1925-2007)

LIST OF CHARACTERS

Berlin, Germany (1991)

Chicago Post-Dispatch (*CPD*) Staff

- Mollie MacAlister, Arts and Entertainment Editor, Phee Swensson's daughter

- Burt Baumgartner, the *CPD*'s Berlin Bureau Chief

- Jason Webb, the *CPD*'s Berlin Bureau photographer

Maestro Horst Ebinger (age 67), chief conductor of the Berlin Symphony Orchestra

- Adrian Stugart, Maestro Ebinger's assistant

- Inge Ebinger, Maestro Ebinger's wife

Algona, Iowa (1944-1945)

- The Swensson Family

  - Phyllis "Phee" Swensson (age 17-18)

  - Frank Swensson, Phee's father, pastor of St. Peter's Lutheran Church

- James "Jamie" Swensson, Phee's older brother, member of The United States Army Band

- Gustav "Gus" Swensson, (age 10-11), Phee's younger brother

- Tristan "Tris" Swensson (age 10-11), Phee's younger brother

- Mollie "Sweet Pea" Swensson (age 8-9), Phee's sister

- Mary Swensson, Phee's mother (deceased)

- "Daisy", Phee's diary

- Phee's Extended Family and Friends

  - Elmer "Bee" Nelson, Phee's grandfather

  - Nancy "Nannie" Nelson, Phee's grandmother

  - Christa Rasmussen, Phee's best friend

    - Jack Rasmussen, Christa's father

    - Peggy Rasmussen, Christa's mother

    - Adam Vanderwilt, Christa's boyfriend

    - Hilda Vanderwilt, Adam's mother

  - Edith "Mrs. Z" Zetterholm, Phee's piano teacher

    - Harold "Doc Z" Zetterholm, Edith's husband, the Swenssons' family doctor

- Town Folk (Algona and Spirit Lake)

- Dorothy Cooper, the Swenssons' next-door neighbor

  - Charlotte Cooper, Dorothy's daughter, Mollie's best friend

- Dr. Herbert Winfield, Winfield Drug Store pharmacist

  - Johnny Winfield, Herbert's son

- Helen Engstrom, Frank's friend

  - Claire Engstrom, Helen's daughter

- Mrs. Goodwin, Algona High School choral teacher

- Camp Algona Military and Civilian Personnel

  - Lieutenant Colonel David McNabb, Commander

  - Captain Edward "Ed" Mattson, U.S. Army Chaplain, Frank's friend

    - Corporal Roy Phillips, Chaplain Mattson's assistant

    - Julie O'Reilly, Chaplain Mattson's secretary

  - Sergeant Ben Jackson, in charge of the camp theater building

  - Corporal Bickford, a guard

  - Private J. Mattingly, a Military Police (MP) guard

- Camp Algona Prisoner of War Personnel

  - Major Heinrich Schmidt, Lutheran Chaplain

  - Sergeant Horst Ebinger (age 20-21)

Contents

1

SUNDAY 19 MAY 1991

EN ROUTE TO BERLIN, GERMANY

As ALITALIA FLIGHT 406 prepared to depart Rome's Fiumicino International Airport, Mollie MacAlister, sitting just behind the wing in seat 17A, knew—just knew—she was going to puke.

Oh, Mollie, why did you drink all that Prosecco at the party last night? she moaned to herself. After taking a few deep breaths—it helped a little—she pulled open the seat pocket in front of her. *Oh, good—the barf bag's there.*

The captain made the obligatory announcement, first in Italian, then in English, and the cabin crew prepared for takeoff. In less than ninety seconds, the Boeing 737 began its two-hour flight to Berlin-Tegel. After popping a stick of Juicy Fruit in her mouth, Mollie closed her eyes and whispered a brief prayer as the plane's wheels lifted off the runway. "Dear God, make it a safe one, thanks a bunch. Amen."

While the plane climbed to its cruising altitude, Mollie decided she needed a distraction from her hangover, so she reached for the tattered in-flight magazine just behind the barf bag. *Of course—somebody's already done the crossword.*

As soon as the captain turned off the seat belt sign, Mollie retrieved her briefcase from the overhead bin, intending to go over her notes from her London and Paris meetings. But then she decided that could wait. With the briefcase open on the tray table, she pushed aside a few reporter's notebooks and cassette tapes and pulled out a large envelope holding several mementoes from her mother's young life. *I've got everything with me, Mom—everything I'll need this week.* Last November, when Mollie spent Thanksgiving at her dad's home in Denver, he asked her to remove her mother's belongings from their bedroom. Reluctantly, she agreed, and soon found all these items in a cardboard box buried in a drawer beneath a couple of colorful scarves and a dozen pairs of old pantyhose.

Mollie wanted to look at the contents of the envelope one more time before she landed in Berlin—the telegram, letters, photos, music, a *Time* magazine article, an odd-looking necklace, and a teenager's diaries. First, she pulled out the black and white glossy photos. It was obvious they'd been handled often over the decades. When she turned them over, she saw her mom's handwriting, familiar yet not familiar, identifying the people and places captured in each photo and the dates they were taken. *I wonder if all these people are still living.* Mollie knew some of them were, probably several. Tomorrow night, she'd meet one of them for the first time. It was the sole reason she was flying to Berlin today.

Superbly handsome Marco the flight attendant stopped at row 17 with the beverage cart just as the airplane, now somewhere over the Italian Alps, began bouncing like a baby on its grandfather's knee. *I sure could use a ginger ale!* The seat belt sign came back on just as Marco handed Mollie a full can of moderately cold Schweppes. As he quickly pushed the cart back to the galley, she took a couple of sips, then returned to her deep breathing exercises while trying her best to focus on the other items in the envelope. She'd already read the diaries twice cover to cover, so she left those alone and reached for the necklace. While holding it in her hand, she gently rubbed the small silver object with her thumb, then turned it over and smiled when she saw I L D carved on the back. One day this week Mollie would wear this necklace, and when the Maestro saw it, he would surely remember.

The plane continued to shake and bounce erratically, and before long, Mollie's willpower gave up the ghost. As discreetly as possible, she reached for the small paper bag, spit out her gum, turned to her left—*oh, aren't the mountains lovely . . . they look like the Rockies back home*—and puked.

2

MONDAY 20 MAY 1991 - PART 1

MOLLIE'S MEETING WITH BURT Baumgartner, the *Chicago Post-Dispatch*'s Berlin Bureau Chief, was at ten thirty this morning. She slept in till eight, took a quick shower, donned her almost-but-not-quite-ripe black pants suit and semi-wrinkled white oxford shirt, and found her way to the hotel's sunny breakfast room. When she traveled, Mollie usually ate a big breakfast so she could forego the noon meal. But she was having lunch with Burt today, so she skipped seconds on everything but coffee.

Mollie had been the Arts and Entertainment Editor at the *Chicago Post-Dispatch*—the *CPD*—for almost ten years, but this was her first face-to-face meeting with Burt. From their earlier phone conversations, she had him pegged for a short, rotund, somewhat greasy, late-forties/early-fifties kinda guy with a great sense of humor. She knew his second wife, a native Berliner, was the manager of a brewery pub not far from Burt's office.

"Well, if it isn't Mollie MacAlister in the flesh," Burt said as he got up from his cluttered desk to shake her hand. He appeared to be in his early fifties, but he wasn't short, he wasn't greasy, and he wasn't particularly rotund.

"Hi, Burt," she said with a smile, "it's so good to finally meet you."

"You, too, kid. Are you all settled in at the Zürich?"

"I am." She set her briefcase on the floor between the two chairs facing Burt's desk. "It's very nice, great location."

"Wunnerful, wunnerful. Please, have a seat. Do you want some coffee?"

"Better not. I've already had three cups this morning."

Burt returned to his chair. "So, are you all squared away for the concert and interviews?"

"I think so. I'll pick up my ticket just before the concert tonight. I've arranged to meet Maestro Ebinger in the Green Room afterwards."

"What time is your interview tomorrow?"

"Ten o'clock, at his studio. We'll meet after lunch, too."

"Do you want Jason to show up first thing tomorrow? I've got him scheduled for a shoot at the zoo at one o'clock."

"Gosh, I'm not sure. Maybe I should check with Herr Ebinger to see what he prefers. It might be better to do it Wednesday or even Thursday."

"You can let me know tomorrow."

"Better write myself a note," she said as she reached into her briefcase for a pen and a reporter's notebook. "I might get so involved in the interview I'll forget about pictures."

For the next hour, the two colleagues chatted about the arts scene in Berlin. Mollie also let Burt in on some of her ideas for her feature length article about Maestro Ebinger, chief conductor of the Berlin Symphony Orchestra. She expected it to be published later this year in the *CPD Sunday Magazine* section.

As she expected, Burt invited Mollie to his wife Karin's pub for lunch. It was a few doors up the street, and they arrived just before the lunch crowd. Waiting for them near the entrance, Karin led Mollie and Burt to a table at the back of a long, narrow room, and she made sure they weren't neglected. It was a bit noisy, but they managed to continue their conversation over *Würstchen* and sauerkraut. After taking two aspirin earlier to mitigate her lingering hangover headache, Mollie was ready for a good German beer. One glass was enough, though.

Just before one o'clock, Burt looked at his watch and pushed back his chair. "I've got a meeting in a few minutes," he said. "Better get back."

"I should be going, too," she said. "I'm hoping to see the Checkpoint Charlie Museum this afternoon."

"Good choice. If I had to recommend one museum for a first timer, that would be it."

"I'll take the U-Bahn back. Which way to the nearest station?"

"It's just up the street. I'll walk with you."

"Better not. It's in the other direction and you need to get back."

"Alright, if you're sure."

"I'm sure. Thanks for lunch, Burt. Everything was delicious."

"Glad you enjoyed it. Karin will be pleased."

They stopped to say auf Wiedersehen to Karin on their way out. Burt held the door for Mollie, then wished her luck on her interviews with the Maestro. "If you need me, call any time, for any reason, even after hours," Burt offered. "I have a feeling this is going to be one heck of a story."

"Thanks, Burt. I hope you're right."

"Oh, and don't forget to let me know about Jason," he said as he backed away. "I'm pretty sure any time Wednesday should work."

"I'll let you know tomorrow."

Mollie strolled to the U-Bahn station and was soon back at the hotel. She dropped off her briefcase, stopped at the concierge desk to ask for a city map, and walked to the Checkpoint Charlie Museum which was about fifteen minutes south of the hotel. Mollie spent a good two hours there, getting a better grasp of what Maestro Ebinger's life might have been like, living and working behind the Berlin Wall—die Mauer—for almost twenty-eight years. Wandering through the exhibits, she kept her reporter's notebook handy, adding more questions to her already substantial list. She hoped there would be time for all of them this week.

Mollie took a different route back to the hotel and was glad she did because she encountered a thirty-foot section of die Mauer that had not yet been demolished. As with most of the Wall's western-facing facades, it was almost completely covered with colorful graffiti. Some of it had been chipped away by enthusiastic souvenir hunters. In fact, two young men with chipping hammers were working nearby, tossing their blue and red and white and green and yellow and orange pieces of history into a small paper sack. One of the men turned to Mollie, smiled, and offered her a small green piece.

"*Dankeschön*," she said before dropping it in her shoulder bag.

On the way to the hotel, Mollie stopped at a supermarket to pick up some bread and cheese and a chocolate bar. Back in her room, she suddenly felt a little anxious about her upcoming interview sessions with Maestro Ebinger. She'd composed her initial list of questions for him a year ago, before he traveled to Chicago to guest conduct the Chicago Symphony's final concert series of the season. Mollie was scheduled to interview Herr Ebinger after his final performance, but a family emergency required him to return to Germany the day they were to meet.

So now, here she was, with a head full of knowledge about the man she'd meet later tonight in the Schauspielhaus Green Room, knowledge she didn't have a year ago. Thanks to her mother's diaries and the other items she'd found in that box last November, she already knew much about the remarkable man who was once a prisoner of war at Camp Algona in Algona, Iowa, her mother's hometown.

Tonight, Mollie would shake the hand of the man her mother loved so many years ago, and maybe tomorrow morning, she'd begin to understand why.

3

MONDAY 20 MAY 1991 – PART 2

BERLIN'S SCHAUSPIELHAUS WAS DESIGNED as a theater hall in the early 1800s by the famous Prussian architect Karl Friedrich Schinkel. Heavily bombed near the end of World War II, it lay in ruins until efforts by the East Berlin government to rebuild it could finally begin in the 1970s. Under the direction of Maestro Horst Ebinger, the hall's grand re-opening gala concert by the Berlin Symphony Orchestra took place on October 1, 1984. Mollie knew the acoustics in the main concert hall were among the best in the world. With that in mind, she expected to enjoy every moment of tonight's performance.

After collecting her complimentary ticket at the box office, Mollie climbed the wide marble staircase to the mezzanine level. The space was crowded, and Mollie thought she might be a little underdressed in her simple black cocktail dress. She wore her longish auburn hair up tonight so the black and gold earrings that matched her necklace were on full display.

"*Meine Damen und Herren, bitte gehen Sie zu Ihren Plätzen.* Ladies and gentlemen, please proceed to your seats." When the pleasant chimes sounded, Mollie returned to the orchestra level and followed signs to the door nearest her reserved seat on the left side, about halfway back from the stage. The hall was beautiful, with brilliant chandeliers hanging from the high ceiling and white busts of famous composers and musicians placed between the entrances on both sides of the hall. Mollie sat under Mozart's gaze. On the stage behind the orchestra were risers for the large chorus that would perform on the second half of the program, and high above the stage was the massive pipe organ. Tonight's concert was all Brahms. From her mother's diaries, Mollie already knew Johannes Brahms was Maestro Ebinger's favorite composer, at least that was true in 1945.

The concertmaster walked out from stage right and acknowledged the polite applause from the standing room only house. While he tuned the orchestra, Mollie reached in her purse for her reporter's notebook and scribbled a few quick notes describing the scene around her. Suddenly, a vigorous applause commenced, and she realized she'd missed the Maestro's entrance. At center stage, he bowed quickly, ascended the podium, and immediately began the opening piece, the *Academic Festival Overture*. Mollie listened but was not focused on the music as intensely as most of the people sitting in the hall. She watched this man with an entirely different perspective than she did last June at Orchestra Hall in Chicago, when she and her mom sat eight rows back in the center of the orchestra level. It was clear Maestro Ebinger garnered much respect and admiration from his musicians. She knew he was an outstanding leader, but since last November, she'd also known he was a man who was worthy of her mother's love forty-six years ago.

Brahms's *Piano Concerto No. 1 in D Minor,* Op. 15, with Herr Ebinger performing as soloist, was conducted by the BSO's associate conductor, Adrian Stugart. The three-movement work lasted more than forty-five minutes. While Mollie was entranced with the emotional performance, she couldn't help but envision her teenaged mother sitting next to this man, performing Dvořák at the concert at Algona High School or Brahms at Camp Algona a few months later. And then there were all the times they rehearsed and played together, just for fun. Mollie had known these details for a while now, but she still found it all quite extraordinary.

After intermission, Mollie returned to her seat just as the concertmaster walked out and tuned the orchestra for *A German Requiem,* Op. 45. The chorus members were already in place behind the orchestra, the men in tails, the women in long black skirts and white blouses. Mollie took a quick count. There were over one hundred singers on stage. Several of the men in both the chorus and the orchestra looked old enough to be World War II veterans, and she wondered if any of them had been prisoners of war in America, too.

As Mollie jotted down her final thoughts at the *Requiem*'s peaceful ending, the audience responded with an enthusiastic standing ovation, encouraging Maestro Ebinger to return to the stage four times. He motioned for the orchestra members to stand each time and acknowledged the chorus and soloists as well. His smile was wide and genuine. Herr Ebinger loved his audience and they him, no doubt about it.

To give the Maestro plenty of time to get to the Green Room, Mollie waited until the hall was almost empty before she stood to leave. She waved to Herr Mozart on her way out, then grabbed the attention of a nearby usher. "*Sprechen Sie Englisch?*" she remembered to ask.

"Yes, can I help you?" the young man replied.

"I've made arrangements to meet Maestro Ebinger in the Green Room. Can you help me find it?"

"Certainly. This way, *bitte.*"

The Green Room was near the end of a long hallway behind the stage. The usher pointed to the door. "Here you are, ma'am. Have a pleasant evening."

"*Danke,*" she replied.

There were at least a dozen well-dressed people inside, most holding glasses of sparkling wine. As she stood in the doorway, she saw the Maestro standing near an elaborately framed painting of the Schauspielhaus, engaged in a lively phone conversation. He soon turned to face Mollie and smiled, finished his conversation, and walked quickly across the room.

"You must be Ms. MacAlister!" he said, extending his hand. "Welcome! So, you have traveled to Berlin at last. Please, enjoy a glass of Champagne with us."

Oh my, he's even more handsome up close! Mollie shook the Maestro's hand with a confidence that belied her rapid pulse and general nervousness. "Yes, I'm finally here," she said, reaching for a glass on the nearby table. "Thank you so much for inviting me. The concert was quite wonderful."

"*Ja*, I believe it was a hit, as the young people like to say." His brilliant blue eyes gleamed as he smiled. "I am relieved our season's final concert was a success." Then, as he moved back into the room, he said, "Please have a seat so we can talk. I have arranged to meet with some friends for a late dinner, but I would like to spend time with you now. Can you stay?"

"It's awfully nice of you to ask," she answered, "but don't let me keep you from your plans. We'll have plenty of time this week."

"Of course. We will meet tomorrow at my studio at—is it—ten o'clock?"

"That's right, at ten."

"I will meet you on the plaza. The entrance is a secret. Only a few can know about it."

"Goodness! I didn't realize I was so special."

"I can know already that you are," he said with an almost imperceptible wink. "And here is my assistant, Adrian Stugart. We have worked together for almost . . . twelve years."

"*Ja*, twelve years in August," Herr Stugart said as he shook Mollie's hand. "Ms. MacAlister, I assume?"

"That's right," she said. "It's nice to meet you."

"We hope your time in Berlin is productive," Herr Stugart said. "You have chosen a good time to come."

"Yes, I have," she agreed.

Herr Ebinger asked about her flights, her hotel, all the typical small talk you'd expect at their first meeting. Mollie couldn't help but stare at the handsome older gentleman. She was just beginning to understand her mother's attraction to him.

At an opportune lull in the conversation, Mollie stood. "I should go. I've had a pretty big day. Thank you again for the ticket."

Maestro Ebinger stood and extended his hand. "So, we will meet again tomorrow. Get some rest. Auf Wiedersehen!"

"Auf Wiedersehen!" Mollie replied. She left her empty glass on the table, then followed the corridor back the way she hoped she came.

She was not at all good with directions, which often frustrated her ex-husband, Ewan. After a couple of wrong turns, she found the almost empty lobby, and as she left the building, she stopped to admire the Schiller Monument near the bottom of the steps. She might need to know something about that Schiller guy for her article, so she'd check that out later.

Mollie walked quickly through the partying crowds back to the hotel. When she got to her room, she found the other half of the chocolate bar she'd bought this afternoon and broke off a small piece. Grabbing the remote, she turned on the television and learned that Michael Jordan, from her beloved Chicago Bulls, was just named the NBA's MVP. It was a perfect ending to a marvelous day.

As Mollie climbed into the comfortable king-size bed, she brought along one of her mom's diaries. She turned to the August 25, 1944 entry and, for the third time, read about Phee Swensson's seventeenth birthday. It was a Friday.

4

FRIDAY 25 AUG. 1944 - PART 1

ALGONA, IOWA

"Dad, hold still!"

Frank grumbled incomprehensibly while he shifted his weight in the chair.

"Sit up straight. I'm almost done."

There was more grumbling, and this time he added an exaggerated sigh.

"Just a few more seconds."

"I think you're done," he said. "Let me see. Did you leave anything up there?"

"You'll see in a minute."

Phee Swensson and her dad were in the parsonage kitchen on this sunny August morning. A white sheet was draped around his shoulders while his daughter cut his hair and trimmed his beard. Frank had finally agreed, as a gift to Phee on her seventeenth birthday, to let her do it. It was his first haircut since his wife Mary died back in December of '42. Mary had always cut Frank's hair, and he had almost always complained. But she managed to convince him that a pastor's appearance was very important. After she became too ill to do it, he wouldn't let anyone touch his head. His thick wavy silver-gray hair grew long, and he looked more like one of the apostles than the pastor of St. Peter's Lutheran Church. Frank's congregation tolerated his shagginess because they understood it was one of the ways Frank dealt with his grief. Most had faith he'd eventually relent and would show up one Sunday morning, freshly shorn.

"That should do it," Phee said as she laid the shears and the comb on the table. "Why don't you have a look. I'll run up and get the hand mirror so you can see the back."

While she was away, Frank walked to the pantry where a mirror was fastened to the inside of the left-hand door. At first glance, he was shocked to see a man who looked like someone he used to know. "Yeh, I guess I needed this," he whispered, almost convinced.

When Phee returned, Frank took the mirror, turned around to view the back, then tousled his hair with his hand.

"Dad! Stop it! Let it be." She grabbed the comb from the table and fixed the tousling.

Frank smiled at his daughter. "Thanks babe, ya done good." Removing the sheet from his shoulders, she gave it a couple of shakes. He stretched his long arms towards the ceiling, then gave Phee a hug. "Happy birthday, Phyllis Anne."

"Thanks, Dad. You look very handsome. I think Mom would be pleased, don't you?"

Frank returned to the pantry mirror, stroked his beard, then nodded. "I'll ask her later when we have our nightly chat."

Phee gathered up all the hair-cutting materials and headed back to the stairs. "I'll get that swept up in a minute," she called over her shoulder.

"Don't bother," he said, reaching for the broom next to the ice box. "I'd like to give all this hair a proper burial."

While she picked up after her dad and three younger siblings in the bathroom, Phee thought yet again about how much her mom did for all of them. Not just cleaning up the bathroom, but millions of things, like cooking and laundry and shopping for groceries, nursing them when they were sick, and making their Halloween costumes. After her mom died, Phee at times took on a bit too much. "How did Mom do it?" she often wondered.

But today was Phee's birthday, and after getting lunch on the table, the rest of the day and evening was for her. She'd open her gifts later this afternoon, and tonight her best friend, Christa Rasmussen, would treat her to supper at Carter's Café. They'd also take in a movie and more than likely visit Polly's Ice Cream Shoppe before calling it a night.

After lunch with her dad, ten-year-old twin brothers Gus and Tris, and Mollie, her precocious eight-year-old sister, Phee spent more than an hour practicing piano in the living room. Her weekly lessons with St. Pete's organist, Mrs. Zetterholm, were on Monday afternoons, and she promised Mrs. Z she'd have the second movement of the Beethoven sonata memorized by her next lesson. Phee had studied with Edith Zetterholm since the Swenssons moved to Algona ten years ago. For the past year or so, she'd been trying her hand at composing, intending to perform three of her own songs on her senior recital at St. Pete's in November. Music was her life, at least it was when she wasn't busy doing everything else.

Just after four thirty, Mollie bounded in the front door carrying a sack of tomatoes from Mrs. Cooper's garden. The Coopers lived next door, and Charlotte Cooper was Mollie's best friend. Charlotte's dad was a pilot in the Army Air Corps and had been overseas for almost a year. Her mom, Dorothy, brought in extra money working as a seamstress. Her most prized creation was Mayor Kimball's daughter's wedding dress from last summer. People still talked about it—the women did at any rate.

"Whatcha got there?" Phee asked when Mollie got to the kitchen.

"Tomatoes from Mrs. Cooper. She said there's more if we need 'em."

Phee peeked in the sack. "I think these will do us just fine."

"When are ya gonna open your presents?"

"Soon as Dad gets home. Shouldn't be long."

"I haven't wrapped mine yet. Don't come in the living room. I'll do it in there."

Phee smiled as she reached for the leftover tuna casserole in the ice box, happy she didn't have to cook supper for her family on her birthday. Thankfully, after her mom died, the church ladies stepped in and volunteered to bring food to the parsonage once a week during the school year. It was usually soup or a casserole and a vegetable dish, sometimes a Jell-O salad, and, when there was enough sugar on hand, a homemade dessert. When the ladies first suggested this weekly visit, Frank hesitated to accept their kind offer. But he soon realized Phee needed help, and so, he gratefully relented.

"Is that tuna casserole?" Frank asked as he walked in the back door after spending the afternoon in his office.

"Just putting it in the oven," Phee said. "Mollie brought Cooper tomatoes home, so you'll have those too."

"Great! Are you ready to open presents?"

"It's up to you guys, but Christa will be here at six. I'll need time to get ready."

"That's right, you're going out tonight."

"Supper and a movie. Better call the boys down. Mollie's wrapping in the living room."

Frank walked to the bottom of the stairs and yelled up. "Boys, time for presents! C'mon down to the dining room." He stopped at the hall closet, reached behind all those winter coats, and brought out a beautifully wrapped box. The boys scurried down the stairs with their gifts and they all joined Phee at the dining room table.

"Open mine first!" Mollie pleaded.

"If you insist," Phee said, reaching for the crudely but lovingly wrapped package that felt very much like a book. She held it up to her ear and shook it gently. "Nothin' loose in here."

"That's 'cause books don't shake," Tris said.

"Tris!" Mollie cried. "Don't say that!"

"Tristan James, shame on you," Frank admonished. "How would you feel if someone gave away your gift?"

"Nobody will 'cause nobody knows but me," he said, crossing his arms over his chest.

"Never mind," Phee said. "You know I'll love everything." She unwrapped the package and found *A Tree Grows in Brooklyn* by Betty Smith.

"How did you know I wanted this?" she asked.

"Because you keep checking it out at the library," Mollie replied. "Dad helped me buy it at Carlyn's."

"Well, I love it. Thank you, Sweet Pea."

"Who's next?" Frank asked.

"Me," Gus said, pushing his package across the table. "Hope you like it."

Phee shook this one too, and this time there *was* noise. "Aha! I hear something in there." Gus beamed as she unwrapped his gift. "A pencil box! It is a pencil box, isn't it?"

"Open it and see," he said.

She did. It was. "Gosh! There must be a dozen pencils in here!"

"If twelve makes a dozen, then you're right," he said.

"I can sure use these, and I love the box. Thanks, Gus!"

"Mine's next," Tris insisted. "You won't guess in a gazillion years."

"Hmmm," Phee mused. "Feels like a magazine."

"Nope. Prepare to be amazed."

She gently unwrapped the package and found a book of English folk songs for piano and voice that had once belonged to her mom. She was overwhelmed with emotion as she held it against her heart, desperately wanting to feel her mom's presence.

"Look up there on the corner," Tris said, pointing. "It was Mom's when she was Mary Nelson."

"Where did you find this?" Phee asked while tears welled up in her eyes.

"I got it from Nannie at the lake last month," he admitted. "She was going to give it to you then, but I asked her if I could give it to you today instead. She thought it was a great idea."

Brushing a tear from her cheek, Phee said, "I don't know what to say."

"Say thank you and move on," Gus suggested.

Phee chuckled. "Good idea. Thank you, Tris. Who's next?"

Frank pushed his gift across the table. "Before you open that, I have a letter for you from your favorite older brother."

"From Jamie!" Phee cried. "I wonder if he's still in England. I'll open it in a minute. I'm very curious about this box. Nice job wrapping, Dad."

"Yes, well, I had some help."

Phee removed the ribbon and paper, lifted the lid, and found a beautiful leather—shoulder bag—purse?

"It's a music pouch," Frank said. "Edith helped me find it. She thought you'd get a lot of use out of it."

"I certainly will. Thanks, Dad, I love it! I'll be sure to take it to my lesson on Monday." Phee looked at her watch. "I'd better get ready. Christa will be here soon."

"Are you going to a movie?" Mollie asked.

"Yeh, after supper. *The White Cliffs of Dover* is still on at The Call."

"Will you be out late?" Frank asked. "Don't forget, Ed's giving us a tour of the camp tomorrow morning." Army Chaplain Edward Mattson and Frank had been good friends since seminary, and Frank was thrilled when he learned Ed would be stationed at the prisoner of war camp that opened earlier this year about a mile west of Algona.

Phee was not enthusiastic about spending time at Camp Algona tomorrow. "You know, I forgot all about that," she said, fibbing just a tad. "I suppose I don't have a choice."

"He invited all the Swenssons. We will all be there."

"What time?"

"He wants us there at ten o'clock."

"Alright—I guess. And, to answer your earlier question, I don't think we'll be out too late. We'll hit Polly's after the movie, as usual."

"Just wake me when you get in. I'll be in my chair."

"You don't need to wait up for me, Dad. I'm seventeen now."

"I'll wait up for you when you're seventeen plus seventeen. You can count on it."

"Whatever you say," she said with a smile. "Thanks, everybody. I love all my presents. You really outdid yourselves this year."

"You get yourself ready for your date with Christa," Frank said. "I'll get supper on the table in a little bit. Don't go far, kids."

Phee placed her gifts in the box with the pouch and headed upstairs to her bedroom. Before she changed, she plopped down on her bed and opened the letter from Jamie. It had been a while since they'd heard from him, and Phee was thrilled to have a letter all to herself. She adored her older brother and missed him like crazy.

Jamie, a fine trumpet player, was a member of The United States Army Band. He was initially stationed at Fort Myer in Virginia, but in June last year, the band was sent to North Africa, and earlier this year, they were transferred to England. Like all V-Mail letters from military personnel, his were censored, so he couldn't give his family any details about his current situation. But each letter they received from Jamie told them he was alright, and that's what mattered more than anything else.

While she changed into one of her mom's favorite dresses, Phee wondered about the camp tour tomorrow morning. What would they see? Who would they meet? She was a little worried about Nazis living so close to town. On the other hand, it was an army camp, and Jamie was in the army. So, there was a connection—sort of.

5

FRIDAY 25 AUG. 1944 - PART 2

ON WEEKENDS, ALGONA'S TEENAGE couples often found themselves hanging out on Lover's Lane. For many years, it was located near a country road west of the city limits, just south of Highway 18, where it was quiet, peaceful, and secluded. Kids could sit in their cars and talk, kiss and cuddle, watch the sun set, and gaze at a million stars. They could listen to the wind blowing through nearby cornfields, and all summer long, a chorus of frogs and crickets would serenade them from the banks of nearby Dennison's Creek.

But all that had changed dramatically over the past several months. Where acres and acres of cornfields once stood, there was now Camp Algona, a prisoner of war camp built from the ground up for German POWs who'd been captured in North Africa and Italy, and, since D-Day, in France as well. A year ago, no one in Algona had even heard of POW camps. Now there were hundreds across the country. Last April, the initial group of five hundred prisoners arrived at the Algona train station and marched over three miles to the camp under heavy guard. In May, six hundred more joined their comrades, and more arrived over the summer. With over three hundred U.S. Army personnel stationed at the camp, the impact of its presence in Kossuth County was substantial.

After the movie, Phee and Christa stopped at Polly's for ice cream treats. The girls had been best friends since fifth grade when the Rasmussens moved to Algona from Wisconsin. Christa's parents, Jack and Peggy, owned Rasmussen Hardware down on South King Street. During the summer, Christa worked at the store full time, and she was behind the counter most Saturdays during the school year. Her older brother Danny, her only sibling, was serving overseas. Christa was as close to Danny as Phee was to Jamie, maybe closer. She wrote to him faithfully, hadn't missed a week since he left for basic training over a year ago.

"Should we hit the old lane?" Christa asked as they strolled back to the car.

"Why not," Phee answered. "It's Friday night and it's my birthday."

Even though it was Friday night, the girls knew there wouldn't be anybody else parked on the old Lover's Lane. A few months ago, Algona's teenagers found a new Lover's Lane on the east side of town where it was quieter and not exposed to the bright lights from the camp. There would be plenty of necking going on over there tonight, and Phee and Christa didn't mind missing all that one bit.

"When's Adam getting home?" Phee asked. Christa's boyfriend, Adam Vanderwilt, had been away all summer working on his uncle's farm down near Pella.

"I got a letter yesterday. He said he'd be home next Wednesday. I've already told him we'll be at the fair on Thursday."

"Can you believe it's already time for the fair? Boy, the summer sure has gone fast."

"Not for me," Christa lamented. "With Adam gone and working all the time, it hasn't gone nearly fast enough."

"Of course, I've been working on my recital music all summer. I'm sure that's helped the time speed by."

"How's it going, the memorizing, I mean?"

"Pretty good. The Beethoven's almost ready. I'm struggling with the Mendelssohn for some reason."

"I'm sure you'll have all those notes in your head in plenty of time."

"Hope you're right. I've been practicing at church quite a bit this summer. That's really helped."

Christa pulled off the road and parked the car facing Camp Algona's bright lights.

"What do you think all those German boys are doing right this moment?" Phee wondered.

"I sure hope they're not playing checkers and drinking beer," Christa said.

"I doubt they're drinking beer. Do Germans play checkers?"

"Who knows. I know a lot of 'em are working on farms around here. I hope they hate it."

"I'm sure it's better than sitting on their butts all day, planning their escapes back to Germany or France or wherever. Dad's friend, Ed Mattson, is giving us a tour of the camp in the morning. He's the chaplain out here."

"I have no desire to see it. You can take notes."

Phee chuckled. "Don't count on it. Dad's already been out a couple times. He said they'll have an orchestra and a band for the Nazis, and a choir too. Imagine that! And they've got a library and art stuff. Dad said Ed wants me to play out here, like for memorial services or something. I'm not sure I'll have time."

"Then don't do it. You're right—you're a busy girl."

Changing the subject, Phee asked, "So, what time should we head down to the fair on Thursday?"

"Let's ride our bikes," Christa suggested. "Dad's closing the store at noon. Pick me up at home at one."

"That'll work," Phee agreed, glancing at her watch. "I should get home. Dad insisted on waiting up."

On the way back to town, Christa told Phee about Danny's latest letter. He didn't say much, but they gathered he was somewhere in France and managing to stay safe. His letters were like Jamie's, always upbeat, no matter what.

"Thanks for everything," Phee said as Christa pulled into the driveway. "I had a great time tonight."

"See you at church. Oh, and watch out for those Nazis. I bet there are some cute ones out there."

Phee waved as Christa drove away, then opened the front door as quietly as she could. She found her dad asleep in his chair, just as he'd promised. Tommy Dorsey's band was playing softly on the radio in the corner.

"I'm home, Dad," she whispered while touching his shoulder.

"Oh, hi . . . how was it?" Frank asked as he sat up and rubbed his eyes.

"Great. Supper was great, the movie was great, and Polly's was best of all, as usual."

"Glad you had a good time," he said as he stood. "Guess I'll head up. Oh, and I told the kids we'll leave the house at a quarter to ten tomorrow."

"Alright," she sighed.

"We only have to do this once, Phee. It'll be fine."

"I guess," she said, following her dad to the stairs. "I've got a lot to tell Daisy tonight. I'll be up for a while."

Phee had been keeping a diary—she called it Daisy—since she started high school three years ago. Daisy was a good friend. Phee told Daisy everything. Tonight, she'd tell her about her wonderful day. But what about tomorrow? Would it be wonderful, too?

6

SATURDAY 26 AUG. 1944

THEIR RIDE TO CAMP Algona took less than ten minutes. Frank drove while Phee sat up front and the three kids were in the back. They traveled west on Highway 18 about two miles, then turned south into the camp entrance and pulled up to the small gatehouse.

"It looks like a playhouse!" Mollie cried as Frank slowed, then stopped. One of the MPs on duty came out to greet them.

"Good morning, sir," said the MP with a bit of a southern drawl. The patch over his right shirt pocket identified him as PVT J MATTINGLY. He leaned over to look inside the car. "Welcome to Camp Algona. I'll need to see some identification."

"Oh sure, right," Frank replied as he reached into his back trouser pocket for his wallet and pulled out his driver's license. "Here ya go."

"Thank you, sir. And what is the purpose of your visit today?"

"Chaplain Mattson's invited me and the kids out for a tour of the camp."

"Is your gun loaded?" Gus shouted from the back seat.

"Hush!" Phee said under her breath, clearly irritated at both Gus and her dad. *I'm not a "kid"!*

"It sure is, young man," Private Mattingly replied. "You're about to enter a United States Army prisoner of war camp. All military police and guards are armed."

"Sorry," Frank said, "my boy is very inquisitive."

"Me too!" Tris chimed in.

The Private smiled. "I'll have to make a phone call to the Chaplain's office to let him know you've arrived. It'll take just a second."

"Sure," Frank said, "no hurry." He turned to look at the twins and Mollie. "Let's come to an agreement, shall we? It'll work best if you speak only when spoken to while we're here. I understand you'll be curious about things, but too many questions will slow us down. Does that sound reasonable?"

Grudgingly, they all answered, "Yes, sir."

"Good, and I don't want you wandering off in here. We'll follow the Chaplain and stick together."

"Dad, will we see any Germans?" Mollie wanted to know.

"I'm sure there's a chance. Civilians aren't allowed to mingle with the prisoners. I read about that in the paper."

"Are we . . . sivilleons?" she asked.

Frank chuckled. "Yes, Sweet Pea, we're all 'sivilleons,' except your brother James Edward, obviously."

Private Mattingly handed Frank his license and the required visitor pass. "Mister Swensson, you should keep the pass on your dash. I've called over to the guardhouse. One of my colleagues will be right out to escort you to the headquarters building. Chaplain Mattson is waiting for you there."

"Excellent! Thanks for your help, Private."

"Yes, sir, happy to be of service. Enjoy your visit."

Private Mattingly raised the gate, and in a matter of seconds, an MP driving a Jeep pulled into the road just ahead of them. Frank followed closely behind, and in less than a minute, they reached the parking lot directly in front of the headquarters building. Frank pulled into the one unoccupied visitor space.

"There's the Chaplain," Frank said as he saw his friend coming out the door. "Wait here while I get the low-down."

"Okay," Phee said, then turned to face the kids. "Don't forget what Dad said about keeping quiet. The fewer interruptions, the sooner we'll be on our way home."

"What's the matter, Phee?" Tris wondered. "Aren't you excited? I think it's neato! We're in an army fort!"

Phee sighed and mumbled, "Whoopee."

Frank motioned for Phee and the kids to join them. The boys threw open the back doors and ran, while Phee and Mollie walked together, hand in hand.

"Welcome to Camp Algona!" Ed exclaimed. "It's great to see all of you. Phee, we met years ago, but you might not remember. You sure look a lot like your mom. I swear I'm looking at her eyes."

"And her nose," Phee said. "And I'm afraid I don't remember meeting you. I must have been pretty young."

"You were about to turn three, if I recollect correctly," Frank remembered. "Ed, these two redheads are Gus and Tris, and over here's my favorite blond, Miss Mollie."

"Dad calls me Sweet Pea sometimes," Mollie said proudly.

"He does, huh?" Ed said. "I like that. So, shall we get started with our tour? I thought we'd drive around the perimeter first so I can show you how everything's laid out. Then we'll come back here, and I'll take you through some of the buildings on the American side."

"Neato! We get to ride in an army car!" Gus shouted as they walked towards the shiny green Ford parked in the Chaplain's reserved space. Frank and Mollie sat up front with Ed while Phee sat in the back between the boys.

There were three compounds housing German prisoners inside the stockade, and as they passed Compound 1, they saw several POWs outside the barracks kicking soccer balls or just enjoying the warm day. Mollie, forgetting her dad's earlier instructions, asked, "Are those Germans?"

"Yes, they are, Mollie," Ed answered. "We have close to two thousand prisoners here now and more are coming. I expect we'll have all three thousand beds occupied before long."

Frank was curious. "So, what happens when all those beds are full and more prisoners are expected? Will you build more barracks?"

"No, we have a number of branch camps in Iowa and Minnesota," Ed explained, "and there are plans for more. We'll ship out some of the prisoners here to make room for new ones. I'm not privy to how the decisions are made, but the army seems to know what it's doing."

As they drove farther north, they came to a large pasture where several horses stood grazing, their tails flicking away the flies. "Hey look!" Tris shouted. "They've got horses out here!"

"We sure do," Ed said. "They help the guards patrol the perimeter of the stockade, and I've seen a couple pulling supply wagons."

"I wanna be a guard," Mollie whispered as she leaned across her dad's lap to get a better look.

After returning to the headquarters building, Ed took them through the officer's mess, a day room, the post exchange and snack bar, the motor pool building, the fire station, and the corral where the kids got to pet one of the horses.

On their way back to Ed's office, they approached one of the gates to the stockade where they saw two men leaving the compound. The shorter of the two was dressed in khaki prison garb, with PW stenciled on the legs of his pants and the front and back of his shirt. The other, an American, wore a typical khaki army uniform. Ed recognized the men. "There's my assistant, Corporal Phillips, with Sergeant Ebinger. Frank, Ebinger's the prisoner I was telling you about the other day. Looks like they're on their way to the theater. I thought I'd show you that building before we're done so Phee can check out our new piano."

Tris grabbed his dad's arm and whispered, "I thought we weren't supposed to be near the Germans."

Ed overheard. "It's alright, he's being escorted. Let's head inside, shall we?"

When they got to Ed's office, he introduced everyone to his secretary, Julie O'Reilly, and asked her if she'd take the kids to the snack bar while he and Frank and Phee walked over to the theater.

"I'd love to!" she said.

"Thanks, Julie," Ed said. "We'll meet you back here in about thirty minutes."

Frank and Phee followed Ed out the back door and across the street to the theater which was, like most of the camp's buildings, a wooden structure painted a light gray with a pitched roof. Next to the theater was a large parking lot which could be used by civilians who visited the camp for special ceremonies and services.

"Frank, I'd like to introduce the two of you to Sergeant Ebinger while we're here."

"Sure, I'd like to meet him," Frank said, noting Phee's frown.

"Phee, we found out the Sergeant's an excellent musician. He was in a band in the Afrika Korps and was captured about a year ago. He'll be in charge of the prisoner orchestra and dance band, and they'll have a chorus, too. He said he'd need an accompanist to assist during their rehearsals and concerts."

"Concerts, huh—like, for the POWs or the Americans?" Frank wondered.

"Both, we think. We're not yet sure how it's going to work."

"So, the other day you mentioned the possibility of Phee accompanying the chorus," Frank remembered as they reached the theater's lobby door.

"That's right," Ed said, then he turned to Phee. "We've been having some discussions about that. One of the prisoners was lined up to be the accompanist, but he was just transferred to one of our branch camps up in Minnesota. We contacted Edith Zetterholm—"

"She's my piano teacher," Phee interrupted.

"That's what she said. She's not available but mentioned you were certainly capable. I don't want you to feel any pressure, Phee, but we could sure use your help."

Phee thought for a moment, then shrugged her shoulders. "I'm not really sure. It would depend on how much time it would take to learn the music, how many rehearsals. I'll be awfully busy when school starts."

"Sure, I understand. Your schoolwork would always come first."

"If Phee decides she can do it," Frank said, "I'd be all for it, as long as there's a guard or two around. How's his English?"

"It's good. I find speaking with him isn't a challenge at all. In any case, I'd like you to see the piano. It was just delivered yesterday, a Chickering, I believe it is."

While the men continued their conversation outside the lobby door, Phee suddenly realized she'd been presented with an opportunity that deserved some consideration. Playing for the chorus here at the camp would certainly give her extra performance time. And what about the adventure of it all?

While Ed held open the door, they heard someone playing the piano inside. "That must be Sergeant Ebinger," he said.

Phee was stunned. *Beethoven!*

Ed peaked through the small window in the door into the hall. "Let's have a seat inside and listen for a minute," he whispered.

He's playing Beethoven!

They found chairs in the back of the hall. The dark-stained baby grand piano sat in the center of the stage. Only the lights over the stage were on, highlighting the Sergeant's wavy blond hair.

I can't believe he's playing Beethoven!

Corporal Phillips was speaking with another American soldier down on the floor level near the stage. They appeared to be discussing how the space might be used for concerts and other performances.

I'm sitting here listening to a prisoner of war play Beethoven!

The music stopped, and Sergeant Ebinger spoke to Corporal Phillips in German. The Corporal replied in German, then the Sergeant stood to lift the lid of the piano to its widest position. He returned to the bench and continued playing, scales this time. After another minute, Ed stood and said quietly, "Let's go down and I'll introduce you to everyone."

Phee was a little nervous, but she followed Ed and her dad down the center aisle, and as they approached the stage, Corporal Phillips saw them, smiled, and stood at attention. Sergeant Ebinger stopped playing and turned to watch the approaching visitors.

"Chaplain Mattson," the Corporal said, "I didn't see you back there, sir."

"I'd like to introduce some friends from town. Reverend Frank Swensson, this is my assistant, Corporal Roy Phillips." They shook hands and Ed continued. "And this is Frank's daughter, Phyllis . . . Phee. Phee's a very talented pianist, and I thought she might like to try out our new instrument."

Phee shook the Corporal's hand and answered more timidly than she intended. "Hi." *Nice smile. Look at those dimples!*

"And this is Sergeant Jackson," Ed continued. "He's in charge of our theater."

"Nice to meet you both," the Sergeant said. "So, how'd our new piano sound from back there?"

"Sounded great to me," Ed said. "What do you think, Phee?"

"Uhm, it's nice, very nice."

Aware of Sergeant Ebinger's stare from the stage, Phee was a bit flustered. She felt a strong urge to turn and walk away when Ed asked, "Phee, would you like to meet Sergeant Ebinger?"

She looked at her dad who smiled and nodded. "Sure, I guess so."

Ed turned to the prisoner. "Sergeant Ebinger, please join us." He jumped down from the stage, and Phee reacted with an unexpected start, taking a small step back. "I'd like you to meet Reverend Frank Swensson and his daughter Phee. Frank is pastor at St. Peter's Lutheran Church in Algona. Frank, Phee, meet Sergeant Horst Ebinger."

Horst? That's a weird name!

"How do you do?" they said while shaking hands with the Sergeant.

"So, what do you think of our new piano?" Ed asked.

Sergeant Ebinger, finally taking his intense blue eyes off Phee's face, turned to Ed. "I do like it. The . . . touch of it is good. It should be . . . *gestimmt*?"

"Tuned?" Roy suggested.

"*Ja*, tuned, for a regular time. And the . . . weather, the atmosphere here in the building should be kept the same, as much as possible."

"And it should be covered when it's not being used," Phee blurted out. *Oh, God, what a stupid thing to say!*

Sergeant Ebinger, almost smiling, agreed. "*Ja*, that is true."

"Phee, why don't you give it a spin?" Ed offered.

Frank gently touched her back. "It's alright, go ahead."

She walked past Sergeant Ebinger and up the four steps to the stage, took a seat, then played a few chords and a C major scale in octaves. Thinking that might not be quite enough, she added "That Moment in Rio," one of her original compositions. It was a short piece, and when she finished, there was polite applause from three of the four men standing nearby. Sergeant Ebinger kept his hands on his hips. Phee blushed and turned to them when she heard Sergeant Ebinger say, "And do you agree with my conclusion for the new instrument?"

"I do. I like it."

Corporal Phillips looked at his watch. "We should get back. It's almost lunch time."

"And Ed, we'd better rescue Julie from those kids," Frank added. "It was nice meeting you gentlemen. Auf Wiedersehen."

Sergeant Ebinger smiled when he heard Frank's German salutation. "And to you, Reverend Swensson," he replied, "*und* Fräulein Swensson . . . auf Wiedersehen."

The Corporal and the two Sergeants left through the west stage door, and Ed, Frank and Phee walked back up the aisle to the lobby.

"That wasn't so bad, was it?" Frank asked.

"I guess not," Phee said. "It's nice, the piano, I mean. I look forward to playing it again." *Maybe.*

On their way back to town, Mollie and the twins went on and on about what they saw at the camp this morning. Gus loved all the cars and trucks and Jeeps. Tris thought the mess hall smelled great, and the snack bar was almost as good as Polly's. And Mollie would be perfectly happy if she could spend all day with the horses.

For the benefit of her family, Phee admitted she thought the camp was very impressive in its design and thought they'd done a nice job with the landscaping. But tonight, when she wrote to Daisy, she'd focus on the prisoner with the striking blue eyes. Phee didn't expect to be so curious about that German man, but she was.

Thurs. Aug. 31, 1944

—Dear Daisy—

What a fun day! The last hurrah before school starts on Monday. Christa and I rode our bikes down to the fair after lunch and had a swell time wandering around the exhibition hall (sure love all those flowers!) and the 4-H barn (but oh, that smell!). We rode some rides but not as many as we usually do. The soldiers from the camp made the lines longer. Anybody in uniform can get in for free this year. So, we took our time sharing our banana split at Polly's booth. Yum! Christa wanted to know about our tour of the camp last Saturday, so I filled her in on all that. I almost didn't tell her about meeting Sgt. Ebinger, but then I did. "Is he a blue-eyed blond Nazi?" she asked, and I said "Well, as a matter of fact." Ha! I told her I'll be playing my recital out at the camp the week after I play it at St. Pete's. (Oh yeh—I forgot to tell you I told Chaplain Mattson a couple days ago I'd do it. He seemed really pleased.) On our way back to our bikes, we decided to stop and ride the ponies, and who should be in line in front of us but Cpl. Phillips, the fellow Dad and I met at the camp theater last Saturday. And you won't believe this, Daisy. He told me Sgt. Ebinger's been asking about me! Holy smokes! I'm pretty sure I turned red as a beet. Ugh! The Cpl. said he'd tell the Sgt. he saw me today, and all I could think to say was "Tell him hello." How lame! Anyway, I rode home and got supper started. We played hearts afterwards.

And life goes on. G'night.

7

MONDAY 4 SEPT. 1944

TODAY WAS FRANK'S USUAL day off and the first day of school for all the children in Algona. The twins, starting fifth grade, and Mollie, starting third, were back at Bryant Elementary over on East North Street. Mary always walked the little kids to school on the first day, and today, for the second time, Frank did the honors. Phee was at school early this morning as she began her last year at Algona High.

The church ladies delivered two tasty-looking casseroles earlier this afternoon, and Frank put one of them in a slow oven so it would be plenty warm enough for supper. They also brought three jars of homemade applesauce which Frank really appreciated because the Swensson fruit cellar was plumb out of applesauce.

"Smells good in here!" Phee called out when she arrived home after her piano lesson. "I guess the ladies stopped by."

"They did indeed," Frank said from his chair in the living room. "We might have enough for the week. They were extra generous today. Better get the kids going on that thank you note."

"Good idea. I'm gonna run up and change."

"Mollie's upstairs and the boys are out on their bikes. I told 'em to be home by six."

Phee looked in on Mollie and found her lying on her unmade bed, reading one of the library books she checked out on Saturday.

"We'll be eating soon. Better get washed up."

"I'm almost done with this chapter. Be right down."

Phee changed her clothes, then returned to the kitchen to get supper on the table. Frank stood at the sink listening to the six o'clock news just starting on the nearby radio. He stared out the window, then leaned over to turn down the volume. "Ed Mattson called today," he said.

"Oh, yeh, what'd he want?"

"Apparently, your presence is requested out at the camp to meet with the POW we met, Sergeant Ebinger I think it is."

Phee was taken aback, but she played it cool. "You're kidding, right?" she asked as she sliced two large, juicy tomatoes from the Coopers' garden.

"Nope. According to Ed, the request came from the German Chaplain—Schmidt. I met him last month."

"Did Ed say why?"

"He did. We'll talk about it after supper."

Just then, the twins careened their bikes into the back yard, dismounted and let them fall to the ground. They ran up the steps and through the back door. "Are we late?" Gus asked, slightly out of breath. "We rode like the wind!"

"Your wind's a little flimsy tonight," Frank said as he glanced at the clock over the sink.

Phee walked to the stairs to yell up to her sister. "Mollie! Get yourself down here!"

"Coming!"

As everyone settled at the table, they paused to say the blessing, then Frank opened the conversation with the inevitable, "So, tell me about your first day of school."

"I'll go first," Mollie offered. "I really like Miss Gregory. She's very pretty. She told us all about herself 'cause she's new and all."

"And what did you learn about Miss Gregory?" Phee asked while passing the tomatoes to Gus.

"Well, she grew up in Bloomfield. That's in Iowa but a long way from here."

"It is," Frank said. "It's very close to Missouri, our southern neighbor."

Mollie continued. "Anyway, she was in the high school orchestra. Let's see, what did she say? Oh yeh, she played . . . Jell-O?"

Phee chuckled. "I think you mean cello. I wonder if she still plays. Christa said the orchestra is short on cellos this year."

"She didn't say. She went to college in Cedar Falls. And now she's here. Oh, and she has three older brothers and they're all in the army, just like Jamie."

"So, besides learning all about Miss Gregory's life, what else did Mollie Serena learn in school today?" asked her dad.

"I learned we're gonna have spelling tests every Friday."

"I guess we know what you'll be doing on Thursday nights," Phee said.

"Who's next?" Frank asked. "Gus? What can you tell us about your teacher?"

"We got Mrs. Wellman. She's okay, I guess."

"Just 'okay'?"

"Well . . . she has a moustache," Gus said, glancing at his brother. "Denny Vestergaard said she must be a Nazi spy!"

Both boys burst out laughing. Their dad did not approve. "Gus, we do not comment on people's appearance. Repeat after me, both of you."

The boys attempted to stifle their laughter while repeating, "We don't comment on people's appearance."

"Let's not forget what I said and move on. Were you capable of learning anything at all on your first day of fifth grade?"

Feeling only slightly chastised, Gus answered, "I guess I learned I'm really gonna like our vocabulary lessons. Words are neato!"

"Do you have anything to add to this conversation, Mr. Tristan?" Frank asked.

"Sure. I'll do better than Gus in arithmetic this year. That's no surprise, though."

"Time will tell," Frank said. "And now, Phyllis Anne, the first day of your last year at Algona High. Give us a synopsis."

"Synopsis!" Tris interrupted. "It can be our Word of the Day."

"What does it mean?" Mollie asked.

"We'll learn about it when Phee finishes her synopsis," Frank said.

"Well," Phee began, "what I *can* tell you is that I'm going to be awfully busy. I'll have lots of homework, especially English and Algebra and History. And you know what that means."

With obvious disappointment, both boys admitted, "More work for us."

"Righto!" Phee said with a big grin. "Chorus and glee club concerts will be in October and December. And then, of course, there's . . ."

". . . your recital," Mollie said sarcastically.

"That's right," Phee agreed. "Dad, if it's alright with you, I'd like to stay at church to practice after choir on Wednesdays and after Luther League on Sundays. Just an hour, probably. It'll really help to have that time alone."

"I see no reason why you shouldn't. I can be home with the kids. Anything else you want to tell us about your day?"

"Hmm . . . oh yeh, they put new curtains in the cafeteria, and they painted it yellow. Very cheery."

"Thank you, Phee," Frank said, "that's a perfect synopsis. So, who can tell me what it means?"

Tris shot his hand in the air. "I think it means . . . a short list of things, like, 'number one, I did this today, and number two, I did that today, and number three, I learned this today'."

"Excellent!" Frank said. "Anyone else?"

Phee added, "A synopsis is like a summary, or an outline, not a lot of details."

"We've got it," Frank said. "Who wants to add it to the list?"

"I will," Gus said as he grabbed a pencil from the drawer next to the ice box. "I'll have to guess on the spelling."

"Give it a try," Frank said. "It starts with an S."

Since Jamie was a little boy, the Swenssons had made a habit of identifying a Word of the Day during supper. Not every day, but three or four times a week, usually. On the first day of the month, if he didn't forget, Frank taped a blank piece of paper on the ice box door where they kept track of all the new words the kids learned during the month. At the end of the month, he removed the paper and put it in a box under his bed. Supposedly, he'd kept every sheet they'd filled since the beginning of time.

They finished their meal, then Phee asked, "Who wants applesauce for dessert?"

The kids enthusiastically raised their hands and Frank said, "Bring it on!"

After dessert, the boys did the dishes, Mollie retreated to her room, and Phee and Frank went outside to the front porch to talk more about Ed Mattson's phone call.

"So, tell me again about Ed's call," Phee said as they sat together on the top step.

"He admitted it's an unusual request," Frank said, "but apparently the camp commander is in on this. There's that rule about civilians not fraternizing with the prisoners, but they thought an exception could be made because Sergeant Ebinger has leadership potential and Ed thinks he's—how'd he put it—pulling away from all the Nazi indoctrination, plus you're both musicians. He thinks you could be a positive influence."

"Really?"

"Yeh, and he'd like you to audition for the Sergeant."

"Audition?"

"Just to see if the two of you could work together. As I understand it, you could play one of your recital pieces, sight read a hymn, maybe follow his conducting."

"Would he come into town?"

"No, Ed said you'd meet in the camp theater for just an hour, no more, and there would be a guard present. I told him I'd call tomorrow with your answer."

Phee stood and took a couple steps down the sidewalk, then turned back. "Do you think I should do it?" she asked.

Frank leaned back on his elbows and crossed his long legs. "If I were you, I'd try it, see how it goes. It could be interesting or even fun."

"Maybe."

"I could go with you if that would help."

"It might. Did Ed say when?"

"He suggested a Sunday afternoon."

"Did he mean this coming Sunday?"

"I don't think it matters. Is there anything wrong with next Sunday?"

She sighed. "I guess not. Might as well get it over with."

"I'll call Ed first thing tomorrow."

"Alright, thanks. I'd better get upstairs. I need to read the first thirty pages of *Merchant of Venice* tonight.

As they walked back into the house, Frank asked, "Phee, you would tell me, wouldn't you, if you're the least bit uncomfortable meeting with the Sergeant?"

"I would. Don't worry."

"Okay, good. Think I'll go tune into *Fibber*.

Phee slowly climbed the stairs, remembering, for many months after her mom died, her dad refused to listen to comedy like *Fibber McGee and Molly* on the radio or watch comedies at the movies. He'd listen to the radio, but only for news and weather and classical music programs. He was open to comedy once again—a good sign, she thought.

When she got to her bedroom, Phee realized she'd made the decision to meet with Sergeant Ebinger as soon as her dad first mentioned it before supper. She'd talk to Daisy about it later tonight. That would help.

She plopped down on her bed, Shakespeare's play in hand, and began to read aloud. It was Antonio speaking. "In sooth, I know not why I am so sad."

8

SUNDAY 10 SEPT. 1944

AFTER SPENDING ALMOST TWENTY minutes fixing her hair at the dressing table in her bedroom, Phee reached for her mom's tube of lipstick she'd been saving for special occasions. It was a lovely shade of red, but she blotted her lips twice so they weren't flaming. The black and white polka dot dress she wore to church this morning would have to do for her three o'clock meeting with Sergeant Ebinger at the Camp Algona theater.

When she got downstairs, the twins and Mollie were just heading out to the Coopers next door. "Tell Mrs. Cooper we should be home by five thirty," Phee said as she reached in the closet for her jacket. Her dad was already in the car.

As soon as her feet touched the porch, Phee remembered she wanted to take her music pouch along. Inside the pouch was her recital music as well as a few other pieces she'd worked on in recent years, pieces she was willing to loan the Sergeant if he was interested—if it was allowed, of course. She hurried back in to grab the pouch from the top of the piano.

As they drove north to the highway, Frank glanced at Phee as she chewed her nails. "You're not nervous, are you?" he asked, sensing she probably was.

"No . . . well, maybe a little," she said, putting her hands in her lap.

"We can change our minds, you know. This meeting doesn't need to happen today."

"No, I'm fine. Besides, you're meeting with the chaplains after my meeting with the Sergeant."

As they approached the camp entrance, they saw Private Mattingly exit the gatehouse. Frank stopped the car and smiled.

"Pastor Swensson," said the Private, "it's nice to see you again, sir."

"Good to see you too, Private."

"And what is the purpose of your visit today?"

"We're meeting some folks in the theater at three, then I have a meeting in Chaplain Mattson's office at four."

"Is there someone I should call to let them know you've arrived?"

"Why don't you give Chaplain Mattson a ringy dingy," Frank suggested.

Phee rolled her eyes and heaved a big sigh.

After a short while, Private Mattingly returned to the doorway and handed Frank the visitor pass. "Miss O'Reilly said to drive on to the theater and she'll meet you there. One of my colleagues will be here in a moment to escort you."

"Thank you, Private."

"Yes, sir. Have a nice afternoon."

A Jeep arrived from the guardhouse and Frank pulled up behind it after Private Mattingly raised the gate. Phee unconsciously put her finger in her mouth, began to chew, then immediately removed it and sat on her hand.

When they arrived at the empty parking lot next to the theater, Frank pulled into a space that didn't have a RESERVED sign and turned off the engine. As they opened their doors, they saw Julie O'Reilly hurrying across the parking lot.

"Pastor Swensson, Phee, it's so nice to see you both again," she said as she approached the car.

"I'm surprised you're working on Sunday," Frank said as they walked to the lobby door. "Surely you get a day off now and then."

"'Now and then' is about right, but I don't mind. I love my job."

"Why don't we go in and get some lights on?" he suggested.

"I believe all the switches are up on stage," Julie said. "Let's get all the curtains open first. That should help."

The stage was still set up from this morning's church service, and there were at least two hundred chairs set in rows on the main floor. The piano, with its lid closed, was sitting on stage left. "Let's see what I can do here," Julie said when they got to the stage. As she flipped the last switch, the door in the back of the hall opened and Sergeant Ebinger and Corporal Phillips walked in. The Sergeant wore his prison garb and carried a parcel Phee was certain did not contain music.

Corporal Phillips, with his ever-present smile, called out from the back. "Sorry we're a little late. They called a surprise inspection right when the Sergeant was leaving the barracks."

"We're just getting settled," Julie said. "I'll leave you to it."

"Thanks for your help, Julie," Frank said. "We'll see you in about an hour."

When the two men got to the stage, Frank shook their hands and Phee didn't. But she did say, "It's nice to see you both again."

Sergeant Ebinger, looking somewhat serious, said, "I have brought some sweets for the children in your home . . . from our mess hall."

Phee was surprised he knew about the kids. She smiled and accepted the package. "That's very nice. I'm sure the children will enjoy them."

"And you may also enjoy them if you like."

"Yes, I expect we all will. Thanks."

"So, we should get this show on the road," Frank said. "You kids get started with your meeting. Corporal Phillips and I will sit in the back and have a deep discussion about the meaning of life."

The Corporal chuckled, the Sergeant looked confused, and Phee was embarrassed. "Ignore him," she said, shaking her head. "He's trying to be funny, or profound, or both."

"Profound?"

"Uhm, deep? Philosophical?"

"*Ja, philosophisch.* I know it."

While Frank and Corporal Phillips found seats in the back of the hall, Phee reached for her music pouch. "I brought some music. You can borrow it if it's allowed."

"Borrow?"

"That's right. You can keep it for a while and then return it to me, like a library?"

"*Bibliothek.* That I also know. Show it to me, *bitte.*"

Phee pulled out everything she'd brought except her original songs. "I brought my recital music. That's for November at St. Pete's and here at the theater the next week."

"Recital?"

I thought Ed said his English was good. "Yes, my senior recital. I'm a senior in high school." Thinking he might need more information, she added, "It's my final year, before college or university."

"And your music studies will continue?"

"Probably. It's . . . complicated. Eventually, yes, I will attend college. My dad will insist."

"And will your mother also insist?"

Now sitting on the piano bench, Phee stared at the keys while brushing her hand lightly across them. "My mom died almost two years ago. She had cancer." He didn't respond, so she added, "But we're fine. We're getting used to not having her around, I guess. We still miss her."

"It is sad when someone . . . I am very sorry for you, for your family."

Phee smiled. "Thanks. Maybe someday I'll tell you about my mom."

At that moment, Phee realized she was no longer nervous or apprehensive or intimidated. Perhaps a little, but mostly not.

They spent the rest of their time talking about and playing music. Phee asked the Sergeant to play some of the Beethoven sonata she heard him playing the day they met. He chose the first movement of the *Pathétique.* Sergeant Ebinger wanted to look at the pieces Phee had composed so she played those, humming along as she did. Phee learned he began studying piano with his mother when he was eight. She was curious to know more personal information but decided to leave that for another day.

"I would like to ask you for . . . how you say . . . a favor," said the Sergeant as he stood next to the piano.

"A favor?"

"I am organizing a . . . choir, a chorus of singers . . . with my comrades. We will call it the *Männerchor*. In Deutschland it means 'the choir for men' or perhaps 'male choir.' It is just the beginning now. We will wait for music to arrive. Until then, we sing *Volkslieder*, the songs we know in our hearts."

"How many are in your group?"

"Until now, we have *vierzig* . . . forty singers who have agreed to join us. I would like to have more, but not many."

"So, you wanted to ask a favor?"

"One comrade I selected who can play the piano for our group, he was sent to another camp in . . . Minnesota, where he must work with . . . peas."

"A canning factory?"

"*Ja*, it is that. He is gone, so I need to find another. I would like it to be you."

"Me?" Phee feigned surprise, even though she knew from Ed Mattson it was a possibility. "How would that work?"

"I have spoken to Corporal Phillips, and he has spoken to others, I cannot say for sure. They would make it possible, he said."

"Gosh, I don't know. I'll have to think about it."

"I would expect it. We will perform before Christmas, in December, here in the theater. The date has not been chosen until now."

"That's after my recital, so . . ."

"We can speak again, if you can agree to meet in a future time from now."

Phee smiled. "Sure, why not."

One of the lobby doors opened, and in walked the two Chaplains, at least Phee assumed it was Chaplain Schmidt with Ed Mattson. She looked at her watch and realized their meeting had lasted longer than an hour. "Oh, gosh, we've gone over. Here, why don't you take this music. My name's on each piece so you'll remember they're mine."

The Sergeant smiled. "I will not forget the music belongs to you."

In the back of the hall, Corporal Phillips shook Frank's hand, then walked to the stage. "Sergeant Ebinger, we'd better go," he said. "Miss Swensson, I hope we'll see you out here again soon."

Phee looked at the Sergeant and smiled. "Yes, I'll come again, for sure in November for my recital, but maybe sooner."

"Great!" said the Corporal. "We'll look forward to it."

"Thank you for our meeting today," said Sergeant Ebinger. "Auf Wiedersehen."

"Auf Wiedersehen," she repeated.

The two men left through the west stage door, then Phee grabbed her pouch and the package of sweets and joined her dad and the two Chaplains at the back of the hall.

"Phee, this is Chaplain Heinrich Schmidt," Ed said. "He's the Chaplain for Sergeant Ebinger's outfit in the Afrika Korps. Chaplain Schmidt, this is Frank's daughter Phyllis who prefers to be called Phee."

"A lovely name for a lovely Fräulein," he said.

"Thank you," Phee said while shaking his hand. "It's nice to meet you."

"Did you enjoy your time with Sergeant Ebinger?" Ed asked.

"I did. He's very talented. He'll be a good leader for the groups."

"Indeed," said Chaplain Schmidt, "it is good to have him in the camp. The men respect him, and that is most helpful."

"So, shall we head back?" Ed asked. "Phee, Julie said she'd be happy to stay with you while your dad's tied up."

"I'd like that. Thanks."

While they walked to Ed's office, Phee thought about the last hour. Her impressions of the Sergeant? He was rather sophisticated and well-educated but was somewhat reserved and perhaps a little sad. He didn't show any signs of anger, though, which was somewhat surprising to Phee. She expected him to be angry about the turn his life had taken. It would be helpful if he wasn't angry because Phee was quite sure she couldn't be friends with an angry Nazi. She was pleased she could communicate with "the enemy" and thought the experience was probably worthwhile. But should that communication continue? She wasn't sure.

9

MONDAY 11 SEPT. 1944

HAROLD AND EDITH ZETTERHOLM and their ten-year-old son, Paul, lived in a large English Tudor on Algona's west side. Affectionately known as Doc Z to most of his patients, Harold had been a general practitioner in Algona for almost fifteen years. He met Edith at a potluck supper at St. Pete's one snowy February night. They married, and a few years later, adopted a baby boy. They named him Paul after Harold's brother who was killed in the First World War. Funny thing was, their son Paul truly looked a lot like Harold. No one would ever guess he was adopted.

Edith Zetterholm was an attractive woman, short in stature but strong in nature and will. She grew up in the Twin Cities and, after graduating from the University of Minnesota, took a teaching job at Bryant Elementary in Algona. She loved teaching, but just before they brought Paul home from the hospital where he was born, they decided it would be better for the family if she resigned her position at Bryant so she could be home with the baby. Eventually, she began teaching piano privately, and this fall had sixteen students ranging from beginners to more mature players like Phee.

Phee's lessons took place in a small room off the living room where Edith's Steinway baby grand was placed against an interior wall. On the opposite wall was a six-foot bookcase full of music books, and a crystal chandelier hung from the high ceiling. There were two windows on either side of a glass door overlooking the small garden on the north side of the house. A tall fence surrounding the garden prevented curious neighbors from observing piano lessons.

Arriving a few minutes early for her lesson, Phee laid her bike on the well-manicured lawn and waited on the front steps next to a large empty flowerpot. Someone, probably Edith, had recently removed the red and white geraniums that had bloomed there over the summer.

At four-thirty on the dot, Phee rang the doorbell. "Hi, Mrs. Z, it's me!" she called through the screen door.

"Hi, Phee!" Edith answered. "I'm in the kitchen. Be out in a minute. Go ahead and get warmed up."

When Phee got to the piano room, she dropped her weekly check in the box on the nearby bookcase. Since the beginning of the war, Edith had been buying war bonds with her lesson money—a "worthy cause," she said.

Phee sat, closed her eyes for a few seconds, then began playing her scales, three octaves up and down: C major, D flat major, D major, E flat major, E major . . .

During E major, Edith came in through the open french doors and waited for Phee to finish F major. "Good. Now minor, starting with D this time."

Phee liked minor scales. Usually, she started with minor, but not today. She was in a good mood and wanted her hands to sound happy.

"That's fine," Edith said, getting down to business. "So, how's the memorizing coming along?"

Phee groaned. "Okay, I guess. I still have more than two months. I'll get there."

"I know you will. So, here's your next goal: I want to hear the entire *Pastoral* from memory in two weeks. If you can't do that, you're in trouble. Do you understand why I'm telling you this?"

"I do. I'm close. The trio in the third movement is still giving me fits. The others are coming along, though. I can play the MacDowells and Grieg for you today. Mendelssohn's not quite there yet. But I'll focus on Beethoven for the next couple of weeks."

"And what about your songs?"

"Those are ready. I decided last night I'll do 'Evening Reverie' and 'Sunset Ride' on the first half and save 'That Moment in Rio' for an encore."

"That sounds fine. Oh, and I've had a thought. What if I played 'Rio' and you sang along? I think your audience would really enjoy that."

"Gee, I don't know. I'll think about it."

"Good. Now, let's hear 'Polonaise.'"

Edith's top student continued to impress. She knew Phee would do a fine job on her recital in November. She appreciated the self-assurance Phee almost always exhibited and wished more of her students would demonstrate that same level of confidence. She understood it was a gift, though, and not everyone was blessed with it.

At her hour's end, Phee decided to mention her meeting with Sergeant Ebinger. "So, guess what I did yesterday."

"What did you do yesterday, besides church and Luther League?"

"I met with one of the prisoners out at the camp."

"You did, huh?"

"Yeh. It was Sergeant Ebinger, the prisoner Dad and I met last month. We just talked about music, mostly. He'll be directing all the prisoner music groups and wants me to accompany their . . . what did he call it . . . . choir, or chorus. There's a German word, I can't remember."

"I did get a call from Chaplain Mattson about this recently. Are you going to do it?"

"It depends on my schedule and how much time it would take. I told Ed I couldn't do it before my recital. But you're always telling me to grab any chance to play, and I love accompanying. I trust Ed. He's the one who asked me to meet with the Sergeant."

"It sounds like you have time to think on it."

"And I will. Oh, and there's one more thing."

"Make it short. Harold will be home soon. We can talk while I walk you out."

"It's about playing my recital at the camp. I told Ed I'd do it the Sunday after Thanksgiving. You wouldn't have to be there."

"I'll check the calendar. I'm pretty sure that should work. It's a good idea, Phee, another opportunity to play, and a different audience."

"Yeh, that's what I thought."

"And don't forget, Beethoven this week and next."

"I'll remember. See you at choir."

Phee tossed her pouch in the bike's basket and waved to her teacher. As she pedaled home, she wondered when she'd next visit Camp Algona. Turned out it was sooner than she expected.

10

SATURDAY 30 SEPT. 1944

TWO DAYS AFTER SHE told Mrs. Z she'd perform her recital at Camp Algona, Ed Mattson called the parsonage to ask Phee if she could play for the camp memorial service planned for this afternoon. He also invited Frank to give the invocation. They would honor the Kossuth County men who had died in service to their country since Pearl Harbor, and the public was invited to attend.

It was raining, not a gully washer, and there was no thunder or lightning. Just a gentle, cold fall rain that was not going to let up before the three o'clock service in the camp theater. Frank decided he and Phee and the kids should leave plenty early in case the traffic was bad. As they crossed over Highway 169 on their way west, they saw brake lights up ahead and a long line of cars moving very slowly. Quite a few people, many with black umbrellas, walked towards the camp along the shoulder on the south side of the road.

"Will you look at that," Frank said. "Traffic's already backed up."

"You don't think we'll be late, do you?" Phee asked. Frank glanced in the rearview mirror, then slowly pulled to the left into the oncoming lane. Fortunately, there were no cars traveling east at that moment. "Dad, what are you doing?!" Phee shrieked.

"Jeepers creepers!" Gus shouted from the back seat.

"We need to get ahead of all these cars. They'll see my collar and the C sticker. I've got the headlights on. I'll keep it slow."

"I can't watch!" Phee moaned as she covered her face with her hands.

Frank drove slowly west in the eastbound lane, occasionally honking his horn to get the attention of the other drivers and pedestrians. The last mile of their trip seemed an eternity to Phee, but Frank's bold plan worked, and they made it to the camp entrance in good time.

"Oh, my God, I can't believe you did that!" Phee cried, her hands now clenched tightly in her lap.

"I can!" Tris shouted. "Good job, Dad!"

"We can't be late," Frank said, "and besides, I prayed the whole time. It worked, didn't it?"

"It sure did!" Mollie chimed in.

"And what if we'd seen a car coming at us?" Phee asked.

"I would've pulled off and let him pass, obviously."

"Right, running over all those people on the shoulder. Dad, you are crazy."

"And it's what you love about me the most, right?"

Phee gently punched his shoulder. Secretly, she was glad he took the risk, but she'd never admit it.

The line of cars moved slowly past the gatehouse. By the time Frank pulled into the parking lot next to the theater, it was almost full. Yesterday, he talked to Peggy Rasmussen about the kids sitting with her during the service, so he wasn't surprised to see her huddled under an umbrella next to the lobby door.

Peggy smiled at Mollie and the twins. "Hi, kids! We'd better get in out of this rain."

"Thanks for keeping them in line," Frank said as he opened the lobby door. "Why don't you just stay in your seats afterwards and wait for us."

"Sure, that'll be fine," Peggy agreed.

Frank and Phee hurried to the stage where Ed Mattson and Glen McMillan, pastor of Algona's First Presbyterian Church, were talking to a high-ranking army officer they didn't know. Impressive red, white, and blue floral arrangements were placed on either side of the stage floor. The piano was on stage left with its lid closed.

At two-thirty, the doors in the back were opened and people began to fill in the chairs on either side of the center aisle. The first four rows were reserved for family members who'd lost loved ones in the war. Phee saw the Larsons walking down the aisle. Their son Kenny was killed in France on June 7th, the day after D-Day. Frank got the call when the Swenssons were at Lake Okoboji in July, and he had to return home a day early to meet with the family to plan the memorial service. While all war casualties were lamentable, Kenny's death was particularly hard on the congregation. He was a favorite son in every sense of the word.

Ed introduced Lieutenant Colonel David McNabb, Camp Algona's Commander, to Frank and Phee.

"We sure appreciate you helping us out today," the Colonel said. "Captain Mattson speaks very highly of you both."

"It's an honor, sir," Frank said while shaking his hand.

"And Miss Swensson, I understand you'll be performing for us in November."

"That's right, my senior recital, the Sunday after Thanksgiving."

"We'll see if we can't fill the hall on that occasion, too. Looks like we have an overflow crowd today."

"We do," Ed said. "I've got the men setting up chairs in the lobby."

The Colonel looked at his watch. "We should begin right at fifteen hundred hours, after Miss Swensson finishes her prelude."

Phee got settled on the bench and reached for her music—two solemn hymns many attendees would know, and Maurice Ravel's "Pavane for a Dead Princess." It was possible some would know that piece, too.

At seven minutes to three, Phee began the "Pavane." A man in the reserved section stood, turned, and motioned for the people behind him to be still. Very shortly, the only sound in the hall was the mesmerizing music of Ravel. When she finished, she looked at her dad. He smiled and nodded.

The service lasted for just over an hour. It began with a color guard entrance from the back and ended with a moving benediction by Pastor McMillan. Phee avoided looking at the people in the first four rows as Chaplain Mattson read the names of those who were being honored.

Forty-eight soldiers, sailors, and airmen from Kossuth County had died since Pearl Harbor, too many for one county.

Before he left the hall, Colonel McNabb complimented Phee on her performance. "You play beautifully. I'm sure everyone was moved."

"Thanks again for asking me. The service was very nice."

While Phee gathered her music, Frank joined Peggy and the kids who were still sitting near the back of the hall. Before Phee could join them, Roy Phillips appeared through the west stage door.

"Corporal Phillips," she said. "I wondered if you'd be here today."

"I was in the lobby. I sure enjoyed hearing you play, especially that piece right before the service."

"'Pavane.' It is beautiful, isn't it?"

"I'll tell Sergeant Ebinger about it. I bet he knows it."

Phee blushed and smiled. "He might."

"I have something for you," he said, handing her a program from the service. "There's an envelope inside. It's from the Sergeant."

"Oh, really? Uhm, thanks."

"Well, I'd better get back. Hope to see you soon," he said as he backed away.

"Phee, you ready?" Frank called out from the back of the hall.

"Be right there," she said.

When they got back to town, Phee asked Frank to stop at Cal's Grocery so she could pick up a few things for their supper. She wanted to eat early as Christa and Adam had invited her see Bing Crosby's *Going My Way* tonight.

While Phee found what she needed in the store, she thought about the envelope from Sergeant Ebinger. She wouldn't have time look at it until after supper, or more likely, when she got home from the movie. Yes, she'd save it until bedtime, before she wrote to Daisy, just in case she needed Daisy's advice.

PHEE TURNED TO WAVE as Christa and Adam backed out of the driveway and drove away. It was almost eleven o'clock, and the kids were in bed. Frank was in the kitchen, humming one of the hymns she'd played at the service today. As she passed by the piano, she glanced at her music pouch where the envelope from Sergeant Ebinger was hidden away.

"Is that you, babe?" Frank asked.

"It's me," she answered.

"Come tell me about the movie. I 'spect you'll say I need to see it, too."

"Absolutely," Phee said as she got to the kitchen, "it's wonderful. Bing is king!"

Frank moaned and they both laughed. "So, what's so great about *Going My Way*?" he asked.

"Well, two things, no, three. First, everybody is going to see this movie so you don't want to be the only one in town who doesn't."

"Now, wait. I'll probably see it, eventually."

Phee shook her head. "No, better make it tomorrow. Second thing, it's about a Catholic priest."

"Not a Lutheran pastor, huh?"

"Nope."

"What a shame. It could've been so much better."

"Sure. Now let's see. Where was I? Oh, yeh, third thing. There's some beautiful music in this movie. Risë Stevens plays herself—she's an opera singer—and she's wonderful.

"Opera, huh? Not Wagner, by any chance?"

"Hardly. And then there's this wonderful boys' choir. That was definitely worth the price of admission. Oh, and I just thought of a fourth thing. It's going to win the Academy Award for Best Picture this year. Adam and Christa and I agreed, and so did most everybody at Polly's."

"Well, I'll think about it."

"You should take the kids. They'll love it. It ends Tuesday, so you'll have to go tomorrow."

"Okay okay, you've convinced me," he said with a smile.

"How was game night?" she asked.

"We decided to write to Jamie instead. We were all thinking about him during the service today."

"I need to write him, too—tomorrow, after I finish my homework and before Luther League."

"Better hit the hay. G'night, Phyllis Anne."

"G'night. Sweet dreams."

While Frank retreated upstairs, Phee turned off the radio and the kitchen light, then walked back to the living room to fetch the envelope from Sergeant Ebinger. Once upstairs, she brushed her teeth, donned her pajamas, and sat on the edge of her bed. At last, she opened the envelop and found a handwritten note.

29 September 1944

Fräulein Swensson,

Forgive me for sending this letter ~~unexpektidley~~ unexpectedly. It seems a reasonable way to contact you. Corporal Phillips will deliver it to you tomorrow. I would enjoy very much another meeting with you. It is a serious reason, to discuss your agreement to accompany the Männerchor in our first performances before Christmas. It remains my wish if you can agree to it. If you cannot, I must find another. I prefer it is you. When you come to Camp Algona the next, we can discuss the music I have chosen up to now. There will be more, but we must begin to rehearse as soon as possible. My comrades are happy about it and are ~~entosiastat~~ enthusiastic to begin our rehearsals. You should contact Corporal Phillips with your answer. I remain hopeful we can make an agreement about this in the next days.

Auf Wiedersehen,

Fw H. Ebinger

Phee read the note again, and once more, before returning it to the envelope and placing it in the drawer of her nightstand. Before she closed the drawer, she pulled out her diary and a pencil. It was late, but she wasn't sleepy. Again, she asked Daisy about the Sergeant's request. Daisy always had the right advice. She told Phee to accept the invitation to accompany the Sergeant's choir, and Phee thanked her for helping her decide.

11

SUNDAY 8 OCT. 1944

IT SEEMED A BIT odd to Phee, how this afternoon's meeting with Sergeant Ebinger was arranged. It wasn't as simple as the last time, when Frank called Ed Mattson to say she'd meet with the Sergeant, and that was it. No, for some reason, today's meeting had to go through several channels before it could be confirmed, and it took three days.

Phee did finally hear from Roy Phillips before choir last Wednesday. He gave her the phone number at his barracks so she could call him any time, day or night. She promised she wouldn't bother him too often and he said it was no bother, no bother at all.

So, this afternoon, Phee found herself driving west on Highway 18, only this time, she was alone. Frank had intended to accompany Phee for this second meeting with the Sergeant, but he had to meet with the family of old Mr. Addison who finally passed away yesterday morning at his home. Ninety-four-year-old Isaac Addison was a founding member of St. Pete's back in 1882. There weren't many of those folks left.

Phee assured her dad she'd be fine without him. She expected Corporal Phillips to be there again, and she couldn't stay longer than an hour because she had to get back for Luther League. When she arrived at the camp gatehouse, she found Private Mattingly on duty once again. "Do you live in this little house, Private?" she asked as he walked out.

He laughed. "No ma'am. I do spend an awful lot of time out here, though."

"Well, it's always nice to see you. I'm here to see Chaplain Mattson, or Corporal Phillips, or both. We're meeting in the theater."

"I'll make a quick call to the Chaplain's office. Be right back."

While he made the call, Phee adjusted the rearview mirror so she could check her hair. *Oh no, is that a pimple?!*

The Private returned with the visitor pass, and Phee placed it on the dash. "Thank you, Private."

"You're welcome. One of my colleagues will be right out to escort you to the theater. The Chaplain said he'd meet you there." He lifted the gate and Phee followed the MP's Jeep the short distance to the theater, then parked close to the lobby door.

She decided to wait for Ed inside. As soon as she opened the outer door, she heard piano music coming from the hall. *It's not Beethoven this time.* Peeking through the window, she saw Sergeant Ebinger sitting at the piano. There wasn't a guard nearby and she thought it odd he was alone. Just as she decided she wouldn't go in without an escort, Sergeant Ebinger stopped playing and called out, "Fräulein Swensson? Are you here?"

Oh, poo! He saw me! Should I go in? Oh, what the heck. "Yes, Sergeant," Phee replied as she opened the door. "I'm a little early."

He stood and said with authority, "*Nein.* You should be on the stage with me now to begin our meeting."

"Is there a guard here?"

"Corporal Bickford is coming. I expect him soon."

"Chaplain Mattson's coming, too," she said, relieved to know a guard was on the way.

"*Ja?* I will say then, you should be safe from all harm."

Phee hoped he was kidding. She joined him on the stage.

"It is a pleasure to see you again, Fräulein. You are looking well."

Phee blushed ever-so-slightly, hoping neither the blush nor the pimple was obvious. "What were you playing just now?"

He returned to the piano. "Do you like it? I have written it since you were here before. It is not complete. I cannot find an ending that suits me. You can help me with it."

Just then, the lobby door opened, and Ed Mattson walked in. Sergeant Ebinger stood at attention. "Phee, Sergeant Ebinger, I'm so sorry for the delay. Where's the guard?"

"He's on the way, we think," she answered.

"That's good," Ed said. "I can't stay long. Believe it or not, I've got a meeting about the Halloween party. I'm not sure why they need input from the Chaplain, but I'm on the committee." He was interrupted by the guard's arrival through the west stage door. "Corporal Bickford, I'm glad you're here. I need to get back."

"Yes, sir. Corporal Phillips brought me up to speed. I'll stay until the Sergeant and Miss Swensson wrap up their meeting."

"Good—thank you, Corporal," Ed said as he got to the lobby door. "Phee, tell Frank hello and we'll try to get together soon."

"I will. Thanks, Chaplain Mattson."

As Corporal Bickford left the stage, he pulled a small book from his trouser pocket. "I'll be back here with my book. Be sure to let me know if you need anything."

"We will," Phee replied.

"Fräulein Swensson," Sergeant Ebinger said, returning once again to the piano bench. "Before we begin, we must discuss your agreement to accompany my choir for the Christmas concert."

Phee hesitated, even though she'd decided to do it. She wanted the Sergeant to understand it could very well be an imposition on her time. She'd make it work, somehow, but she didn't want to show too much enthusiasm, at least at the beginning. "Right," she said, "about that—"

"You can agree to it, *ja*?"

"Yes, but—"

"*Wunderbar!* It is the expected answer. I can show you the music I have chosen until now. Some will be *a cappella*, and some—"

"Maybe."

"Maybe?"

"I won't be able to think about learning anything new until after my recital. We'll have to wait."

"We cannot wait. The learning will be . . . too much in a short time."

"Alright, but let's not talk about it today."

For a second or two, the Sergeant seemed annoyed with Phee's reluctance. But then he smiled, and for the first time, Phee realized he was rather handsome. Before this moment, she'd considered him somewhat nice looking, attractive enough. His wavy blond hair, steel blue eyes, and prison garb were always reminders she was in the presence of a German POW. But now, she wondered: could this prisoner of war be a teacher, or a friend, or both?

"*Ja*, we can wait for a small time," he said, "but you should expect to come here again to discuss it."

"I can arrange that. I'll let Corporal Phillips know. I have his secret number."

The Sergeant smiled. "Ah, then you have much power with the Corporal."

Phee shook her head and chuckled. "It's just his phone number. I'll call him to arrange our next meeting."

"And now we can make my composition better together." The Sergeant played his piece, and they both tried to find a fitting ending to it. He didn't particularly like most of Phee's ideas, but they led him to a different approach which pleased them both.

"You should write it down before you forget," she suggested.

"I will make notes. I can for the most remember what I have done." He reached for a pencil and a fresh sheet of manuscript paper. While he wrote, he paused to tell Phee that he received his supply of paper from the YMCA representative. "*Doktor* Hill visits us over some time. He will bring what we need for our orchestra and dance band, the instruments, and the music we perform. He is . . . *ein Engel vom Himmel* . . . an angel from heaven."

"*Ein Engel vom . . . Himmel?* I like that.

The Sergeant continued with his notetaking while Phee reached for her music pouch. When he finished, she said, "I brought some more music today. I've worked on these for about three years. They were two of my mom's favorites."

"I would like to hear them, *bitte*." He rose from the bench and Phee took his place. First, she played part of the Haydn, then the Debussy. When she finished "Clair du lune," he smiled. "You play with much emotion. You are thinking of your *Mutter, ja*?"

"How did you know?"

"I can hear it. Did you play these for her?"

"I did. When she got sick, she'd lie on the couch in the living room where our piano is, and I'd play for her whenever she asked me. She asked me a lot."

"My *Mutter* also prefers a house with music."

"Do you have brothers and sisters?"

"*Ja*, there is one brother, Erich, and one sister, Anika. They are younger."

"Are they musical, too?"

"Anika has studied the piano with *Mutter*. I believe my brother's talents . . . come from another place."

"Do you hear from them?"

"I do, but not . . . regular. It is sometimes difficult for letters from Deutschland to come to our camp."

"I have three brothers and one sister," Phee said.

"Such a grand family. And are you the eldest?"

She told him about her siblings and her grandparents and mentioned Jamie's deployment to North Africa and the UK but didn't say anything more in case she shouldn't. She wanted to ask about his father, but when she looked at her watch, she saw it was almost four thirty.

"Oh, look at the time. I'm sorry, I really should go. I have to be back at church for Luther League at six."

"Luther League? It is a religious group?"

"Yes, it's for the high school teenagers.

"*Ja*. We also have groups for the *Jugend*—the youth."

"We get together once a week during the school year, play games, sing, serve Easter breakfast, visit shut-ins, go caroling before Christmas, stuff like that."

"Caroling?"

"We walk to houses in the neighborhood and sing Christmas carols to people. It's lots of fun." She looked across the hall to Corporal Bickford and whispered, "Looks like he's asleep!"

The Sergeant walked to the edge of the stage and spoke in a full voice, "Corporal, we have completed our meeting."

Corporal Bickford sat up with a start, letting his book fall to the floor. "Yes, you have," he said as he reached for the book. "Sorry. I must've—"

"Thank you for staying with us today," Phee said.

"Certainly, any time. Shall I escort you to your car, ma'am?"

"Sure, that would be fine."

She turned to the Sergeant. "This was fun. Thank you for inviting me, Sergeant Ebinger."

"And I thank you for your assistance with my music, Fräulein Swensson. It was much help."

Taking a chance, she softly asked, "Do you think we could call each other by our first names?"

At first, Sergeant Ebinger seemed surprised at the suggestion, but then said, "*Ja*, we should do it. I am Horst and you are . . . Phee?"

"That's right, Phee, and I'd love to hear your piece with the new ending soon."

"I can do it, and I will make a good name for it."

"Sergeant," Corporal Bickford said as he got to the stage, "please stay here while I walk Miss Swensson to her car."

When they reached the lobby door, Phee turned to wave, then followed Corporal Bickford out to the parking lot. While she drove back to town, she hummed the melody of Horst's song, still fresh in her mind. Eventually, it would be in her heart, but she couldn't know that now.

12

TUESDAY 31 OCT. 1944

HALLOWEEN IN WARTIME ALGONA was different from pre-war years. The city fathers decreed that trick or treating from house to house would not take place. Kids were disappointed, as were many adults who enjoyed welcoming the cleverly costumed children onto their porches and into their living rooms. The ongoing sugar rationing meant handing out candy, fudge, and cookies to neighborhood youngsters wasn't possible again this year, so families found alternatives to the traditional holiday experience.

The twins and several classmates were invited to the Zetterholms' for a party tonight. Paul and his parents had gone all out to decorate the already-scary-enough basement in their home on North Jefferson. Over the weekend, they carved a dozen jack-o-lanterns, and courtesy of farmer Ted Ogren's nearby cornfield, there were dried corn stalks propped up in each corner and tied around each pillar. Harold supplied rolls of gauze so Edith could "spin" spider webs, and she and Paul cut spiders from black construction paper she'd saved over the years just for Halloween. But the *crème de la crème* was Skelly the Skeleton. Harold brought him home from his office earlier this afternoon. Paul was sure their party was the only one in town with a real live skeleton on display to scare and amaze. They hung Skelly in the farthest corner and placed a small lamp on the floor behind him, backlit for full effect.

Mollie was invited next door to the Coopers' for the third-grade girls' party hosted by Charlotte's mom and her sister who drove down from Burt. Frank offered to help the ladies with the party, and he and Mollie left the house at five thirty.

Since Frank and the three kids would be eating at their respective parties, Phee decided a peanut butter and jelly sandwich and a tall glass of milk would suffice for her supper. She practiced for an hour, did most of her homework, then started a letter to Jamie. She wanted to tell him about her new friend Horst. Settling on the couch with the V-Mail form and a book to write on, she began.

Dear Jamie, Happy Halloween! Nobody here is trick-or-treating tonight. They put the kibosh on it, again, because of rationing. Dad's at the Coopers' with Mollie (the angel, courtesy of St. Pete's), and Gus (the pirate) and Tris (the lion) are at Paul's. I got my practicing and homework out of the way (mostly). So, you know about the POW camp, about Dad's friend Ed Mattson, about my playing for the memorial service last month. What you don't know (unless Dad has told you) is that I've also been out to the camp to meet with one of the POWs. I know it might sound strange, but it's really not anything special. His name is Sgt. Ebinger and he leads the prisoner orchestra and dance band and chorus (he calls it the m annacore—sp?). He's also a very good pianist, and I guess that's how it all got started. Dad and I met him in August when Ed was showing us the camp theater. They'd just had a baby grand delivered and Sgt. Ebinger was trying it out (playing Beethoven, believe it or not) when we walked in. I got to play it too. So anyway, early last month, Ed called to ask if I'd be willing to spend an hour with the Sgt. at the theater. Long story short, I did, and I've met with him once more since then. Dad went along the first time and had a nice chat with Cpl. Phillips (Ed's assistant). The Sgt. was in a band, believe it or not (percussion), and was captured in '43 in N. Africa. Could he have been near you, do you think? Wouldn't that be something?! Anyhoo, I was a little nervous at first, but once we started talking about music, everything seemed OK. There's always a guard nearby so I feel safe. I volunteered to accompany the mannacore for their Xmas program. I'll go out again next Sunday to get the music for that. Just wanted you to know about all this. Running out of room—better wrap this up. Stay safe, and don't forget I love you oodles and gobs. Phee XOXO

Frank and Mollie walked in the front door at seven fifteen, and the twins were dropped off about ten minutes later.

"I wrote Jamie tonight," Phee said as Frank joined her in the kitchen. "Can you take it to the post office tomorrow?"

"Sure. Did you tell him about the kids' costumes?"

"I did. And I told him about Sergeant Ebinger."

"You did, eh?"

"Yeh, just about meeting with him, and that I'll accompany the chorus in December."

"You know they don't celebrate Halloween in Germany."

"I didn't know that. How was the party?"

Frank sighed. "Too many shrieking eight-year-old girls, I'm 'fraid."

"Yeh, no kidding. Think I'll go up and ask the kids about their parties."

On her way upstairs, Phee thought about Jamie, how proud of him she was, playing in The Army Band, bringing joy to people over there who really needed it. When he was first deployed, she worried about him almost constantly. After a while, though, she realized he probably wasn't in harm's way. Phee prayed for Jamie and all the soldiers and sailors and airmen almost every night because she figured they needed all the prayers they could get. And she also prayed for her new friend, Sergeant Ebinger—Horst. She was pretty sure he needed them, too.

13

SUNDAY 5 NOV. 1944

"*HALLO*, FRIEND PHEE," HORST said as he hurried to the stage from the lobby after greeting Corporal Bickford, once again the guard on duty. "I am sorry to be late." He carried a large envelope containing all the music Phee would need to learn for the *Männerchor* concerts next month, now on the camp calendar for the 21st and 22nd of December.

"Hello, friend Horst," Phee said from the piano bench. "You're not late; I'm early."

"There are small snowflakes in the air," he said as he joined her on stage. "It will help us remember *Weihnachten* while we look at our music."

"*Wei*...?"

"Christmas, of course."

"Oh, sure, I knew that," she fibbed. "I don't think it's supposed to snow much. We can get a lot of snow in November. How 'bout where you're from?"

"We do not see snow in Potsdam in this month or other months. It rains often and there are always clouds blocking the sun. I do like the sunshine here in our camp."

"So, your hometown is Potsdam?"

"*Ja*, I have lived there for all my life, until North Africa."

"Where is Potsdam?" she asked.

Horst reached into the envelope and pulled out a piece of manuscript paper and a pencil. "I will make a map." Phee walked around to stand next to him—not too close—while he drew a crude outline of Germany. "Here you can see Deutschland. You will know Berlin, I am sure."

"I know it's in Germany."

"It is . . . here, in the north, in the state of Brandenburg, and Potsdam is . . . here."

"So, it's southwest of Berlin?"

"*Ja*, it is not far, close for the bombs."

"Oh, gosh, is your family there?"

Horst tapped the pencil on the piano lid while he considered his family's fate. "My mother and sister are in Wittenberg with my father's sister. It is, perhaps, one hundred kilometers to the south and west . . . here. They are safe there. My mother wrote to say my brother has been drafted. He is only sixteen years old until the next spring."

"That seems awfully young."

"They will find young men and old men to fight until the end. It is not good."

Phee saw that Horst was distressed about his brother's predicament, so she changed the subject. "Can we look at the music you brought?"

He pulled out several pieces from the envelope and laid them on the piano. "Of course. I have everything now. *Doktor* Hill mailed it since the last week. So, we have Rheinberger, Wagner, Brahms—they are *Volkslieder*, folk songs, arranged by Herr Brahms—Schumann, Bruckner, and the carols you will know, *ja*?"

"I know a lot of carols, hopefully the ones you've chosen."

"You will accompany all the carols except "*Stille Nacht*." For that we will have a *Streichquartett* . . . string quartet."

"That'll be nice."

"And for my beloved Brahms . . ."

"Your beloved Brahms?"

"*Ja*, Herr Brahms, since I was a boy, learning to play the piano."

"I know he wrote symphonies, but I'm not familiar with them or his other works."

"You must listen!" Horst was serious; Phee was surprised.

"Okay, I'll see if I can—"

"And I should make it for you . . . an assignment, for our next meeting, to listen to Johannes Brahms' First Symphony, and if you have a longer time, his Second."

"You're giving me homework?" Phee asked, trying her best not to laugh.

"It will help you to be a better accompanist."

"Can it wait till after my recital?" she asked, doubtful a dose of Brahms symphonies would improve her accompanying skills.

He hesitated, clearly wanting to say "*nein,*" but instead, he said, "*ja,* but you will not come for a rehearsal before listening."

"If you insist. What else will I play besides the carols?"

They looked at all the pieces the *Männerchor* would perform next month. Even though half would be *a cappella*, Horst wanted Phee to be familiar with everything so she could play along at the rehearsals.

Just as they finished their conversation about the December concerts, Phee realized they'd been alone in the hall the entire hour. "I thought Corporal Bickford would come in after you arrived," she said. "Do you think he's asleep again?"

"Perhaps we should make his name . . . Sleepy Bickford," Horst suggested.

"I like that," she whispered. "It'll be our secret."

"And when you see Corporal Phillips, you can say I was a gentleman today. He would want to know it. You can make a call to his secret number."

Phee chuckled. "I might just do that."

"We should make an appointment for our first rehearsal with the *Männerchor*. If we can agree with the time, it will be official with the calendar."

"I think the first Sunday in December should work," Phee said as she began to gather up the music. "It's a week after I play my recital here."

"Very well," he said, "it will be here on the stage at . . . fourteen hundred . . . for you, two o'clock. I will ask Corporal Phillips to contact you when it is arranged."

"I'd appreciate it. Thanks."

"And now, Corporal Sleepy can walk with us to the car."

When they got to the lobby, they found Corporal Bickford resting his eyes while leaning back in his chair.

"Corporal, we have finished our meeting," Horst said.

The Corporal opened his eyes, smiled, and stood. "Fine, fine. I'll walk you out."

On the way to the car, Horst asked Phee about her recital preparations. She explained that she would practice every day at St. Pete's the week before the recital, then the day before, she'd perform everything for her teacher. She also told him about singing "That Moment in Rio," the piece she played the day they met in August.

"I would like very much to hear it," Horst said as they got to the car. "It is . . . how you say . . . in the works for some of us to attend."

"Oh, I hope you can. I'll ask Dad to say something to Chaplain Mattson. They kind of owe me since I played for the memorial service in September."

"I believe you can be . . . *überzeugend* . . . persuasive.

Phee opened the car door and tossed her music pouch on the seat. "Thank you, Horst. Guess I'll see you in a few weeks."

While "Sleepy" Bickford turned his back and lit a cigarette, Horst reached for Phee's mitten-covered hand, pulled it to his lips, and gently kissed it. She was quite surprised and didn't know how to react, so she didn't.

"Auf Wiedersehen, friend Phee."

"Auf Wiedersehen, friend Horst."

Phee stopped at the gatehouse to turn in the visitor pass, then drove away while singing "That Moment in Rio" at the top of her lungs. Singing her song made her happy and knowing her friend Horst might get to hear her recital later this month made her even happier. She was confident Ed would approve the request because—*he does owe me.*

14

MONDAY 13 NOV. 1944

THIS AFTERNOON WAS PHEE's final piano lesson before her recital. Earlier, when Edith arrived at St. Pete's, she moved the piano to the center of the chancel area, in "concert position." The ebony five-foot-eight Baldwin baby grand was a magnificent instrument, one of the nicest pianos in town. It was a gift to the church from the Johnson family in memory of their parents and grandparents. The Johnsons claimed the piano once belonged to Herbert Hoover's cousin's wife's brother. There was no provenance, so there was room for doubt. But Phee was grateful to have such a fine instrument at her disposal.

Phee went straight to church from school and was almost late. She came in through the back of the sanctuary, breathless. "So sorry! Glee Club ran late. I tried to sneak out."

Sitting on the organ bench, Edith had just finished practicing the piece she'd play for next Sunday's prelude. "You're not late," she said, turning off the organ and pulling the cover down over the keyboards. "Have a seat and catch your breath. I have something for you."

Phee tossed her music pouch on the front pew and plopped down next to it without removing her coat or scarf or mittens. She laid her head on the back of the pew and closed her eyes. "I'm so tired," she moaned.

"Can't Dad call the school office to tell them I'm sick this week? I've never done it, not once in all these years. Maybe Thursday, Friday?"

Edith smiled. "I doubt your dad would fall for it. Let's figure out a way for you to get more sleep this week. We could have the boys and Mollie over to our house after school, maybe stay overnight on Friday or Saturday or both. I'll talk to Frank." She reached for a large box leaning against a nearby chair, walked down the steps, and sat next to Phee. "Here, I found something for you. We'll call it a senior recital gift."

Phee sat up, removed her mittens, then her scarf and coat. "Gosh, Mrs. Z, you didn't have to do that."

"I know, but I really wanted to. I hope you like it."

Phee noted it was a Younkers box. She removed the lid, peeked under the white tissue paper, and gasped. Slowly, she stood while lifting a stunning royal blue velvet formal dress from the box. It was the most beautiful dress she'd ever seen. And then, she began to cry. It had been a while, and she had a good one.

Edith took the dress, laid it gently on the pew, and gathered Phee in her arms. She let her cry for a while without saying a word. There were tears in her eyes, too.

Finally, when Phee could talk, she pulled away and said, "It's so beautiful. Where did you find it?"

Edith pulled a handkerchief from her skirt pocket. "In Des Moines," she said as she dabbed her eyes. "You might remember Harold and I went down in August for a conference at Iowa Lutheran, just for overnight. I had plenty of free time, so I went shopping.

"At Younkers?"

Edith nodded. "I didn't intend to find a dress, but I ended up walking through the formal department and I saw this one on a mannequin, or one just like it. I could see you wearing it." Phee reached for the dress and held it up so she could have a look. "Oh yes, definitely."

"Looks like it'll fit just fine," Phee said. "I'll try it on as soon as I get home. I won't show it to anyone till Sunday. Does Dad know?"

"He does. I wanted him to know in case he had plans of his own."

Phee chuckled. "I'm pretty sure Dad wouldn't have thought about this. He'd find something else, like . . . a ukulele. Definitely not a dress."

"He was very appreciative, said it's something your mom would have done."

"Yeh," Phee said with a sigh, "she could've made this. I was going to wear Mom's favorite dress on Sunday. I'm sure she'd like this one a lot better."

"There's something else in the box."

Phee removed all the tissue paper, finding a package of Hanes nylons underneath. "Nylons! Where did you find these?"

"I've been holding onto them for a while, and I found them in a drawer last week. That dress deserves real nylons."

"Oh, yes, it does, but—"

"No buts. I'm more than happy to donate them to a worthy cause."

"Oh, Mrs. Z, you are too good to me," Phee said as she hugged her teacher once again.

"I'm not, but thank you for saying so. Now, let's put it back in the box and get down to business."

It took Phee almost an hour to play through all the pieces on her program. They ran through "That Moment in Rio" while Edith played and Phee sang. Overall, the teacher was pleased with her student's concentration and determination. The earlier emotional event seemed to have cleared Phee's head.

When they finished, Edith said, "Phee, I'm satisfied with where you are today. If you can stay focused the rest of this week, you'll come in here for the dress rehearsal and sail through everything."

"Hope you're right. I'm feeling pretty good about everything. I'll practice in here every day this week. Dad said he'd keep the heat on for me."

"Sounds good. Now, I want you to try to relax, get enough sleep, eat well, spend as much time as you can on your own. You're going to do just fine next weekend."

"And the weekend after," Phee said, reminding Edith of her performance at Camp Algona the following Sunday.

"Absolutely. Now, let's get you home. Try on the dress tonight and let me know how it fits."

Edith turned off the sanctuary lights, they grabbed their coats, and walked up the aisle to the narthex. When they opened the heavy red door, they stepped outside into a swirl of snowflakes.

"Oh, look!" Phee shouted. "Goody goody!

Edith groaned. "Oh phooey, not what I wanted to see tonight."

"Well, I love it!"

"Lucky you. Get on home now."

"I'll let you know about the dress, and thanks again."

"You're welcome, dear."

With her music pouch slung over her shoulder and the box holding the beautiful dress under her arm, Phee walked quickly to the parsonage, whistling "Winter Wonderland" as the white stuff began to stick to the withered grass. So far, the street and sidewalks and church parking lot were just wet. If it kept up overnight, someone who was not Phee would be shoveling in the morning.

Phee decided the dress from Mrs. Z would be her "good luck charm." She'd need to keep it clean so she could wear it at Camp Algona on the twenty-sixth. She must remember to ask her dad if he'd talk to Ed about allowing the POWs to attend her recital. Not all of them, obviously, just a select few, including her friend Horst.

But first, she would play her recital in the sanctuary at St. Peter's Lutheran Church at four o'clock next Sunday afternoon. She would look beautiful, but more importantly, her performance would be beautiful, too. Tonight, she was more confident than ever.

15

SUNDAY 19 NOV. 1944 - PART 1

IT WAS UNUSUALLY QUIET in the parsonage this morning. The twins and Mollie had stayed overnight at the Zetterholms', and Harold had dropped them off at home after breakfast so they could get dressed for church. Frank instructed them to remain silent unless it was an emergency and then only whispers should be uttered. They all walked quietly out the front door at nine thirty. As far as they knew, Phee was still asleep upstairs.

But she wasn't. She heard the door close and hoped she could drift back to sleep. No such luck. Her attempts to not think about her recital were in vain. First of all, her beautiful new dress hung mere feet from where she lay. It had been there since last Monday evening when she tried it on, found it to be a perfect fit, and decided she just had to show it to everyone.

The second reason she couldn't stop thinking about her recital was because the music was so much a part of her now. Every day for months, either through her fingers touching piano keys or the residual sounds remaining in her head after the touching had ended for the day, she felt and heard Beethoven, Grieg, MacDowell, Mendelssohn, and Swensson. She wondered if the music would ever leave her. Today it seemed impossible, but perhaps, eventually, it would fade like the fading of her grief after her mom died. She was so sure that could never happen, but it did.

When she got to the bathroom, she turned on the bath water and wrapped her head in a towel so her hair, which she'd washed yesterday, stayed dry. She didn't always want a bubble bath, but this morning she did. She leaned back in the tub, letting her arms float, slowly wiggling her fingers, praying those fingers would land where she needed them to land later today.

Toast and jam, along with a generous bowl of hot oatmeal, sounded good to Phee this morning. She turned on the radio to catch the news at the top of the hour. It was pretty much all war news again since the election was over.

While she sat at the kitchen table, the phone rang. She took another bite of toast and walked to the phone in the front hall. "Hello," she said with a toasty voice, "Swensson residence."

"Phee? It's Nannie. Bee and I thought you'd be home this morning."

Nancy and Elmer Nelson, Phee's grandparents, lived in Spirit Lake, about sixty-five miles north and west of Algona near the Minnesota border. They owned Bee's Bungalows, a small summer resort on nearby West Lake Okoboji. Bee got his nickname after being stung by five bees one summer afternoon when he was a young boy. For years, the Swenssons spent three or four days around the fourth of July at Bee's Bungalows, celebrating not only the Independence Day holiday, but also the twins' birthday which fell on the fourth. The Swenssons and the Nelsons were very close, possibly more so since Mary died.

"Hi, Nannie! Yeh, Dad gave me the morning off. I'm just having breakfast."

"Oh, well, I don't want to keep you."

"I'm almost done. Hope you're not calling to say you can't come today."

"Oh, no, we'll be there at three thirty. That's our plan, anyway. I'm calling to let you know we're bringing some folks along."

"Great! Do I know them?"

"No, it's Helen Engstrom and her daughter Claire. She's Mollie's age, I think. Helen's a member of our church."

Phee remembered her conversation with Bee at the lake last summer when he mentioned a woman whose husband had been killed at Pearl Harbor. Might that woman be Helen? Bee thought she and Frank might hit it off. "I'm glad you'll have company. Hope you can stay for the reception."

"We plan to. Are you doing alright, dear?"

"I'm pretty relaxed now but ask me again in four or five hours."

"I've been praying for you all week, Phee. I'm so proud of you, I could just burst."

"Thanks, Nannie, that means a lot. I'm so glad you're coming."

"Now, you get back to your breakfast. We can talk after the recital."

"Can't wait! 'Bye!"

Phee returned to the kitchen table and finished her now lukewarm oatmeal. Yesterday, Edith told Phee to spend no more than thirty minutes warming up today. She decided to do that now, before everyone got home.

AT TWO O'CLOCK, THERE was a knock at the front door.

"I'll get it!" Mollie yelled, running from the kitchen where she and Gus were playing crazy eights. She opened the door to find a smiling Christa holding a small suitcase.

"Hi, Moll!"

"Hi, Christa! Phee's upstairs gettin' ready."

"She won't be ready till I've worked my magic."

"Your magic?"

"Yep, you'll just have to wait and see."

Christa hurried past Mollie and bounded up the stairs and around to Phee's closed bedroom door. She knocked three times.

"Who is it?" Phee asked timidly.

"It's your personal dresser slash stylist slash makeup assistant. Open up!"

Phee opened the door. "Get in here!" She grabbed Christa's arm and pulled her into the room. "My hair's a disaster!" she cried as she slammed the door shut. "It won't stay up. What am I gonna do!?"

"Calm down," Christa said, tossing the suitcase and her coat on the bed. "Sit—let me see."

Wearing her bathrobe and slippers, Phee sat on the small bench at her dressing table, looked in the mirror, and began to cry. "Oh God, Christa. I need to be at church in an hour and look at me!" She buried her face in her hands and moaned.

"Stop!" Christa said. "Sit up. Let me see what you've done."

Phee sat up straight with her hands in her lap. Christa lightly touched her hair, then walked around to the other side and back again, pondering the disastrous hair situation.

"Yeh, I see what you mean. I guess there's no hope."

Phee was startled. "Really?!"

Christa punched her shoulder. "I'm kidding! Now, come on. Who's better with hair than me, you know, who doesn't do it for a living?"

"Nobody's better than Christa," Phee mumbled.

"Right, nobody. Now, what are you trying to do?"

"I want it up, close to my head so it doesn't bounce all over the place while I'm playing. A bun, I suppose, or a braid or two braids. What do you think?"

"Braids are good. Let me see what I can do." Christa gave Phee's longish auburn hair a thorough brushing. "Get ready to hand me bobby pins when I ask for 'em."

It took Christa almost fifteen minutes to salvage Phee's hair. "Where's your hand mirror?" she asked as she stuck the last bobby pin in place.

"It's in the bathroom next to the sink."

"I'll get it, you stay put." When Christa returned with the mirror, she said, "Here, turn around. Whadaya think?"

With mirror in hand, Phee swiveled around on the bench to have a look. "Uh-huh . . . uh-huh . . . hmmm . . ."

"Well!?"

She stood, grabbed her friend, and shouted, "It's perfect! I love it!"

"Whew! What a relief!"

"I could never have done it myself, not in a million years!"

"Obviously. Now, time for some makeup—rouge, powder, lipstick, the whole shebang."

"You don't think a little lipstick is enough?"

"Not today, my dear girl. This is the biggest day of your life . . . so far. You're already gorgeous, but we can enhance it a bit." Once more, Christa worked her magic. Phee liked the result and hoped her dad wouldn't think it was too much.

"So," Christa said, looking around the room. "Where's that dress I've been hearing about all week?"

"I'll get it. Close your eyes." Phee grabbed the dress from the closet. "Open!"

"Holy cow, you're right! It's gorgeous! Are you ready to put it on?"

"Let me get my shoes. Dad shined 'em for me last night. They look almost new, don't they?"

"They sure do. Better put 'em on first." Christa helped get the dress over Phee's head, then zipped it up in the back. She stepped back to assess. "I think you're all set."

"Oh wait, I forgot earrings." Phee sat once again at the dressing table. "Dad gave these opals to Mom for their tenth wedding anniversary."

"They're perfect."

"Oh, Christa, you are the absolute *best* best friend in the entire world. I can't thank you enough. You saved my life today."

"Oh, I wouldn't go that far. I saved your hair, certainly, but hardly your life."

They both laughed while Phee gave Christa a hug and sent her on her way. Before she went downstairs, she took one last look in the full-length mirror on her closet door. Satisfied with her reflection, she gave herself a wink, then walked to the landing while softly humming "That Moment in Rio." She was ready.

16

SUNDAY 19 NOV. 1944 - PART 2

Just before three o'clock, the twins and Mollie escorted Phee across the parking lot to the church. Frank's office, just inside the back door, was serving as the "green room" for the recital. The Zetterholms arrived with a box containing two hundred programs Harold had printed at Jensen's Printing in Fort Dodge. If there were any left over, they'd be handed out at Camp Algona next Sunday.

"Phee, how lovely you look," Harold said as he stuck his head in the office.

"Thanks. Do you have the programs?"

"I do. Where would you like them?"

"In the narthex, please. The twins will hand them out."

"I'll take them back there now. Boys, I'll put the box on the balcony steps."

"Can I have one?" Mollie asked. "I want Phee's autograph."

"Oh, my," Phee said, "aren't I special?"

"You most certainly are," Frank said as he opened his desk drawer. "Here's a pencil."

"Phee, when you're done with that, we should go in," Edith said.

When they got to the sanctuary, they walked all around it, just to get a feel for the space. Phee even walked up to the balcony, hoping some of the guests would choose to sit up there. They met back at the piano, which had been tuned after yesterday's dress rehearsal, and decided it wasn't quite in the right position. They moved it about twelve inches to the west. Phee sat on the bench while Edith opened the lid.

"How does it feel, the dress, I mean?" Edith asked.

Stretching her arms out to her sides and over her head, she nodded affirmatively. "Feels great."

"The pedals? No interference?"

Phee placed both her feet on the piano's pedals. "It's good, no problems." She glanced at the altar where the two fall-colored floral arrangements from this morning's service remained on either side of the gold cross. Off to the side was a single red rose in a bud vase. "Who brought the rose?" she asked.

"I thought Frank would have told you. He asked me to put it up there after church this morning. It's for your mom."

Phee walked to the altar, took the bud vase in her hands, and smelled the rose. "I love this. Bless his heart."

"Why don't you go ahead and play a few scales, but don't overdo."

When they returned to Frank's office, Phee gave her dad a hug. "Thanks for the rose," she whispered in his ear.

"You're welcome," he whispered back.

"Phee, I'll come get you when it's time," Edith said. "Just stay here and relax if you can."

"I'll try. Thanks, Mrs. Z."

After Edith left, Frank reached into his desk drawer and pulled out several pieces of paper. "I think now's a good time for you to see these," he said. "Have a seat."

"Telegrams?" Phee said when she saw the familiar yellow and brown Western Union papers.

"Yeh, they were all sent here this week. Would you like me to read them?"

"Sure," she said, sitting in one of the chairs next to Frank's desk.

The first one was from Christa's brother Danny—very sweet. The second one was from Jamie—even sweeter. The third was from Frank's sister Mabel in Kentucky, and the fourth from Mary's sister Millie in

Minnesota. The last one was from Corporal Roy Phillips and Sergeant Horst Ebinger.

"Dad, wait, let me see that one." Phee was more surprised, and pleased, than she let on. He handed her the telegram and she read it aloud. "'To Fräulein P. Swensson; stop; Congratulations for a successful piano concert at Saint Peter on Sunday; stop; we hope the music flows easily from your fingers; stop; save some for Camp Algona in one week; stop; best wishes from Cpl Phillips and Sgt Ebinger; stop.'" Phee looked at her dad. "Well, isn't that nice?"

"It is, very nice. Better go check on the kids. I won't come back, so I guess this is it." Frank hugged his daughter and wished her well. "My dearest Phyllis Anne, I'm so very proud of you. I hope you know that."

"I do, Dad."

"So's your mom."

"I know."

"Good luck, babe. Love you so much."

"Thanks, Dad. Love you, too."

Phee glanced at the clock on the wall. It was five minutes till four. She looked at the telegrams laying on Frank's desk and picked up the one from the Corporal and the Sergeant. She read it again, then once more, and smiled.

PHEE STOOD ALONE NEAR the door leading into the sanctuary. She didn't peek inside because she didn't want to see the size of the crowd until she was at the piano, ready to play. Edith gave her introductory remarks, welcoming everyone to the recital, telling them a little bit about Phee's musical journey, and inviting them to the reception in the fellowship hall. When she finished, the audience applauded vigorously as she walked to the door where Phee waited.

"Okay Phee, you're on."

Phee took a deep breath and walked quickly to the piano as the applause continued. She turned towards the audience and bowed. *Good grief, it's almost full!* She turned, sat, and waited for the applause to fade away. It took a few seconds, then, except for an occasional cough, it was very quiet in the sanctuary. Phee's hands were in her lap, palms down, fingers spread. She closed her eyes, bowed her head slightly, and prayed *Dear God, help me make beautiful music. Amen.*

She raised her hands to the keyboard, positioned her right foot on the damper pedal, glanced at the rose on the altar, returned her gaze to the black and white keys, and began.

THERE WERE SIX PIECES on the first half of the program, but they were all short, so even with the applause and bows after each one, Phee was back in Frank's office thirty minutes after she played the first notes. Before long, Edith joined her.

"It's going very well, Phee. I'm awfully pleased with the turnout. Harold said they ran out of programs, but right at the end so I don't think anyone had to go without."

"We'll need to have more made for next Sunday."

"Don't worry, we'll take care of it."

Phee walked to the window behind Frank's desk and looked out to the neighbor's yard. "I started feeling a little anxious after the Grieg. And then I imagined Mom sitting in the front pew, smiling at me and nodding and saying, 'You're doing great, Phee. Keep it up.' I could just hear her. And then I was calm, not a bit anxious."

"I'm glad," Edith said. "I had a feeling she'd be here today." She looked at her watch. "I should probably get back out there. I'll see you on stage for 'Rio.'"

Phee followed her teacher back to the sanctuary door. Before she walked through, she glanced at the front pew. *Yep, Mom's still there. Good!*

WHEN PHEE FINISHED THE Beethoven, the audience rewarded her with a standing ovation. Some shouted and a few whistled—in church, for

Pete's sake! Phee returned to the piano for a third bow, then motioned for Edith to join her. It was time for the encore.

Before they began, Phee thanked everyone for coming and for their support. She singled out her dad, her siblings, and her grandparents. And she thanked Mrs. Edith Zetterholm who, she said, had to be the best piano teacher in the entire universe.

"Some of you might be wondering about the red rose on the altar. It's in memory of my mom, Mary Swensson. Mom insisted I start piano lessons when I was seven. I was reluctant, to say the least, but I didn't have a choice. She made sure I practiced all the time, or almost. Mom knew I'd eventually fall in love with the piano, and she was right. I can't imagine my life without it. It's a gift from God, and I'm pleased I was able to share that gift with all of you today." After more enthusiastic applause, Phee concluded. "So now, Mrs. Zetterholm and I will perform one more of my songs. I call it 'That Moment in Rio.' It's a Latin song, a love song, I guess. It's short, but it repeats. Feel free to join me the second time through."

NOT EVERYONE STAYED FOR the reception, and it was a good thing. The fellowship hall was crowded, and they ran out of cookies and punch before everyone got served. Phee and Edith stood near the bottom of the stairs, greeting everyone who came down.

"Looks like we've seen the end of the line," Edith said.

"Thank goodness," Phee said under her breath, "I've been smiling so much my cheeks hurt!"

Edith offered some advice. "When you get home, eat a little something, then take a long hot bath and go right to bed. Try to relax and soak it all in. We won't have a lesson tomorrow unless you want to meet, just to talk."

"Let's not," Phee decided. "I could use the break."

"Okay, good; no Phee lesson on Monday."

"I'd better spend some time with Bee and Nannie before they have to drive back. If I don't see you before you leave . . ."

"Go take some time with your family."

Phee hugged her teacher, then strolled through the tables to the far side of the room where Frank and the kids were sitting with Bee and Nannie and their guests from Spirit Lake. Helen Engstrom and her daughter Claire sat across from Frank and Mollie. In the center of the table between them was a plate of cookies. "Are those for me?" Phee asked as she placed her hands on her dad's shoulders. He reached for her hand and kissed it.

"They most certainly are," Nannie answered. "We grabbed extras because we knew they'd run out. The punch was gone by the time we got to it. Want some coffee?"

"No thanks, I'll get some water from the kitchen."

"I'll get it!" Mollie volunteered. "You can sit in my chair."

"Thanks, Sweet Pea. So, Claire, are you in third grade this year, too?" Phee asked as she sampled one of the cookies.

Claire nodded.

"Claire," Helen said, "can you tell Miss Swensson about your teacher?"

Claire's face lit up. "Miss Nolen. She's new this year. She's really nice. She's from Sioux Falls."

Returning from the nearby kitchen with water for Phee, Mollie said, "My teacher's new too! Her name's Miss Gregory. I like her a lot."

"Sweet Pea, why don't you show Claire your Sunday School room," Frank suggested, "if it's alright with her mom."

"Sure, that would be fine," Helen said, looking at her watch. "Bee, we should probably be on the road in half an hour or so."

"That's fine with me," he replied.

Phee wanted to say "hi" to people, so she excused herself and wandered around the room with her water glass in hand. As she moved from table to table, she kept an eye on her dad and Helen, hoping everything remained copacetic.

Just before six thirty, Bee, Nannie and Helen stood, and Frank told Gus to fetch the girls from the classroom. They all moved through the tables to the front staircase and Phee joined them, grabbing Nannie's hand as they walked up the steps.

"Well, Nannie, looks like I survived the big day."

"You most certainly did, dear. We're so proud of you."

"And I get to do it again next weekend!"

"Heavens! I can't imagine going through this twice."

They stopped at the cloak room off the narthex, then hugs, kisses, handshakes, and goodbyes were shared. Phee noted Frank's and Helen's handshake took a bit longer than everyone else's. And there was laughter; laughter was good.

Phee and Frank and the kids stopped in Frank's office to get their coats.

"I think I'll go downstairs to thank the ladies," Phee said. "See you back at the house."

"Sounds good," Frank said. "Will you want something to eat?"

"Yeh, I probably should, just a quick sandwich would do."

"I'll get something going. You don't need to worry about supper tonight. Oh, and I'll get the rose from the altar."

"Thanks, Dad. Glad you remembered. See you in a bit."

Phee returned to the fellowship hall and found the ladies clearing tables and washing dishes. She hugged them all before climbing back up to Frank's office to get her coat. The telegrams were still on the desk, so she grabbed them before turning out the light. On the way home, she felt relieved and elated and exhausted. She wondered what it would be like next Sunday at Camp Algona. Would Horst be there? She really hoped he would.

Thurs. Nov. 23, 1944 Thanksgiving Day

—Dear Daisy—

What a great day! As usual, I ate too much so I'm feeling a little groggy tonight. We stopped at the cemetery to wish Mom a Happy Thanksgiving before we drove down to Christa's. Everything was delish! We used Jack's parents' Danish dishes—so pretty! Dad used "fervent" in his blessing so we decided that would be our Word of the Day. Conversation around the table was lively as usual. We talked about Danny and Jamie (of course), football (of course), and places the kids hope to travel to someday (baseball fields in Chicago and St. Louis for the boys and Niagara Falls for Sweet Pea). Peggy asked me about my recital out at the camp on Sunday which you know I've been thinking about almost constantly this week. Christa and Mollie broke the wishbone before we left (Mollie got her wish, supposedly) and Peggy gave us a plate of leftover turkey to bring home. Love those turkey sandwiches! When we got home, the kids and I went for a walk while Dad napped (of course). It was cold but sunny—invigorating!

And life goes on. G'night.

17

SUNDAY 26 NOV. 1944

EARLY LAST WEEK, FRANK decided the children didn't need to hear Phee's recital a second time. There was no argument from the twins, and Mollie said if she couldn't see the horses, she didn't care about going back to Camp Algona. The kids were spending the afternoon next door at the Coopers' while Frank and Phee were at the camp.

"Frank, I hope you'll let me drive today," Edith offered as she stepped inside the front door. "My car's almost warmed up."

"Can't think why I shouldn't," Frank replied as he walked to the staircase and called up. "Phee! Edith's here. Time to go. Hup-hup!"

"Be right down!"

For the second time, Phee wore her lucky velvet dress, and once again, Christa came by to help with her hair and makeup. It was Phee's choice to wear her hair down today, and Christa found a way to involve braids again. Both Frank and Edith approved.

"Phee, you look lovely," Edith said as Phee reached the bottom step. "I think I like your hair down even better."

"And I think you're beautiful either way," Frank said. "You'd be beautiful with no hair at all."

"Very funny," Phee said as he helped her with her coat. "I'm so glad Christa could help me again today."

"She did a splendid job," Edith said. "Make sure she's on your thank you list."

"Right at the top."

When they arrived at the camp's gatehouse, Edith explained the reason for their visit to an unfamiliar MP and was handed the required visitor pass. It was two twenty when the gate was opened for them. The recital would begin in forty minutes.

After Edith parked the car, they entered the lobby where they saw orderlies preparing for the reception. White linen cloths covered a long table where four large trays with a variety of cookies were placed near a lovely floral centerpiece. Another smaller table was nearby, with two large coffee urns set on either side.

As she hung her coat on the nearby rack, Edith commented, "This looks nice. They must expect a big crowd."

"How many programs do we have?" Phee asked.

"Harold had Jensen's print a hundred more this week."

"Folks will have to share," Frank said as he opened the door into the hall. "They've got way more than a hundred chairs set up in here."

"I'd better get warmed up," Phee said.

"We'll wait out here for Ed," Frank said. "Might steal a cookie if I can."

An orderly looked up and smiled at Frank. "Help yourself, sir. I won't say a word."

Inside the hall, Phee noticed the back two rows of chairs had been cordoned off with RESERVED signs. She was curious, but her focus was on the piano and the beautiful floral arrangements that were placed on both sides of the stage near the steps. She took a seat on the piano bench. When she finished her D minor three-octave scale, Ed, Frank, and Edith came in from the lobby.

"Phee, you look lovely!" Ed said as he walked down the center aisle. "Do you need more time, or can we open the doors?"

"You can open."

"I should fill you in on what to expect at three o'clock. We've got a group of prisoners coming. They'll be seated in the back two rows. I hope that's alright."

Goody! "Sure! The more the merrier."

"You and I will take a seat on the front row. I'll go up first to say a few words. Shouldn't take more than a couple minutes, then it's all you. How'd the piano sound? We had it tuned yesterday."

"It sounds fine. Thanks, Ed."

"Think I'll go find a seat," Frank said. "Knock 'em dead, kiddo."

"Thanks, Dad. I'll try."

"WELCOME TO THE CAMP Algona theater," Ed began, speaking loudly from center stage. The POWs had just finished filing in. Not wanting to know if Horst was among them, Phee didn't turn to look. "My name is Captain Edward Mattson, and I'm the American Chaplain here at Camp Algona. We're glad you're here, and a special welcome to our visitors from Algona. You're in for quite a treat today."

Edith reached for Phee's hand and gave it a gentle squeeze.

"You may be wondering how today's recital came about," he continued. "As some of you know, Miss Swensson's father, Frank, is the pastor at St. Peter's Lutheran Church here in Algona. Frank and I became close friends at Augustana Seminary back in . . . well, more than a few years ago.

"My wife Ellen and I spent a lot of our free time with Frank and his wife Mary when we lived in the same apartment building in Rock Island. After graduation, we went our separate ways. Frank and Mary stayed in the Midwest, and Ellen and I found ourselves in Pennsylvania. Eventually, we moved to Delaware with our two daughters while Frank and Mary and their family moved here.

"After Pearl Harbor, I knew the army would be looking for chaplains. When I found out they were building a prisoner of war camp here, I jumped through a few hoops and was assigned to Camp Algona. This past August I heard Phee, who's a senior at Algona High, playing our piano here on stage and was quite impressed. I asked her if she could take time out from her studies to play for us. Obviously, she said yes. Ladies and gentlemen, please welcome Miss Phee Swensson to the stage."

The hall was well over half full and there was enthusiastic applause. Phee, smiling broadly, walked up the steps, shook Ed's hand, turned, bowed, and sat. She didn't look for anyone in particular. Now was not the time for distraction. Now was the time for Grieg.

AT INTERMISSION, PHEE RETURNED to her seat next to her teacher. "Do you think I should explain about 'Rio' before we do it?" she asked.

"Certainly, just like last week."

Just then, Corporal Phillips walked up and extended his hand. "Miss Swensson, brah-vo!"

"Hello, Corporal, I'm so glad you're here. Mrs. Zetterholm, this is Corporal Roy Phillips from . . . I'm sorry, I don't know where you're from."

"I'm from Idaho, born and raised. How do you do, ma'am?"

Edith stood to shake his hand. "It's very nice to meet you. I'm Phee's piano teacher."

"Corporal Phillips is Chaplain Mattson's assistant," Phee explained. "We met here in the theater last summer."

"How long have you been here?" Edith asked.

"I arrived back in June, about a week after the Chaplain."

"Well, I hope you're enjoying your time here. Now, if you'll excuse me, I'd like to find a glass of water. Phee, would you like one, too?"

"Half a glass would be fine. Thanks."

As Edith headed to the lobby, Corporal Phillips leaned towards Phee. "Sergeant Ebinger's here. He'd like to speak with you if you can spare a minute."

Phee turned to look at the prisoners. She saw Horst sitting in the back row next to a guard.

"Sure, I guess I can." She followed the Corporal back along the side aisle. As they approached the Sergeant, he stood and offered his hand.

"Fräulein Swensson, I am pleased you can hear my compliments for your performance."

"Thank you," she said, smiling broadly. "I'm glad you're here."

"You play with much feeling and emotion. I enjoyed your compositions. We should look at them together at another time, perhaps."

"Perhaps."

"And you will have your first rehearsal with the *Männerchor* in one week, *ja*?"

"Yes, it's on my calendar. Two o'clock, a week from today."

"*Wunderbar!*" he said with a wink.

"I'm sorry, I really need to get back."

Horst stood erect, then, with a soft click of his heels, bowed his head briefly.

Phee began to walk away, then turned back when she remembered to say, "Oh, and thank you both for the telegram. It was such a nice surprise."

Edith returned with the water. Phee took a quick gulp, then climbed the stairs to the stage for the second time and enjoyed the applause. As she came up from her bow, she saw Horst's smiling face and was encouraged to play Beethoven in a way that would please him.

Wed. Dec. 20, 1944

—Dear Daisy—

I'm beat! It was a long day with school, and then the Männerchor dress rehearsal was after supper. Last night I told you we heard on the radio that the Germans had started a counter-offensive (I think that's it) somewhere in Belgium. We talked about it at school today and some kids were saying it doesn't look good for the Allies. Here we all thought the war would be over soon, and now it looks like that might not be the case. I asked Dad when I got home from school if he thought they might cancel the four concerts at the camp because of all this. He thought they should go on as planned, and they will, thank God. Before the rehearsal began tonight, Horst came over to tell me that they (the POWs) knew what was happening in Belgium, at least enough to say the war was over for their side. He said they all felt it was Hitler's "last act of desperation" (he really did say that) and the Allies still had the upper hand. He didn't want me to worry about it. Isn't that nice? I was relieved to know the POWs weren't hanging on to some hope for victory, at least it seems the members of Horst's groups aren't. Oh, war is horrible! Guess I haven't said that for a while. Horst didn't mention his brother, but I'm sure he's worried about him. The rehearsal didn't last too long, about an hour. We're ready. Horst seemed satisfied at any rate. On the way out of the theater, I stopped to look at the nativity scene they've put up on a table in the lobby. Some of the prisoners carved and painted it and there's a beautiful backdrop behind it. It's so lovely. I wish we could display it at church.

And life goes on. G'night.

18

FRIDAY 22 DEC. 1944

"MOLLIE SERENA, GET YOUR butt down here! We need to leave *now*!"

Phee was at her wit's end. It was ten past five—she was supposed to be sitting at the piano on the camp theater stage at five thirty— and her sister was still upstairs getting ready. At the supper table earlier, Mollie said she couldn't decide what dress to wear to the concert. Gus said, "wear what you've got on"; Tris said, "nobody cares"; Frank said, "just so you wear *something*"; and Phee said, "you'll look beautiful no matter what you wear."

Phee ran up the steps two at a time, and when she got to Mollie's bedroom door, she saw that her sister had narrowed her choice to two dresses—the brown one with the lace collar and the blue and gray plaid one. Both were lying on her unmade bed, side by side. Phee took a deep breath and spoke in the calmest voice she could manage, "Mollie, please, I can't be late. We need to leave right away. Let me decide for you."

Sitting in a chair across the room, Mollie sighed. "Okay . . . I guess."

Phee walked over to the bed, grabbed the plaid dress, and tossed it to her sister. "Here, it's perfect, you'll be the belle of the ball. If I were you, I'd wear your blue sweater too. You'll need it."

"I'm sorry, Phee. I just couldn't decide."

Phee looked at her sister with a deep sense of sadness. Their mom should be here, helping Mollie choose what dress to wear. "It's fine, Sweet Pea. Just hurry as fast as you can. Dad and the boys are already in the car."

It took Mollie about two minutes and thirty seconds to put on her dress and sweater. She bounded down the steps, skipping every other one, and landed two-footed at the bottom. "I'm ready!" she shouted.

Phee helped her with her coat, pushed her out the door, and remembered at the last moment to unplug the Christmas tree lights. She'd already accepted the fact that she'd be late, but hopefully, just a little.

While Frank drove, Phee closed her eyes and breathed deeply. The boys and Mollie were excited about the beginning of Christmas vacation. Everyone but Frank hoped for lots and lots of snow. A white Christmas would be perfect, but any day next week would be fine, too. If four or five inches of the white stuff covered the ground, Phee and the kids would go sledding at Wildwood Park just as soon as they could get there.

Phee removed the mitten from her left hand and chewed her nails, trying to think of a good excuse for being late. She had a feeling Horst did not tolerate tardiness any more than Algona High's principal, Mr. Campbell, did.

When Frank got to the gatehouse, Private Mattingly stepped out, and Phee feared he'd want to chat. But, thankfully, he didn't this time. He extended a friendly greeting while handing Frank the visitor pass, then opened the gate. Frank drove irritatingly slow to the theater and parked almost as far away from the lobby as he possibly could and still be in the lot. Phee was exasperated.

"Sorry," she said as she opened the car door, "gotta run. See ya later." Inside the lobby, she saw all the chairs in place for the expected overflow crowds. The choir was already on stage, with Horst leading the warm-up from the piano. Phee walked quickly down the center aisle. When Horst saw her, he stood and walked to center stage without an acknowledgement or comment. Several choir members were grinning from ear to ear, poking their comrades in the side to get their attention. Fräulein Swensson had arrived at last.

As she took her place on the piano bench, she saw an envelope on the music rack. Written on the front was her name in now familiar handwriting. She placed it inside her pouch after removing the music for tonight's performances.

Horst wanted to start the Wagner, the "Pilgrim's Chorus" from *Tannhäuser*, and asked for a B flat. After they sang through the first twenty measures, the lobby doors opened, and people began to enter. Phee watched for her family and finally saw Frank. "Please don't sit in the front," she mumbled. They didn't, unless the second row was considered the front. Phee sighed, smiled, and waved discreetly.

Horst conferred with his assistant, then walked over to the piano. "Is everything alright?" he asked.

"Oh, yes, it's fine. My sister was . . . slow."

"She must be the same with my sister. It seems she is late for everything."

"She was so excited about coming tonight, then couldn't decide what dress to wear. Imagine—she's only eight!"

"And they are here now?"

Phee nodded. "Uh-huh, there, in the second row."

Horst turned to look at Frank and the kids. Frank smiled and nodded, while Mollie and the twins were stunned with wide eyes.

"I would like to meet the children at the end," he said.

"Sure, that would be nice."

"I should prepare my mind for our performance. Do you have everything you need?"

"I do, thanks."

As he turned and walked away, Phee motioned for her dad to come to the stage. "Horst wants to meet the kids afterwards. They'll clear the hall for the second concert pretty fast, so it'll have to be quick."

"Right. Say, we haven't talked about how you're getting home. Do you need me to come back to get you?"

"Oh gosh! How did I not think about that before now? You might have to."

"Let me talk to Ed. He's sitting a couple rows back. I'll see if he can give you a lift."

"Let me know."

BEFORE THEY BEGAN "SILENT Night," the final piece on the program, six guards holding white candles walked single file down the center aisle and stood across the front of the hall facing the audience. Only the two Christmas trees on either side of the stage and the guard-held candles illuminated the hall. At the end of the carol, the full house gave the *Männerchor* a standing ovation. Horst took several bows, acknowledging the choir, Phee, soloists and instrumentalists, before the applause finally died away.

"Well, what did you think?" Phee asked when Frank and the kids got to the stage.

"I liked the candles," Mollie said. "I 'specially liked the carols at the end."

"I thought you might like those the best," Phee said. "How 'bout you boys?"

"It was kinda strange hearing songs I know with words I couldn't understand," Tris said.

"Yeh," Gus added, "I guess they couldn't sing in English, could they?"

"We shouldn't expect Germans to sing in English, even if they're fluent," Frank said. "Personally, I prefer the German."

Horst appeared through the crowd to greet Frank and meet the children. "Pastor Swensson, it is a pleasure to see you. I thank you for coming."

"You're welcome. Your choir is magnificent."

"*Vielen Dank*. I appreciate your kind words."

"I especially enjoyed the Wagner. I'm partial to Wagner, right, Phee?"

"Oh, yes. We get to listen to Wagner quite often at home."

Horst smiled. "It is a favorite of mine. There is much emotion in the music."

"Sergeant, let me introduce my sons, Gustav and Tristan."

"Hello, young men. I enjoy your names very much. They are very ... Teutonic, and Wagnerian."

The twins were perplexed.

"And this is Mollie, my youngest."

"Hello, Mollie. I am pleased you heard our concert. I will say how lovely you are looking."

Mollie took refuge under her dad's arm but managed a broad smile.

"She's a little shy tonight," Phee admitted.

"Well, we should be on our way," Frank said, extending his hand. "Sergeant, again, bravo on a fine performance. I hope we can hear them again."

"And you will," he said. "Please, have a nice holiday at your home. *Fröhliche Weihnachten.*"

"*Und ein . . . frohes Weihnachtsfest . . . auch für Sie,*" Frank answered.

Horst smiled, clicked his heels together, bowed slightly, then returned to the stage.

"He's nice," Gus said. "I kinda forgot he was the enemy."

"Me too," Tris added.

Mollie held onto her dad's hand. "I like his eyes. They're bluer than blue!"

Phee laughed. "They are, aren't they? Well, you need to skedaddle. Dad, what did Ed say about my ride home?"

"Oh, yeh, he said no problem. You should stay here till he comes for you. Will that be alright?"

"Sure, that'll be fine."

DURING THE SECOND CONCERT, when she wasn't playing, Phee sat very still on the piano bench with her hands in her lap. Her focus wasn't on the choir and the music they sang. It was on Horst, and it suddenly occurred to her that she admired him—his technique, his talent, his obvious devotion to his ensemble. There was a lot to admire.

After the concert, an army photographer approached the stage and asked Horst and his choir to remain in place so he could take more formal photos of the group. When he finished, Horst dismissed his men. Then the photographer turned to Phee. "Miss Swensson, Colonel McNabb wants these photographs for the camp records. Do you mind staying for a couple minutes?"

"Yes, I can stay."

"Great. I'd like you to remain seated. Sergeant, if you could stand behind Miss Swensson, I'll take a few from here and a few farther back. Yes, that's good . . . right there . . . great . . . there you go . . . very nice . . . let's try one with you both looking at the music. Yes, you can smile if you like . . . good . . . got it . . . perfect." He returned to the stage. "Chaplain Mattson will have copies of everything if you'd like to see them."

He turned to leave, and as Phee gathered her music, she remembered the envelope in her pouch. "I found this earlier," she said to Horst. "Is it from you?"

He smiled. "Perhaps."

"Should I open it?"

"*Ja*, you should do it now."

She pulled out a card with a lovely winter scene on the front. The text at the top was in German. "A German card? How did you—?"

"We made our request to *Doktor* Hill some time ago. In the next month, he brings boxes of cards for all of us."

"It's very pretty. You'll need to translate, though."

"I will, but there is more inside."

Phee opened the card and was stunned to find two ten-dollar bills. There was a handwritten note on the left side, opposite the printed German message. She shook her head slowly, then looked at Horst with tears in her eyes. "Oh, gosh, I'm sorry. I just . . . I'm overwhelmed. This is too much, Horst."

"Read my words," he insisted.

She took a deep breath and then read aloud, "For Fräulein Swensson, we thank you for joining our performances to celebrate Christmas at our camp. We enjoy your excellent talent and hope you will consider performing with us again in the new year. Please accept this gift of

American money with our sincere appreciation. Merry Christmas from the Camp Algona *Männerchor* and our esteemed leader Sergeant Horst Ebinger." She chuckled. "'Esteemed'."

"I can read the German words now," Horst said. "Here, at the top, 'Greetings of the Season'." He opened the card and continued. "And on the inside, 'Best wishes for a wonderful holiday season, and a very happy new year.' It is not so clever, I suppose."

"No, it's lovely. But really, this wasn't necessary. How did they—"

"My comrades made the decision alone. They . . . how you say . . . made a collection from the money they earned from their labors."

"It's a very generous gift. And I've just thought of something I can spend it on."

"Something you want, or something you need?" he asked.

"Both, maybe. Remember that homework assignment you gave me last month?"

"*Ja*, to listen to my beloved Brahms's First Symphony. I have not forgotten."

"Neither have I, but I'm having trouble finding a recording. So, I'll use some of this money to buy it. There's a store in Fort Dodge that might have it. If not, I should be able to order it. I'll find it, somehow."

"It is a good plan. You should like it very much. It is magnificent music."

It was nine thirty. Still no Ed. In fact, there was no one in the hall except the two of them.

"Chaplain Mattson's supposed to drive me home."

"He will come to the lobby door. We should wait there."

When they got to the lobby, Phee admired the nativity scene once again. "This is so beautiful."

"Some of our comrades were building it in the last months," Horst explained.

"They are . . . *Holzschnitzer* . . . wood carvers in our homeland before the war. Colonel McNabb likes it very much."

"So do I." Phee looked out the window towards the parking lot. She hoped Ed would be delayed just a little longer. She was comfortable now, alone with Horst, not intimidated at all. "I'm glad the choir sang 'Lo

How a Rose.' It was my mom's favorite. We used to sing it at church every year on Christmas Eve."

"*Es is ein Ros entsprungen.*' My mother also likes it very much. It is a German carol, did you know?"

"I assumed all the carols they sang tonight were German."

"All but one. 'Still, Still, Still' comes from Austria."

"That's almost German, isn't it?"

"Almost, but not."

Phee saw a car enter the parking lot. "Looks like the Chaplain's here." She turned to Horst and offered her hand. "Thank you, Horst. This was so much fun."

He took her hand and gently kissed it. "*Fröhliche Weihnachten.* Merry Christmas, Fräulein Swensson."

"*Fröhliche Weihnachten,* Sergeant Ebinger."

When Phee got to Ed's car, she turned and waved. *I think I'll write a song about the nativity scene—a carol, or a lullaby. Yes, that's it—a lullaby for baby Jesus.*

19

MONDAY 25 DEC. 1944

It was half past midnight when the Swenssons returned home after the late Christmas Eve service. Frank and Mollie got the milk and cookies ready for Santa. No longer believers, Gus and Tris let Mollie have her moment with Santa and didn't tease her about it. Their agreeable attitudes might have resulted from Frank's sit-down discussion with them on Saturday when he reminded them it wasn't so long ago when *they* believed in Santa Claus.

Frank put the milk and cookies on the bookcase in the living room where all seven stockings—Mary's and Jamie's included—were hung. After the kids went up to bed, Frank and Phee stayed behind to fill their stockings with oranges and apples and small toys and socks. Santa always left socks. Phee had some things for Frank's stocking, but she'd deliver those after he went upstairs.

Phee grabbed the milk glass and cookie dish from the shelf and sat on the couch. Standing near the tree, Frank found two ornaments he thought needed adjusting.

"Do you want some milk and cookies, Santa?" she asked.

"Nah, I'm fine. Just making sure some of these aren't gonna jump ship."

"Some crowd tonight, wasn't it? I guess you saw all the Kimballs. They filled a pew and a half!"

Frank leaned down to pick up some tinsel off the floor. He tossed it onto an upper branch, then heaved a big sigh.

"You alright, Dad?" Phee asked.

"Oh sure, right as rain. Just . . . missin' your mom."

Phee set the milk glass on the coffee table, then stood and embraced her dad. "I know, me too."

"Phee, you've been such a big help to me these past two years. I owe you so much."

"Dad, you don't owe me a thing."

"Are you sure you're not missing out, you know, spending more time with your friends, going to the movies?"

"I'm going to the movies tomorrow—later today, I guess."

"But, I mean, with your friends, on a date."

"We've talked about this before, Dad. I'm not interested in the boys at school right now, not more than friends, anyway. And I do go to the movies all the time, or often enough."

"That may be, but I still want to know when I ask too much."

"I know you do. And, since you brought it up, there is something . . ."

He stepped back. "Oh, okay, shoot."

"I want you to go to bed so I can finish stuffing the stockings."

Frank laughed, a little too loud, so Phee whispered, "Shhh! You'll wake the kids!"

"Sorry, I'll go up," he said softly.

"I guess we'll get the usual wake-up call in the morning."

"You can count on it."

"Love you, Dad."

"Love you, too, Phee. Nighty-night."

Phee finished the milk, then walked to the hall closet where she'd stashed her dad's gifts. Besides socks, there were two others, both acquired with Ed Mattson's help. She dropped everything into Frank's stocking, unplugged the tree lights, turned out the lamp next to the couch, and headed upstairs.

PHEE WAS IN A deep sleep, and, for the first time, she was dreaming about Horst. They were alone in the gymnasium at the high school. He wore a tuxedo and all she had on was her well-worn pink bathrobe and slippers. He was about to take her in his arms—

But then the music from downstairs blasted away, plenty loud enough to interrupt everyone's peaceful slumber. Almost immediately, the three kids remembered it was Christmas morning. Mollie stopped in the bathroom before bouncing happily down the stairs to the living room. Meanwhile, the twins made a beeline for the basement to use the icky toilet only the male members of the family dared to flush.

It was Wagner they heard from the Victrola in the dining room, Wagner at full volume, and Phee would never know if Horst was going to kiss her because Richard Wagner interrupted that moment forever.

Phee donned her bathrobe and slippers and visited the bathroom before sauntering down to the living room.

"Aha, she lives and breathes!" Frank said. "Better get in here and see what Santa brought."

Phee yawned and stretched. "Santa came? How 'bout that. Guess he forgot socks this year, though, huh?"

All three kids held their new socks high over their heads and yelled, "No he didn't!"

"Did Santa bring you anything, Dad?" she asked, settling on the couch.

"It does appear there's something in my stocking." He brought it to his chair and reached inside. The fruit and socks were on top, so he pulled those out and reached deeper, finding a small, wrapped item.

Tris was impatient. "Open it!"

He did and held up a key fob designed with an army chaplain insignia. "It's for my keys. Santa must have shopped at the PX out at the camp."

"Santa doesn't shop," Mollie said with authority. "He makes everything at the North Pole!"

"Maybe he contracted out for this one," Frank suggested.

"Is there more, Dad?" Phee asked.

"I think . . . no . . . wait. There is something else in here." In the bottom of his stocking, he found a long, slender item, wrapped in the same paper. He held it up to his nose and smiled.

"What is it?" Mollie wanted to know.

Frank grinned. "I can tell ya it ain't candy."

"Open it!" Gus yelled.

Frank removed the colorful paper to expose a cellophane wrapped cigar.

"Santa brought you a cigar?" Gus wondered.

"He most certainly did!" Frank smiled at Phee, understanding his friend Ed was most likely responsible for his two unique Santa gifts.

"Can we open our presents under the tree now?" Mollie asked.

"Not until Phee empties her stocking," Gus said, handing it to his sister.

She reached in and pulled out an orange, an apple, socks, and one more thing. "Oh look! Lipstick! Just what I wanted!"

"Mrs. Claus told Santa to get that color for you," Frank said. "Hope you like it."

"I do! My very own lipstick. Thanks, Santa!"

When it was time to open the gifts under the tree, the youngest, Mollie, opened her gifts first and the oldest, Frank, opened his last. The boys were patient, and it took a good half hour for all the packages under the tree to disappear.

"I hope Jamie got our box," Frank said, blowing on his hot coffee.

"I'm sure he did," Phee said. "I bet the army tries really hard to get packages to everybody on time, especially for Christmas."

"I'm starving," Tris admitted. "Let's eat!"

"Dad, we're still going to the movies, aren't we?" Mollie asked.

"Yes, Sweet Pea. Looks like *My Pal Wolf* is the only kids' movie playing today. The Zetterholms saw it on Saturday, liked it just fine."

In the kitchen, Phee turned the dial on the radio until she heard Christmas music. "Good, this will be better breakfast music than Wagner."

106   SALLY JAMESON BOND

"Nothing is better than Wagner," Frank said.

While they ate, Frank told everyone they'd visit their mom after the movie. Phee wondered how long they'd keep it up, all of them visiting Mary together. It was hard because it was always a reminder she was gone, but it wasn't as hard now as it was the first year. *I don't even think about her every day now. Is that okay?* Then Phee realized—*I think about Horst every day. Is* that *okay?*

IT WAS SNOWING LIGHTLY when they came out from the movie, and when they arrived at Mary's gravestone, it was just beginning to stick to the grass. Nobody wore boots, so Frank decided they'd make it a quick visit. The kids told their mom about their gifts, and Frank spoke about the late service last night. Phee wanted to tell her mom about the concerts at the camp last week but decided to save that for another time. Instead, she told her about the lipstick from Santa. "The color is gorgeous! Mrs. Claus picked it!"

Back at the parsonage, the phone rang just as they walked in. Phee answered. It was Christa, who wanted to know if it was a good time to drive over with Phee's gift. The girls had exchanged Christmas gifts for the past few years. It was usually something small, inexpensive, often silly. Christa usually gave Phee something from her dad's hardware store, and more often than not, Christa's gifts from Phee came from the five and dime downtown. Last month, Phee decided on the perfect gift for Christa but hadn't wrapped it yet because it wasn't exactly wrap-able.

"Sure, we won't eat till about five," she said. "Now's a great time."

Phee stuck her head in the kitchen. "Dad, could you please turn the oven down to two-fifty? I need to run up and wrap Christa's gift."

In less than ten minutes, there was a knock on the front door. "I'll get it!" Phee yelled as she hurried down the stairs. She quickly stuck the crudely wrapped envelope on the tree about halfway up, then ran to the door. "Come in, come in! I see it's snowing harder. Sledding tomorrow?"

Before she crossed the threshold, Christa stomped her feet to get the snow off. She laid Phee's gift on the side table and sat on the nearby chair to remove her boots. "You betcha! Adam said it's supposed to keep snowing all night. We'll get to the park by ten. Wanna meet us there?"

"Sure. I'll have the kids with me."

Frank came out from the kitchen. "Merry Christmas, Christa. Can I get you girls some hot cider?"

"Merry Christmas to you too, Frank. I'd love some cider. Half a cup, though. I won't be here long."

"That sounds good to me, too," Phee said.

"Your tree sure is pretty. I kinda like it over there in the corner."

Frank brought the cider to the living room and set the cups on the coffee table.

"Thanks, Dad," Phee said, then handed Christa her gift. "Merry Christmas. You'll never guess in a million years."

"A million-dollar check?"

"Wrong."

Christa tore into the wrapped envelope, pulled out a single sheet of stationery, and smiled. "Heavens to Betsy! How did you know?"

Phee's note informed Christa she was the lucky recipient of a year's subscription to *Seventeen*, a new magazine Christa had been reading at the library since it first appeared on the shelf a couple months ago. "A little elf told me," she said, "plus, I've seen you reading it at the library. I did check with your mom to make sure they weren't getting it for you. She said she'd never heard of it."

"Of course, she hadn't. Now, your turn."

Phee felt around the edges of the package that felt very much like a book. After tearing the wrapping away, she stared at the book's cover for a moment, then cleared her throat. "This looks interesting—*Berlin Diary,* by William Shirer."

"It's my dad's. Well, it's yours now. I saw it on the bookcase at home and I thought 'Phee should read this book,' now that you're spending so much time with that German fellow, what's his name?"

"Sergeant Ebinger."

"Right. Anyhoo, Dad thought was a great idea, so it's kinda his gift to you. Saved me some dough this year."

"I love it. I'll be sure to thank him properly."

"Well, I should get home," Christa said as she took another sip of cider. "I smell a roast so it must be about time for supper."

"Yep, better get out there and make gravy."

By now, it was snowing heavily, with at least a couple of inches covering everything in sight. "It's sure pretty, isn't it?" Phee asked as she stared out the storm door window. "We'll have a blast tomorrow."

"Yep, ten o'clock. Be there or be square."

The girls hugged and Christa yelled, "Bye, Frank!"

Frank yelled back from the kitchen, "Be careful out there . . . could be slippery."

Phee waved, closed the door, then took her book to the kitchen. Frank had peeled the potatoes, and they were boiling on the stove.

"Whatcha got there?" he asked.

"My present from Christa, and her dad."

"*Berlin Diary*. That's an interesting choice for a seventeen-year-old girl."

"Christa thinks I should read it because of Horst."

Frank stroked his beard. "I've wanted to read that since it first came out. Can I borrow it when you're done?"

"Sure. I bet I can get through it before school starts."

"That sounds good to me. How soon till we eat?"

Phee looked at the stove and guessed. "Let's say . . . forty-five minutes? I'll get the gravy made. Could you get the carrots in the steamer? They're in the ice box."

EATING IN THE DINING room was always a special occasion, and tonight was no exception. The food was yummy, and the centerpiece on the table, which Mary had made a few years ago, was lovely with candles, glistening ornaments, ribbons, and pinecones. Frank chose the Word of the Day: optimistic. He heard it on the radio earlier and decided it was the perfect word for Christmas Day.

"Who knows what it means?" Frank asked.

"I do!" Gus volunteered. "It means . . . thinking something's going to turn out alright. Like, I'm optimistic I'm going to get an A on my spelling test next week."

"Very good," Frank said, "and you'd better get an A. You're an excellent speller."

Gus beamed and Tris added, "I'm optimistic that Jamie will be home by my birthday."

"And what a grand birthday it will be," Frank said. "Now, who wants to add it to our list?"

"I will," Mollie volunteered. "Gus can help me with the spelling."

Phee began clearing the table, but Frank had other plans. "Phee, leave everything. I'll do the dishes tonight."

"But there's a lot."

"I know, but I don't mind. You kids deserve a break."

Phee gave him a hug. "Thanks, Dad, you're the best." She stopped in the kitchen to grab her new book. "Think I'll go up and get started on this."

The *Berlin Diary* dust jacket told Phee she was about to learn what life was like in Germany when Horst was growing up. "*Uncensored.*" *Guess I'm going to learn the truth about the Nazis.* She was a little apprehensive about discovering what Horst's life might have been like before he joined the Afrika Korps band. But it might help her understand some things about him that had thus far remained a mystery.

20

SUNDAY 31 DEC. 1944

The day after Christmas, while Phee and the kids were sledding at Wildwood Park, Ed Mattson called Frank to invite the family to Camp Algona's New Year's Eve party. He said there would be a cocktail hour, dinner and dance, and Frank was delighted to accept the invitation. Phee would need to be back at St. Pete's for the Luther League party, but Frank was confident she could attend both events, and Phee concurred.

Ed had suggested they all meet in his office, so after Frank parked in the theater lot, they all marched over to the headquarters building.

"Hello, everybody," Ed said when they walked in, "so glad you could join us tonight."

"We're always ready, willing, and able to eat on Uncle Sam's dime," Frank said as he tossed his coat on the nearby loveseat.

Just then, Ed's secretary, Julie, stuck her head in the door. "Hello everybody! I was wondering if the children would like to take a ride with me over to the stables."

Mollie was stunned. "Really?!"

"Yes, really, if it's alright with your dad. We'll be back in a flash."

Frank smiled and nodded. "Go have fun with the horses."

"Goody!" Mollie yelled. "I just knew we'd get to see the horses tonight!"

Ed, Frank, and Phee followed Julie and the kids down the hall to the nicely decorated lobby where there was an open bar serving Champagne, beer, and pop. Phee waved to Julie and the kids as they left through the front door, then she grabbed a 7-Up and helped herself to some of the hors d'oeuvres. Just as she popped a grape in her mouth, someone tapped her on the shoulder. She turned to see a smiling Roy Phillips holding a glass of Champagne.

"Corporal Phillips!" Phee said, quickly swallowing her grape, seeds and all. "What a nice surprise. I thought you'd gone home for the holidays."

"No, it's a long way to go for just a few days' leave."

"I guess it is. Care for a grape?"

He chuckled. "No thanks. Uhm, will you be staying for the dance later?"

"I'm afraid not. I've got another party at church. I can't miss it."

"The prisoners are playing, the dance band, I mean, Sergeant Ebinger's group."

"Oh, really? Gosh, I wish I'd known. I'd sure like to, but—"

"Well, if you change your mind, I'd sure like to be your escort."

"That's very sweet. Thank you, Corporal."

"Do you think you could try 'Roy' tonight?"

Phee grinned. "Sure, and I'm Phee. I'll have to check with my dad. I could probably stay for an hour, but no more."

"If he says you can, come find me at dinner. I'd be happy to drive you to your party whenever you need to leave."

"That would be great. I'll let you know what he says."

Right away, Phee wanted to talk to her dad about Roy's invitation. So, she grabbed a few more grapes and walked through the crowd to the bar where Frank and Ed were speaking with Colonel McNabb. The Colonel saw Phee and smiled. "Phee, there you are. Welcome to our party. I've heard rave reviews about your involvement with the *Männerchor* concerts. I sure hated to miss them, but I was out of town both Thursday and Friday last week."

"The kids and I got to hear them," Frank said. "Quite a powerful group."

"Yes, they are," the Colonel agreed. "The dance band will play tonight. That should be a real treat."

"I wish we could stay, but the kids need to get back, and Phee has—"

"Dad, I'm sorry to interrupt. I need to talk to you about that when you have a minute."

"Can we talk on our way over to dinner?"

"Sure, that'll be fine."

Just then, Julie and the kids walked in. Mollie ran up to Frank and gave him a hug. "Whoa there, filly, watch the beer!"

"Sorry. Guess what, Dad? We got to sit on one of the horses!"

"You don't say."

"I'm sure our horses enjoyed the visit," said the Colonel as he glanced at his watch, "but I believe it's time we head over to the theater."

"Right," Ed agreed. "We need to get our coats from my office. We'll see you over there, sir."

"So, what's up?" Frank asked as they followed Ed out the back door.

"Would it be alright if I stayed after dinner, for the dance, I mean, just for an hour?"

"I thought you were going to the party at church."

"I am. I ran into Corporal Phillips—Roy. He invited me to the dance. You heard the Colonel say Horst's band is playing, and I'd really like to hear them. It might be my only chance."

Frank slowed his pace, then stopped. "You need to be at church tonight, Phee."

"But I could do both. I told Roy I had to be at the Luther League party. He offered to drive me back to town."

He took her arm as they walked on to the theater. "Well, I did recently say 'I owe you,' didn't I?"

"Yes, you did."

"So, you tell the Corporal I expect him to deliver you to St. Pete's by nine o'clock, no later. Can you do that?"

"Oh, yes, absolutely! Thanks, Dad!"

The camp theater building had been transformed into an attractive dining space, with tables arranged in long rows in the hall and buffet lines set up in the lobby. Once inside the hall, they all found their seats. Seeing Roy standing near the stage, Phee decided to give him the good news before dinner. "Roy, I can stay!"

He was obviously pleased. "Swell! We'll have a grand time, I promise."

"Do you think you could let Sergeant Ebinger know I'll be here for the first set?"

"I guess I could. I'll tell him when he gets on stage."

"Thanks, Roy. See you in a little bit."

Dinner was wonderful—baked chicken and ham, scalloped potatoes, a fruit salad with fresh pineapple, marinated vegetables, lime Jell-O with grated carrots, and a huge bowl of baby shrimp with cocktail sauce on the side. It had been a long time since the Swenssons had enjoyed a meal like that, probably never. And there were three different desserts!

The stage was already set for the band. At seven forty-five, a dozen fast-working soldiers cleared the tables so they could be folded, stacked on dollies, and moved outside. The buffet tables in the lobby were dismantled, and two bars were quickly set up in their places.

While Phee walked Frank and the kids to the lobby, Mollie turned to Phee and asked, "Aren't you coming with us?"

"No, I'm staying behind, just for a little while. I'll get a ride into town later."

"Have a great time tonight," Frank said, "but don't forget—nine o'clock."

"I won't, and thanks again, Dad. Happy New Year, kids!"

"Happy New Year, Phee!"

When she returned to the hall, Phee saw the band members walking through the stage door with their instruments. She didn't see Horst, but she did see Roy and Ed talking near the stage. As soon as the band was seated, they began their warm-up routines, a cacophony of sound that was reminiscent of a radio in search of a clear station. There were four saxes, three trumpets, a trombone and a tuba, a drummer, and a string bass. The piano was on stage right and Phee wondered if Horst could play dance tunes as well as classical. She probably wouldn't find out tonight because someone who was not Horst sat down and began "tickling the ivories."

At five past eight, Phee got antsy. *Why don't they start? Where's Horst? I don't have much time.* Just then, the stage door opened, and Horst hurried in with music under his arm. He stopped to speak to Ed and Roy, looked up as if searching for someone in the hall, then turned to speak to his musicians.

"There you are," Roy said when he found Phee in the back of the hall. "Sergeant Ebinger knows you're here. You might want to speak to him before we leave. He said he got a letter from home yesterday. Apparently, there's some news about his brother. He seems pretty upset."

"I don't know if I'll get the chance to talk to him," she said. "We'll be on our way to St. Pete's by the time they take a break, won't we?"

"Most likely. I'll try to find out when they'll take their first break."

They started with Duke Ellington's "Take the A Train," clearly a crowd favorite, and Phee and Roy joined the other dancers who were ready to work off some of the fabulous dinner they'd all just enjoyed. The band was tight, Phee noticed, very professional in their execution of the familiar big band sounds. *Whadaya know, Germans have rhythm, too.*

When they finished the first tune, Roy moved through the crowd up to the stage and caught Horst's attention. After a brief conversation, Roy returned to Phee's side. "The Sergeant said they'd break at eight forty-five. He'd like you to be close to the stage then."

For the next half hour, Phee danced with Roy, but her thoughts were with Horst. What had happened to his brother? It had to be bad news if he was upset. For the first time since she met him in August, she was worried about him.

At eight forty-five, the band finished "Twilight Time," a popular Les Brown tune. "Better grab your coat and go up to the stage," Roy said. "I'll go get the car. If I run, it'll take me about ten minutes."

"I'll wait for you by the stage door," she said.

The crowd quieted down when they saw Colonel McNabb walk to the microphone near the piano. "We're so glad you're here tonight," he began. "But before we all dance the night away, we should thank Sergeant Ebinger and his band for providing the music for our New Year's Eve celebration."

Hurry up, Colonel, I don't have much time!

"I know none of us thought a year ago we'd be standing here tonight, dancing to the music of Tommy Dorsey played by a band of German soldiers."

You're right, we didn't. Now please, wrap it up!

"Let's give them another hand, shall we?"

Hurry up, please!

"The Sergeant tells me they'll take a fifteen-minute break, so we'll all catch our breaths and be back for the next set at . . . twenty-one oh five."

Phee met Horst at the bottom of the stage right stairs. "Good evening, Fräulein Swensson."

"Good evening, Sergeant Ebinger. Corporal Phillips said you wanted to speak to me."

"*Ja*, but I would like it to be private. We can speak outside."

"You don't have a coat?" Phee asked as they walked out to the west stage door landing.

"It is in the barracks," he said while rubbing his arms for warmth. "I will be alright. The cold air is . . . how you say . . . invigorating?"

"Yes, definitely invigorating." She hesitated, then continued. "Horst, I'm so sorry, but I don't have much time. Corporal Phillips is getting his car so he can take me into town. I have another party."

"Of course, I am sorry. I want to say . . . my mother has written. My brother Erich is missing, in Belgium."

"Oh, no . . ."

"I have told you about him. He was drafted only some months ago. My mother is very worried."

"I'm so sorry, Horst. Is there anything I can do for you?"

He rubbed his hands together, then reached for Phee's. "It is enough that you know. And you have a father who is good with praying, *ja*?"

Phee smiled and nodded. "Yes, he is. I'll ask him to pray for Erich. I'll ask Chaplain Mattson, too. And I will too, certainly."

"And Chaplain Schmidt, I have spoken to him before now."

"Good. All that will help." She turned slightly to look across the parking lot—no Roy yet—then turned back. "Horst . . ."

Still holding her hands, he raised them to his lips and kissed them. He'd done it before, but this time, there was more. He reached for her face, held it in his hands, and gently kissed her lips. It was a brief kiss, but it took her breath away.

Happy New Year.

21

SUNDAY 7 JAN. 1945

ALL THE CHRISTMAS DECORATIONS in St. Pete's were gone, and for Phee and no doubt others, it was always a letdown when they first entered the sanctuary and there was no tree where there had been a tree, no candles where there had been candles, and no wreaths where there had been wreaths. By next Sunday, though, nobody would notice anything was missing. Visually, things would be back to normal.

Worshipping at St. Peter's Lutheran Church on the first Sunday of the month, communion Sunday, was somewhat unique. During the service, when it was time for the Lord's Prayer, it was spoken in Swedish. In the United States, the churches of the Augustana Synod, of which St. Peter's was a member, conducted church services in Swedish until the mid-1920s when the Synod fathers decided it was time to move on to English. To appease the older members of the congregation, Frank's predecessor, Reverend Otto Carlson, led the Lord's Prayer in Swedish once a month. Not wanting to make waves, Frank continued the tradition after arriving in Algona in 1934. The Swedish was printed in the bulletin for those who couldn't recite it without help.

After a short chat with Christa about their history assignment, Phee ran downstairs to hang up her choir robe and grab her coat. She was always in a rush after church. Most Sundays, there was meat roasting in a slow oven at home, and it was almost always done when she walked in the house. Today it was a pork roast.

When Phee walked in, she saw Mollie reading a book on the couch. She could smell the roast and was glad she remembered to put the leftover scalloped potatoes in the oven before she left the house this morning. They'd also eat peas from the cellar today, even though Mollie hated peas. Phee used to hate peas too until one day, about five years ago, she didn't.

"Where's Dad?" Phee asked as she hung up her coat.

Mollie looked up from her book. "He's not home yet."

"He wasn't in his office."

"I saw him talking to that soldier from the camp. Can't remember his name. We've seen him a few times."

"Was it Corporal Phillips, Chaplain Mattson's assistant?"

"Yeh, that's him, I think."

"I'm going up to change. It would be nice if you'd set the table."

"Sure," Mollie answered, still focused on her book.

I didn't see Roy in church. Wonder what they're talking about?

Every day since New Year's Eve, Phee had thought about the kiss. She was very confused, wondering why it happened and what it meant. Maybe it meant nothing at all. It made no sense for Phee to have feelings for Horst and vice versa. He was a POW, for Pete's sake. There could be no future for them. So, should she avoid spending time at the camp? There was plenty to keep her busy at home and school, plus, she was working on new pieces for college auditions in the spring. Horst could find someone else to accompany his choir. It didn't *have* to be Phee—did it?

She changed quickly and ran down to the kitchen. Mollie was setting the table as requested, and the twins were in the basement working on their dartboard skills. When she opened the oven door to check on the roast, Frank came in through the front door carrying his briefcase. He placed it on the floor next to his chair in the living room.

"Smells good in here!" he called out as he headed upstairs to change. "How soon till we eat?"

"Give me five minutes. Just gotta heat up the peas and slice the roast."

Phee called the boys up and made sure they washed their hands. When Frank joined them at the table, they said the blessing together. Because the casserole dish was too hot to pass, Phee spooned potatoes on everyone's plates.

"No peas for me, thank you," Mollie said politcly, hoping it would help.

"Sweet Pea," said her dad, "we go through this every time Phee puts peas on the table. If you have the word 'Pea' in your name, you gotta eat peas. That's the law in this house."

"But I don't like peas. They're not sweet like me."

"Hardy har har!" Tris chimed in. "You're crazy."

"I'm not crazy, I just don't like peas."

"Tell you what," Frank said. "Why don't we try ten peas today. That's a reasonable helping for someone who says she hates peas."

"I *do* hate peas," Mollie pouted.

Frank continued. "You can fit ten peas on your spoon and get it over with in one gulp. Next time, we'll make it an even dozen."

"You can always hold your nose," Gus suggested. "I do when I have to eat something I don't like."

"What don't you like?" Phee asked. "I thought you ate everything under the sun."

"Well, I'm not crazy about lima beans," he admitted.

"I like lima beans!" Mollie exclaimed. "We should have those next Sunday."

"I'm not fond of peas either," Tris confessed, "but I mix 'em with the potatoes and they're not bad.

While Mollie contemplated the best way to eat her ten peas without gagging, Frank moved on to another topic. "Roy Phillips was in church today."

"Really?" Phee said. "I didn't see him."

"He was the last one in line, so we stayed and talked. He brought me an envelope from Ed."

"Oh yeh, what's in it?"

"Pictures from the concert last month, he said. I haven't opened it yet."

"That's right. The photographer was at the last performance."

"Can we see 'em?" Mollie asked.

"I don't see why not," said her dad. "We'll have a look after we eat. The Corporal also brought us something from the mess hall. Feels like it could be cookies."

"Yay!" yelled the kids while clapping their hands.

Phee smiled as she reached for the pea bowl. "Anyone want seconds?"

"Ish no!" Mollie cried. On the floor next to her chair was a heating duct register, a perfect receptacle for unwanted food. Six of Mollie's ten peas ended up rolling down the duct to the furnace today. She swallowed the other four, one at a time, while holding her nose.

"I'd love seconds," Frank said.

While Phee carried their dishes to the sink, Frank retrieved Roy's goodies and the envelope from his briefcase. Inside the brown paper package were cookies and brownies which they all washed down with milk. It was a jolly way to end their Sunday dinner.

"Can we look at the pictures now?" Mollie asked.

Frank handed the envelope to Phee. Inside she found four five-by-seven black and white glossy prints. The picture on top was taken relatively close to the theater stage and showed the *Männerchor* standing in concert formation with Horst facing them, his arms raised. The second picture was taken farther back so the entire stage could be seen. A smiling Phee, sitting at the piano, was just barely visible on the left side of the photo. Horst, who wasn't smiling, stood on the opposite side of the stage.

The other photos showed Phee and Horst at the piano. In one, they were both looking at the music on the music rack with somewhat serious demeanors. In the other, taken closer—the one Phee liked best—they were both smiling at the photographer.

"Pass 'em around," Frank suggested.

"I'll hold them up so you can see. I don't want sticky fingers touching them."

Mollie's only comment was that she wished they were in color so she could see the Sergeant's blue eyes. The boys lost interest almost immediately, and Frank said, "Looking good, Phyllis Anne. Oh, and I'll keep them in my office for now. Corporal Phillips said Ed doesn't want us to show these around just yet, especially the ones with you in them. Maybe after the war."

"I guess that makes sense," Phee admitted. "Dad, I need to practice. Are you going to nap?"

"Yeh, but not for long. I need to get a couple of letters written today. Can you wait till three?"

"Sure, I've got homework waiting upstairs."

"Boys, you're up for KP duty," Frank said. "Don't break anything."

As she followed her dad upstairs, Phee thought about the pictures from the concert and how much she enjoyed working with Horst and his choir last month. But she was busier than ever now. *I can't commit to it. I just can't.*

At the top of the stairs, Frank turned to Phee. "By the way, I asked Corporal Phillips if he thought they'd want you to accompany the *Männerchor* for their next concert—"

Oh, no!

"—and he said he didn't know but he'd be happy to find out."

When she got to her bedroom door, she turned and said, "Dad, I should probably hold off on that, at least till after graduation. And who knows, maybe they'll all be gone by then."

"I guess it's possible, but it's likely they'll be here for a while. Even if the war ends in the summer, they won't close all these camps right away. At any rate, focusing on your schoolwork and your lessons makes sense to me. I can let Ed know tomorrow."

"Thanks, Dad. Enjoy your nap.

Phee closed the door, reached for her social studies book, and sat on her bed. *I'm glad Dad's keeping those pictures in his office. I really don't need any reminders.*

22

SATURDAY 20 JAN. 1945

TODAY WAS INAUGURATION DAY in Washington, DC. After spending time at his office this morning, Frank came home and turned on the kitchen radio just before eleven so he could listen to President Roosevelt's speech from the south portico of the White House. Thankfully, it was a short speech, as the weather in DC was brutally cold and there was snow on the ground. No parades or parties or dances were planned. There was a war on, and austerity measures were in place, even for the President of the United States.

Phee spent most of the day at Christa's where they were collaborating on a big project for their English class. With Phee away, it was up to Frank to get lunch on the table. After the president's speech, he made peanut butter and jelly sandwiches for the kids and himself. He heard Ralph the mailman on the front porch as he put their milk glasses on the table. Would there be a letter today?

There were two.

"Mail's early, I'll get it!" Tris shouted from the living room. He opened the front door, reached into the mailbox, grabbed a short stack of envelopes, and hurried to the kitchen. "There's a letter from Jamie—and something for Mollie."

Upstairs in her room, Mollie heard her name and came running down the stairs.

"Something for me?! Gimme gimme!"

"Gimme gimme, *please*," Frank ordered.

Mollie, waiting impatiently, added, "Please?"

"I get to read Jamie's letter," Tris declared. "I brought it in."

"Leave it on the table," Frank said. "We're about ready to eat."

Mollie preferred to open her envelope in private, so she sat in Frank's chair in the living room with the letter opener she'd grabbed from the nearby secretary. The postmark said Spirit Lake, so she assumed it was from Nannie and Bee, but it wasn't. It was from Claire Engstrom, an invitation to her birthday party on Saturday morning, February 3rd, at ten o'clock. "I got a birthday party invitation from Claire!" she said as she returned to the kitchen. "Can I go? Please?"

Frank took the invitation from Mollie and looked it over. "Well, we'd have to leave awfully early to get there by ten, and you know how hard it is for you to get up early, especially on Saturday."

"But I will, I promise! I'll go to bed really early!"

Frank grinned. "Tell ya what. Let me check my calendar. We could all go up Friday night, stay over with Nannie and Bee if they'd have us. We'd have to head home right after the party, though."

The twins were agreeable, and Mollie was ecstatic. "Oh, yes, what a marvelous idea!" she exclaimed.

"I'll run over to my office after lunch. If the calendar's clear, I'll call Bee. If he says it's a go, you can send Claire your RSVP."

"RSVP? What's that?" Mollie asked.

"It's an abbreviation for some French words. It means . . . you'd better write me back to let me know if you're coming to my party, something like that."

Mollie got up to give Frank a hug. "Thanks, Dad, it'll be so much fun!"

"I hope it all works out. Now, let's eat. And Tris, go ahead and read that letter from your brother."

"LET'S SEE IF WE can find some pretty stationery in here."

They'd just finished supper, and Mollie and Frank were in the living room staring at an open drawer in the secretary. It was a mess, and Frank was reminded that his wife's propensity for order had a purpose. Without it, they were unable to quickly find that box of pretty stationery he knew was in there somewhere.

"Is it in the bottom drawer?" Mollie asked.

It was. Under some canceled checks, they found a robin egg blue box with the words "Deluxe Stationery" printed in scrolled letters on the top. "Bingo!" Frank said as he lifted it from the drawer. "Should we go to the kitchen to work on this?"

"Sure! Would it be alright if I practiced on regular paper first?"

"That's a splendid idea."

Earlier this afternoon, Frank had discovered his calendar for February 2nd and 3rd was clear. He called Bee and Nannie from his office to see about the whole gang staying over Friday night. Nannie was thrilled, saying, "It's been too long since you were at the house. You're more than welcome."

After supper, Phee and the boys played Sorry! in the living room while Frank and Mollie worked on her RSVP. It took her quite a while to finish, and it was almost eight o'clock when she put the sealed envelope on the table in the front hall.

"Sweet Pea, time for a bath," said her dad. "Make it snappy so the boys can get theirs done. I feel like a long one myself tonight."

"Good thing I took mine this morning," Phee said. "Hope there's enough hot water for ya."

"There won't be, but I'll manage."

After Frank went upstairs to urge Mollie along, Phee went to the kitchen to get started on the ironing. Before bed, she got five of her dad's shirts ironed along with two of her dresses and a few pairs of the boys' pants. She hung the hangers on an iron rod that was fastened above the door between the dining room and kitchen. The rod had escaped all the scrap iron drives because everyone but Phee forgot it was there. She wasn't about to give it up, even for a worthy cause. There was just no other place to hang freshly ironed clothes near the kitchen. Someday, before Phee left for college, Mollie would take over this chore unless there was an adult woman in the house who could and would plug in an iron from time to time.

As Phee got ready for bed, she thought about the four pictures from the December concert that were hidden away in her dad's office. Frank told Ed last week that she couldn't accompany the *Männerchor* until after graduation in May. So, that was done. But the kiss outside the theater on New Year's Eve would not leave her alone. There hadn't been any notes from Horst asking her to meet with him, so maybe the kiss meant nothing. Maybe it was a mistake. Maybe—

Fri. Feb. 2, 1945

—Dear Daisy—

I didn't go to Spirit Lake with Dad and the kids today. My history project that's due Monday got in the way. (I need a good grade on it so I can keep my A going in that class.) After they left this afternoon, I got everything set up on the dining room table. (I put both leaves in so I could spread out.) Not long after I settled in for the long haul, the phone rang. It was Ed Mattson, and he was calling to tell me that Horst had gotten the horrible news that his brother's body had been found in Belgium. Ed said that Horst was pretty upset and had asked to see me. (Oh dear!) His request was approved, Ed said, but I hesitated to say yes because I've been trying to keep my distance since New Year's Eve. I told Ed I wanted to talk to Dad about it before I decided. I called up to Bee and Nannie's after I knew they'd be there, and Dad said it was up to me if I wanted to meet with him or not. Since I was without a car, he wondered if Horst could be brought to St. Pete's and we'd meet there. I thought that was an okay idea, and when I called Ed back, he said he'd make the arrangements. It will most likely be Roy and a guard with Horst, he said. They'll come at 2:00 tomorrow afternoon. I will admit I'm a little nervous. What should I say to Horst? What shouldn't I say to him? Oh, Daisy, I need your help—again.

And life goes on. G'night.

23

SATURDAY 3 FEB. 1945

WHEN PHEE GOT TO the sanctuary a little before two, she stopped by the thermostat to turn up the heat. She also turned on all the lights. It was a cloudy day, so the natural light coming through the stained-glass windows needed some assistance. She walked up the center aisle to the narthex and unlocked the front door for the expected visitors from Camp Algona.

Phee was sitting at the piano when she heard the front door open. She'd been playing her scales, hoping the routine would help calm her nerves. As Roy, Horst, and Corporal Bickford entered at the back of the sanctuary, she stood and said, "Welcome to St. Peter's."

"Hello, Miss Swensson," Roy said as he led the two men down the center aisle. "Thank you for having us."

Phee's attention was focused on Horst. "Sergeant . . . I'm so sorry about your brother."

Horst attempted a smile. "Thank you for saying it. I am glad to be here. The church is very beautiful."

"Yes, it is," Phee agreed.

"Could you give us a tour of the building?" Roy asked. "I'd like Corporal Bickford to have a sense of the layout."

"Sure," she replied. "You should probably leave your coats on, though. I've turned up the heat, but it's still pretty chilly in here."

She led the three men down the back hall past the small library next to Frank's office. Downstairs, they saw the fellowship hall, the kitchen, one of the Sunday School rooms, and the choir room. Before finishing the tour, they walked up to the balcony and climbed the narrow winding staircase to the belfry where there was no bell. Phee explained, when the church was built in 1896, they couldn't afford to install a bell in the belfry. Over the years, it seemed a little too extravagant to spend money on a bell. Other churches in town had bells that could be rung when required, she said.

When they returned to the sanctuary, Roy said, "I'll post Corporal Bickford at the front door, and I'll go down the hall to the library. It's close to the back door. Just come get me when you're ready to leave."

"Thank you, Corporal," Horst said.

"We'll be right here," Phee said as she sat in the pew nearest the piano. Horst sat next to her, a little closer than she expected. She shuddered. "So," she began, "how did you hear about your brother?"

"From my mother, in a letter I received three days ago."

"It must be hard, being so far from home and hearing such awful news."

"My mother is with my sister Anika and my father's sister, Gerda. My father . . ." He turned slightly away, sighed, and began to explain. "Before Herr Hitler came to Germany, my father was a . . . *Rechtsanwalt*. He works in the law."

"An attorney," Phee suggested.

"*Ja*, in Potsdam, near Berlin, as you know." Horst rubbed his face with his hands and continued. "He was very busy in his work, spending many hours away from our home."

"Is he still in Potsdam?"

"*Nein*. He works for the government in Bavaria, at least it is what I know. I have not heard about him for many months."

"He works for Hitler?"

"In some ways, I believe it is true. He is not a . . . *Berater*, an advice giver."

"An advisor?"

"*Ja*, an advisor. We do not know what will happen to him at the end of the war. But I cannot worry about him now. My concern is with my mother and my sister."

"Can you tell me what your mother wrote, about Erich, I mean?"

"He was with *das siebte Armee* . . . how you say . . . the seven . . . Seventh Army. They were fighting in Belgium in December. He was missing then. You know it from before. After some time, his body was found in the snow with his comrades."

Phee knew there were men from Algona in Belgium but kept it to herself.

Horst looked at Phee. "You must know, we want this to end. My comrades, we want it for many months."

Phee was relieved to hear he still felt that way about the war. She was close to finishing *Berlin Diary* and had recently read about the Hitler Youth. If Horst had been a part of that program—he'd not yet mentioned it—it seemed clear to Phee those experiences no longer influenced his attitude about Germany's success.

He continued. "And I am here, even outside the barbed wire, sitting in a beautiful *Kirche* with a beautiful woman in the middle of America, safe from harm. I have enough food to eat and a warm bed to sleep. I can have music almost each day if I choose it—a *Männerchor*, an orchestra and a band with enthusiastic comrades to follow my leading. I can read books, watch films, visit the library . . ."

His list continued, but Phee had missed everything he'd said beyond two words: "beautiful" and "woman."

". . . I can make paintings and jewelry, I can play the nice piano in the theater, and I am trusted to do it alone without a guard most of the time. And now, I know my brother is dead." He sighed. "I have much worry that he suffered."

She wanted to reach for his hand but didn't. "It's possible he didn't suffer, Horst. We should try to imagine he died quickly and peacefully. Surely that can happen, even in a war."

Horst stood and walked slowly up the steps to the altar. Gazing at the gold cross that stood behind a large open Bible, he said, "It has been many years since I have been inside a church."

"Really—how many?" Phee wondered.

"I am not sure. It can be . . . more than ten." He turned to look out at the sanctuary.

"Were you baptized?" she asked.

"*Ja*, at St. Nikolaikirche, a beautiful church not far from our home. It has surely been bombed."

Phee winced. If the church wasn't far from his home— "Is there anything I can do for you, Horst?"

He walked slowly back to the pew and sat. "You have agreed to meet with me today, and I am . . . grateful."

"It's what friends do," she said softly.

For the first time since he arrived over an hour ago, Horst seemed reassured. "So, friend Phee, I must make an apology for the last time we were together."

Oh no! Don't apologize for the kiss! "Surely not. I can't think why."

"It was wrong for me to kiss you and I am sorry for it."

"Oh, Horst, you don't need to apologize for that. You'd just found out your brother was missing, and you were worried for your mother and sister. And it was New Year's Eve. Everybody gets kissed on New Year's Eve, at least they do around here."

He smiled, reached for her hand, and gently squeezed it. "There is one more thing we must discuss. I was told you will not accompany the *Männerchor* for the next months. I am hoping to make a change for your thinking."

Phee, he said you were a "beautiful woman." He's hurting. Say yes. You won't regret it.

"Well, I guess I could change my mind about that. I'll find a way, Horst . . . I will." She hoped for another smile, and she got it.

Phee walked with Roy and Horst to the narthex where they joined Corporal Bickford. She waved as they drove away, locked the door, then returned to the sanctuary to turn off the lights. She felt good about their meeting and hoped music would somehow help her friend Horst get through this difficult time.

Sat. Feb. 3, 1945

—Dear Daisy—

It was kind of an interesting day, not as bad as I'd feared. Horst and Roy and Cpl. Bickford got to church right on time for our meeting at 2. I gave them a tour (including the belfry), then Horst and I sat in the sanctuary and talked while Roy and Cpl. Bickford were guarding the doors. We talked about Erich, as you would expect, and Horst's dad, who's an attorney and works for Hitler but isn't an advisor, he said. He was worried that Erich suffered, so I tried to set his mind at ease. Not sure I was successful. And guess what? He apologized for kissing me on New Year's Eve. He also said he wanted me to accompany the Männerchor on their next concerts. Maybe I shouldn't have agreed to it, but I just couldn't say no. He was so sad about his brother, and he's still worried about his mother and sister. Dad and the kids got home right before supper. They all had a great time. Bee took the boys ice fishing while Mollie and Dad were at Claire's party. Mollie said they played Bingo and she loved it, so it looks like we'll be doing that at her party in April. They brought home a big piece of chocolate cake. Yum! Dad and I had a nice chat tonight about my meeting at church, and about Helen, indirectly. I asked him if he'd ever get married again and he said maybe. "I suppose it's possible" were his exact words. So, there it is. I'm glad, at least I think I am. I want Dad to be happy, and having a girlfriend (Helen?) could help with that. It's too soon to know. Dad promised he wouldn't make a quick trip to Vegas for an elopement. Ha! Church tomorrow, practicing and homework, Luther League tomorrow night. And then it's Monday again! Where do the weeks go?!

And life goes on. G'night.

PS—Today Horst said I was a "beautiful woman"! Can you believe it??!! I about choked!

24

SUNDAY 4 MAR. 1945

IN THE END, PHEE agreed to meet with Horst twice in February to look at the music for the four *Männerchor* concerts, now on the camp calendar for March 23rd and 24th. Their Sunday afternoon meetings were productive, and while she always appreciated any chance to learn new music, it was clear to Phee she enjoyed spending time with Horst more than just about anything now, and this afternoon was another opportunity.

In her pouch with the concert music was one of the photos from the December *Männerchor* concert. This morning after church, Frank agreed to let her have one photo from the envelope he kept in his desk if she promised to return it to him as soon as she got home. She wanted Horst to identify all the singers so she could write their names on the back.

On the way to the camp, Phee and her dad, who was meeting with the chaplains in Ed's office at three, talked about the parent-teacher conferences at Bryant School this past week. Overall, the twins and Mollie were doing very well in their classes. Miss Gregory told Frank she adored Mollie and was pleased with her curiosity and especially her enthusiasm for spelling. It did sometimes take Mollie longer than others to come up with an answer for a given question, but once she spoke, she was more often right than wrong.

According to Mrs. Wellman, the boys were typical ten-year-olds. She said their work was consistently above average and their reading comprehension scores were almost always high. Gus needed to work a little harder on his arithmetic homework, and penmanship was probably Tris's weakest subject. Mrs. Wellman confided to Frank that she was partial to redheads because both her brothers had red hair.

Phee pulled up to the gate and was greeted by her favorite MP, Private Mattingly. "Hello, Private," she said.

"Good afternoon, Miss Swensson. What's your destination today?"

"I'm dropping Dad off at the headquarters building. He has a meeting with Chaplain Mattson at three. I have a rehearsal at the theater, same time."

"I'll give the Chaplain and the guardhouse a quick call, and we'll get you on your way."

While they waited, Frank reminded Phee, "Be sure to tell the Sergeant I approve of his selections for the next concert, especially *'Muss i denn.'*"

"I promise. I'm sure he'll be pleased you approve."

Private Mattingly returned with the visitor pass. "Miss Swensson, Corporal Bickford will meet you at the theater. Have a nice day, folks."

After dropping her dad off, she drove to the theater, arriving just after the Corporal. They walked in together. "If it's alright with you" he said, "I'll just stay here in the lobby and read my book."

"Thank you, Corporal," she said as she pushed open the door into the hall. "We'll be here for an hour or a little longer."

"Friend Phee!" Horst called from the stage. "You have arrived at the appointed time."

"I just dropped Dad off at the Chaplain's office. He said his meeting shouldn't last more than an hour."

"We will rehearse until they are finished, *ja*?"

"Sure. What's up first?"

When they finished looking at all the concert music, Phee remembered to mention, "My dad said to tell you he approves of the pieces you've selected, especially *'Muss i denn.'* He especially likes that one for some reason."

"He should like it. It is very popular for the German people."

"Oh, and I just remembered something else," she said as she began to gather her music. "I brought one of the pictures from the last *Männerchor* concert. I'd like to know the names of the choir members so I can write them on the back, if you think they wouldn't mind."

"I am certain they would not. Shall I look?" Phee pulled the photo from her pouch and handed it to him. "My happy comrades. Should we begin in the front row or the back?"

"The front, I guess. First and last names if you can."

"Of course. The first is Fritz Bauer, then Jurgen Riedel, then Heinrich Theisinger—"

"Hang on," she said, "you'd better spell it."

He continued, spelling the names of all thirty-nine singers in the photo, and Phee was impressed he could recall their names so easily. She didn't mention it, but she hoped to put one or two names to faces when she was here for the dress rehearsal on the seventeenth.

She looked at her watch. "I should go. Dad's probably waiting."

"We can walk to your car," he said, then under his breath, "We will stop to say auf Wiedersehen to Corporal Sleepy. Should we make a bet? Is he sleeping or not sleeping?"

She chuckled and whispered, "Surely he isn't this time. I'll say not sleeping."

Phee finished gathering her music and slipped it into her pouch. As she slung it over her shoulder, Horst touched her arm. She hesitated, then turned to face him, leaning back against the piano. He reached for her hands and drew them to his lips. *Oh gosh . . .* He touched her cheek, moved an errant strand of hair from her eye, and moved closer. *Oh gosh . . .* And then he gently kissed her.

He spoke first, whispering in her ear. "I am sorry."

"Don't be," she whispered back.

"I do not want you to be afraid."

"I'm not."

"I have wanted—"

"Me too."

"*Ja?*"

"Yes." She pulled back and smiled.

"If others know . . ."

"They won't," she said, touching his cheek. "We'll be careful."

"Phee, I—"

"Shhh. Don't talk, just kiss." And again, they did.

ON THE RIDE HOME, Frank was very animated as he told Phee about his meeting with the chaplains. They discussed a possible summer concert involving the prisoner ensembles, the city band, and several local church choirs. Her reactions to the mostly one-sided conversation involved intermittent head nodding and a few "uh-huhs." Ordinarily, Phee would want to hear all the details about Algona's biggest event of the summer, but her mind was miles away until she heard her dad mention Horst's name.

"Huh?"

"I said, how was your meeting with the Sergeant?"

"Oh, fine, I guess."

"You guess? What happened?"

"Nothing happened. We just looked at all the music for the concert. They'll sing some verses *a cappella*."

"Did you tell him about '*Muss i denn*'?"

"Yes, I did."

"Did he say which of the concerts will be for the Americans?"

"Shoot, I forgot to ask. I'm sure Ed will know."

When they got home, Phee managed to get a light supper on the table. After they ate, she excused herself, saying she had homework which she did, but she didn't open her history textbook right away. Before reading about the early Italian Renaissance, she reached for her diary so she could tell Daisy about kissing Horst. It was now very clear to Phee that she had feelings for him—not "maybe a little," not "sort of," not "probably," not even "most likely." Tonight, she had no doubts.

25

SATURDAY 17 MAR. 1945 - PART 1

Normally, on Saturdays, the parsonage mailbox remained empty until at least three o'clock. But today, the mail was delivered just past noon. When he heard the mailbox lid slam shut, Gus pushed his chair back from the kitchen table and prepared to make a beeline for the front porch.

"Stay seated young man," his dad instructed. "The mail can wait till we've finished eating."

"Aw, gee," Gus said, clearly peeved. "It could be a letter from Jamie."

"It might be," Frank said before taking another bite of his ham sandwich, "but we've waited this long, we can wait another five minutes."

"But I'm done," Gus whined.

"I see milk in that glass," Frank said.

Gus picked it up, finished it off, then let loose with a loud burp. "How's that?"

"Gus!" Phee cried. "What do you say?"

"Excuse-me-now-can-I-get-the-mail?"

"You can, but don't run," Frank answered, shaking his head.

In less than a minute, a disappointed Gus returned to the kitchen. He held a single yellow envelope in his hand. "This is all we got. It's for you, dummy," he said as he dropped it on the table next to Mollie.

"Goody! I bet it's from Claire!"

Phee and Mollie spent much of last Saturday creating invitations for Mollie's upcoming birthday party. Besides delivering invitations on Monday to all the girls in her third-grade class, she mailed invitations to Bee and Nannie and to Claire who was now her "second best friend after Charlotte." It appeared Claire had RSVPed.

"Aren't you going to open it?" Phee asked.

Mollie picked up the envelope, held it to her chest, closed her eyes, and prayed, "Dear God, please let Claire and her mom come to my party. It would be really swell. Amen."

Frank and Phee smiled, while Gus and Tris rolled their eyes.

"Okay, now I can open it." She gently pulled a sheet of yellow stationery from the envelope and began to read the letter to herself.

"Well, Sweet Pea, what's the verdict?" Frank asked.

"They're coming with Nannie and Bee!"

"Guess I'll add two more to the guest list," Phee said.

"Oh, I'm so happy. See, my prayer was answered right away!"

Frank chuckled. "It sure was. Good for you."

"I think I'll go write Claire to thank her for coming."

"That would be nice," Phee said. "Boys, you can clean up our dishes. I need to get ready for my rehearsal."

"When will you be home?" Frank asked. "I can heat up the leftovers for supper."

"I'm not sure how long it'll go," she said, checking the ice box to make sure there was enough for their supper. "Looks like there's plenty for another meal. Just set the oven on low and put it in around four thirty if I'm not home."

"Got it. Oh, and try to find out if we're invited next weekend. I keep forgetting to ask Ed."

"Christa might come too if it's Friday. Adam's birthday is Saturday, so they'll be busy that night."

Just before one thirty, Phee grabbed the car key from the bowl on the table in the front hall. "See ya later!" she yelled in case anyone was listening.

THE WESTERN UNION TELETYPE machine that served Kossuth County was kept in a small windowless room at the back of Winfield Drug Store on Main Street. Telegrams during wartime did not necessarily contain bad news. Joyful greetings for birthdays or weddings or anniversaries came through the wires with regularity. Occasionally, telegrams containing best wishes for a successful senior piano recital came off the press. Sometimes, a telegram could bring a smile.

But not in Algona today, when only one Western Union telegram came off the teletype machine in the back of Winfield Drug. While answering a customer's question about a prescription, Dr. Herbert Winfield heard the machine click on in the back room and looked at the clock on the wall. It was almost half past one. As soon as the customer was satisfied and turned to leave, Dr. Winfield walked to the phone on the wall and called home to his fourteen-year-old son, Johnny, who'd been delivering telegrams since his brother, Bobby, left for college last September.

"Johnny, I've got a telegram for ya. Better get over here right away."

He walked back to the teletype machine and gently removed the strip of printed text. As he almost always did before he glued the typed message to the brown and yellow Western Union paper, he closed his eyes and said a prayer for the family who would most likely read it within the hour. Even if it was good news, a prayer never hurt.

But it wasn't good news. It was for Christa's parents, Jack and Peggy Rasmussen. Herbert knew them well. He knew their son Danny was in the army overseas. Even before his eyes behind thick spectacles could focus on the text of the telegram, he knew the Rasmussens' lives would be forever changed today.

After the gluing was done, he folded the paper and slid it into an official Western Union envelope, making sure the recipients' names and address were visible. He returned to the counter and laid the envelope next to the cash register. Ten minutes later, Johnny, wearing his official green Western Union cap and shirt, rode up to the store and leaned his sky-blue Schwinn against the front window.

"It's for Jack and Peggy Rasmussen," Dr. Winfield said as he handed the envelope to his son. "They might be at the store, but I'd run it over to the house first, just in case."

"Alright," Johnny said without a hint of emotion. "Do you need me back here after I deliver it?"

"No, you can go on home. Hopefully there won't be any more today. Tell your mom I'll be home around six."

"I will. See ya, Pop."

Johnny mounted his bike and took off down Main Street. It wouldn't take him long to get to 112 East Lincoln.

CHRISTA WAS HOME ALONE this afternoon. Her parents were in Sioux City at the Western Iowa-Eastern Nebraska Hardware Convention. They attended every year and had been taking the bus to Sioux City since gas rationing began three years ago. Christa expected them home late tonight. If the bus was on time, she'd pick them up at the station at midnight.

At five minutes to two, there was a knock at the front door. Christa got up from the chair in the living room where she'd been reading her assigned pages from Shakespeare's *Romeo and Juliet.* As she got to the front hall, she could see Johnny through the white lace curtain. She knew it was Johnny. She'd seen him riding his bike around town, wearing his green hat and shirt, and she knew why he was knocking.

When she was about three feet from the door, she stopped, didn't move, didn't breathe. Her heart raced, and she began to feel light-headed. *Romeo and Juliet*, which was still in her hand, fell to the floor.

Johnny knocked again, this time a little harder.

Stop knocking at my door! Go away!

Just then, Johnny turned and walked back to his bike which was leaning against the spirea bush next to the steps. As he pulled it upright, Christa opened the door. She looked out the storm door window but didn't speak. Her sad eyes and pale face spoke for her. Johnny walked back up the steps and held out the yellow envelope. Without saying a word, she took it, closed both doors, and walked back to the living room, stepping over *Romeo and Juliet* on the way.

Christa sat on the round leather footstool next to the chair where, only minutes ago, she was reading about those tragic star-crossed lovers. She held the envelope in her hand, wondering what she should do with it. *I shouldn't open it. It's not addressed to me.* And then, she wondered if she should have tipped Johnny because, in the movies, everybody tipped the delivery boys. *I'll stop by the drug store later to give him a dime.*

Suddenly, she felt like throwing up. Dropping the envelope on the floor, she ran down the hallway to the bathroom, raised the toilet seat, and sat on the edge of the tub. After staring into the bowl for a while, she closed the lid and retreated to the kitchen for a glass of water. She drank half, then wet her hands and vigorously rubbed her face.

She returned to the living room, hoping the last five minutes had been a bad dream and she wouldn't find a sad, lonely Western Union envelope on the floor next to the footstool. But she did. Her hand shook as she picked it up. Sitting on the stool, she slowly opened the envelope, pulled out the single sheet of paper, and read the telegram once—twice—three times. She moaned, softly at first, then louder. With her fist tightly clenched, she pounded on her thigh, again and again and again, and finally, she screamed the most painful scream she'd ever heard or felt or imagined. And then, she knew—*I've got to see Phee!*

After stuffing the horrendous news into the pocket of her coat, she grabbed the car key from the hook near the door and ran to her dad's car. She backed out of the driveway without looking for traffic either way. It usually took no more than five minutes to get to Phee's house, but it seemed to take much longer. She had to hit the horn just once when the car in front of her stopped mid-block for no apparent reason. She sped around it and ran the next stop sign.

As she approached the parsonage, she noticed Frank's car wasn't in the driveway. *Oh gosh, maybe nobody's home. Why didn't I call first?*

She pulled up to the curb, turned off the engine, and opened the door. Tears streamed down her cheeks as she ran up the steps and across the porch. "Phee, it's Christa!" she shouted as she pounded on the door. "Phee, are you home?!"

After a few moments, Frank opened the door. "Come in, come in. What's the matter, Christa?"

She rushed past him and stopped when she got to the living room. "Is Phee here?"

"I'm sorry, she's not. She's at a rehearsal out at the camp."

Her shoulders slumped and her head dropped. Under her breath, softly but clearly, she said, "Oh, God, no. She's with that damn Nazi!"

"Come here. What's going on?" She almost collapsed as he held her in his arms.

"Oh, Frank, it's the most horrible thing!"

"Shhh, take a breath. Let's go out to the kitchen. I'll get you a glass of water."

As they walked to the kitchen, Christa removed her coat and dropped it on a chair in the dining room. "I have something to show you," she said meekly. She threw the crumpled piece of paper on the kitchen table.

Frank needed only a quick glance to understand why Christa was here in the state she was in. He picked up the telegram and read it. "Oh, Dear God, Christa, I am so sorry."

Christa buried her face in her hands and whispered, "Danny, Danny, oh, God . . ."

"Where are your folks?"

"They're in Sioux City at the convention," she moaned.

Frank looked at the clock over the sink. "When do you expect them home?"

"Late tonight on the bus. I'm s'posed to pick 'em up at the station at midnight."

"Well, there's no question, we should drive to Sioux City and bring them back. They need to know about Danny, and it would be much better to hear it in person. Problem is, Phee has my car, and I don't expect her home for another couple of hours. I don't want to take your car because of the A sticker."

"Yeh, and it's almost out of gas. Couldn't you call out there and ask Phee to come home now?"

Frank considered her suggestion, then had another idea. He was torn because he knew Phee would want to be with Christa, but he also knew she was in the middle of the only dress rehearsal scheduled for next weekend's concerts. If his idea didn't work out, he'd call his friend Ed and ask him to get a message to Phee to come home immediately. "Drink some of that water while I make a phone call. I'll be right back."

Christa drank while Frank walked to the phone in the front hall. She heard a noise in the basement and realized it was probably the twins and possibly Mollie, too.

When Frank returned to the kitchen, he sat next to Christa and reached for her hand. "I just spoke to Edith. One of their cars is all tanked up, and we can take it to Sioux City. She insisted. The kids can stay with them till Phee gets back to town and can pick them up."

"That's very generous, but could you call out there anyway and ask them to get a message to Phee?"

"I'll call Chaplain Mattson. If he's not available, I'll leave a message to have her call Edith. Chances are we'll be on the road by the time she gets the word."

"Thanks, Frank, I mean it. I don't know what I would have done if you hadn't been home."

"We're going to help you get through this, Christa," he said. "There are a lot of people around here who love you and care about you. Some know firsthand what you're going through right now." He got up and walked to the basement door and called down. "Boys, Sweet Pea, come upstairs, please. We need to get over to Paul's house."

They clamored up the steps, and when Gus saw Christa, he wondered what was up. "You're here and Phee's not. Must be a surprise."

Christa forced a smile. "In a way. Your dad and I are going to Sioux City to pick up my parents."

"Christa, do you need to use the bathroom before we go?" Frank asked.

"Yeh, good idea. Be right back."

"You kids wait for me in the living room," Frank said. "I need to make a call and then I'll talk to you before we leave."

Frank had to leave a message with the camp switchboard operator. Then it was time to tell the kids about Danny. "So, you know Christa's brother Danny is overseas in the army."

"Yep," Tris said while the others nodded.

"Christa got a telegram today."

"A telegram from Danny?" Mollie asked.

"No, it's from the War Department, and it's sad news. I'm afraid Danny's been killed."

They were silent for a moment, then Gus displayed a sensitivity that made his dad proud. "We should give Christa a hug."

Frank smiled. "That's a fine idea, Gus."

"Where did it happen?" Tris asked.

"The telegram mentioned western Germany. I'm sure we'll learn more in the next few days."

Mollie, looking very worried, asked, "Will Jamie die too?"

Suddenly, Frank felt the enormity of the news about Danny Rasmussen. For the past twenty minutes, he'd worn his "pastor's hat" as he attempted to comfort Christa while making logical and sensible decisions about what had to be done in these first hours. But now, Frank thought his heart would burst with sadness. He sat in his chair and held out his arms. "Come here, Sweet Pea." Mollie climbed in his lap, and he continued. "I understand why you'd ask that question. But, no, Jamie is not going to die. He's in the band and they're kept away from the fighting. They're not close to any danger. Danny was in the infantry, in the thick of it—"

"Did God want him to die?" she interrupted.

Rubbing her back, Frank sighed. "Oh, Sweet Pea, you've asked one of the most profound questions people have been asking since the beginning of time. Some day you and I will have a long talk about that.

But for now, we need to believe that Danny's with God and, well, it's likely he'll run into your mom up there in Heaven."

"I sure hope he does," she said.

When Christa appeared from the hallway, Mollie got up to give her a hug. "I'm sorry about Danny, Christa." The boys joined them.

Christa's eyes gleamed as she looked at Frank and said, silently, "Thank you."

"Let's get our coats on," Frank said. "We'll take Christa's car over to Paul's."

The kids were outside in a flash, and Frank and Christa walked to the front door, arm in arm.

"Did you get ahold of Chaplain Mattson?" she asked.

"I had to leave a message. I'm sure Phee will get it. Do you want me to drive?"

"Yeh, if you don't mind. I forgot my purse." She handed Frank the car key, then he remembered the telegram was still on the kitchen table. He hurried through the house to get it, then out to the car where the kids and Christa were waiting.

26

SATURDAY 17 MAR. 1945 - PART 2

PHEE'S REHEARSAL WITH THE *Männerchor* went longer than expected, but she wasn't disappointed since being with Horst was so important to her now. The last song they rehearsed didn't involve piano for the final two verses, so she walked to the back of the hall to listen from there. What she heard gave her goose bumps—close harmonies, perfect diction, at least she assumed it was perfect, and an emotional ending, not loud, but strong and confident.

Horst wasn't aware that Phee had left the stage, so when he lowered his arms and turned to the piano, he didn't see her. A few of the men pointed to where she stood.

"Fräulein Swensson," he said with a firm voice. "You have heard our choir from a different space. What can you say about it?"

"Your singing gives me goose bumps," she said, not quite shouting. German-speaking POWs apparently didn't understand what she meant, so she tried again. "You sound marvelous!"

Horst smiled, motioned for Phee to return to the stage, and turned back to his choir. When he brought the rehearsal to a close, several of the men left through the west stage door. One, who looked to be younger than most of the others, walked over to the piano.

"Fräulein," he said, "thank you for helping us for another time."

It's Gerhard, I'm almost positive. Phee shook his hand and smiled. "You're quite welcome. It's been fun . . . Gerhard."

For a moment, the young man Phee hoped was Gerhard didn't move. And then, he burst out laughing and turned to speak to the few comrades remaining on stage. "Fräulein Swensson is knowing my name! It is . . . marvelous!"

The last choir member to exit the hall was Hans, Phee guessed, wishing she had that photo so she'd know for sure. Horst had remained at center stage, practicing his conducting technique. He sang softly to himself as one arm, then both, moved gracefully in tempo. She loved watching him. Then, for the first time this afternoon, they found themselves alone.

"So, my friend Phee, can you see we had success today?"

"Yes, I can. Can't you?"

"*Ja*, I have confidence now. We will be . . . marvelous for our audience." Smiling, he walked around the piano and joined Phee on the bench but faced the opposite direction. "I have missed you," he said.

She blushed. "I've missed you, too."

"I have thoughts about you at all hours of the day and night."

"Do you? I think about you all the time, too."

He moved closer and whispered in her ear, "I want to kiss you now."

She turned to look across the hall to the lobby, then smiled and whispered, "Okay."

Their kiss was soon interrupted by a sound in the lobby. Horst stood immediately, wiped lipstick from his mouth, and moved quickly around the piano to center stage.

Phee had told her dad she'd be home by four thirty. It was almost five now. While she gathered up her music, the lobby door opened, and Roy Phillips walked in.

"Corporal Phillips," Horst said. "Have you come to escort me to the barracks?"

"Yes and no," Roy said as he neared the stage. "I'm here to deliver a message to Miss Swensson first. It's from your dad. He'd like you to call Mrs. Zetterholm."

"Did he say why?"

"I just got the message from Chaplain Mattson who got it from the switchboard. That's all I know. I'm supposed to take you to the Chaplain's office to make the call."

"Alright, thanks," she said. "Sergeant, I'll see you on Friday. Oh, about the concerts. My family would like to come, so we'll need to know which one."

"*Ja*, it has been decided," he said. "The first concert on Saturday we will sing for the Americans."

"Good. I'll let Dad know."

"Auf Wiedersehen, Fräulein Swensson."

"Auf Wiedersehen, Sergeant Ebinger."

ALONE, PHEE SAT AT Ed Mattson's desk after Roy ushered her in and closed the door. Her hand shook as she dialed Edith's phone number. She had a feeling she was going to hear bad news. She did.

FRANK SWENSSON HAD BEEN a grateful person most of his life. His parents went out of their way to instill the concept of gratitude in each of their children at a young age. He found it useful to focus on gratitude when he was starting out in the ministry. But it was often difficult to feel grateful during Mary's illness. That experience was so overpowering he thought, at least for a while, he'd lost all contact with gratitude. He never doubted God's love for him and his family, he didn't lose his faith, but he wasn't grateful for much of anything as he watched his beloved wife fade slowly into death.

But tonight, on the drive home with Christa and her parents, Frank was overwhelmed with gratitude. He was grateful for his good friends Harold and Edith Zetterholm, who insisted he take their fine Cadillac sedan to Sioux City so he could find and comfort Jack and Peggy Rasmussen. He was also grateful for the opportunity to have a meaningful conversation with Christa while they rode together. In all the years he'd known Christa, he was sure they'd never had a conversation, one on one, for more than ten or fifteen minutes. This afternoon, as they traveled one hundred and forty-five miles to the city on the Missouri River, he learned a lot about Phee's best friend, and no doubt, she no learned a lot about him.

Jack sat to Frank's right, silent except for occasional audible sighs. Peggy and Christa were in the back, holding hands, sniffling, softly moaning every now and then. No one felt much like talking, so Frank was glad there was music on the radio. Whenever the music was interrupted by laughter or war news, he reached for the dial to find more music.

When they left Sioux City, Frank drove east on Highway 20 over to Fort Dodge, then turned north on 169. He was glad they didn't drive past Camp Algona. Seeing the lights from the camp would surely remind the Rasmussens that Germans lived while their son and brother didn't.

"Jack, your car's parked over at the Zetterholms," Frank said as they got to Algona's city limits. "If you don't mind, I'd rather just take you home. Phee and I can get your car back to you a little later. Does that sound alright?"

Jack didn't answer immediately. Most likely, Frank's words interrupted a memory or a thought, and of course, he was still in shock. "Sure, Frank," Jack said, sounding understandably melancholy. "Sounds fine. Thank you."

When they arrived at the house on East Lincoln, Frank opened the trunk and reached for their small suitcase and a paper bag filled with convention paraphernalia and literature. "I've got this," Frank said. "You folks go on in."

Finding the front door unlocked, Peggy and Christa went straight to the kitchen to make coffee and sandwiches. Jack, who had stopped to grab the mail before coming in, stood in the living room looking through the stack and discovered a letter from Danny. He dropped everything else on the floor and stared at it.

Frank, standing nearby, offered a suggestion. "Jack, here, let me have that. You go sit down. We can look at this later. Maybe tomorrow, huh?"

Jack handed the letter to Frank. "I guess so." He glanced at the Blue Star Banner hanging in the living room window. "We'll need a new banner."

The Rasmussen house was one of six on East Lincoln with a Blue Star Banner hanging in the window, signifying a family member was serving in the Armed Forces. A Gold Star Banner was hung in memory of a loved one who had died in service to his country.

Frank gently squeezed Jack's shoulder. "Don't worry about that, Jack. We'll get you a new banner."

Peggy and Christa brought cups and saucers and four sandwiches out to the dining room table. After lighting her first cigarette since hearing the news about Danny, Peggy asked Frank a few questions. Would there be more communication from the War Department? What about a memorial service? When should they have it? What about school for Christa? Could she take a few days off? Did he think it would be alright if they kept the store closed next week?

Peggy didn't ask about Danny's body, and Frank was relieved. When they were ready to talk about it, Frank would tell them Danny's remains would be buried with other American soldiers in an American cemetery, probably in Belgium or France, and after the war, if they preferred, his body could be returned to them. Frank knew how this worked; he'd had to discuss it with several families since Pearl Harbor.

"I'm happy to stay as long as you need me," Frank said as he glanced at his watch. "Is there anything else you want to ask, anything else I can do for you?"

Peggy blew smoke over their heads. "Frank, you've done more than enough for our family today. We'll never be able to thank you properly."

"Peggy's right, Frank," Jack added. "I don't know what we would have done if you and Christa hadn't come to Sioux City. Hearing that news over the phone, then riding back on the bus—"

"Don't say another word," Frank said. "You know I would have moved heaven and earth to make this as easy on you as I possibly could."

Christa walked around the table and gave Frank a hug. "You are a wonderful man, Frank. Thank you so much, for everything."

"Now, you get yourself home," Peggy said, snuffing out her cigarette in the nearby ashtray. "And don't worry about the car. You can wait till tomorrow. Don't think we'll make it to church."

"Of course," Frank said. "Oh, and if you don't mind, I'd like to make an announcement to the congregation. No one will have heard, unless Herb told—"

"Make the announcement," Jack said boldly, then softly, "people need to know."

"Will do. And Monday we can get together to talk about the service."

"That'll be fine, Frank," Peggy said. "Monday it is."

Christa hugged Frank one more time and remembered to give him the key to her dad's car. Frank promised they'd have it back in the morning before nine.

Frank drove the Cadillac back to the Zetterholms. The house was dark, so he left the keys in the car and drove Jack's car back to the parsonage. It was late, but he had a lot to think about. On top of everything else, he realized he would probably need to counsel his older daughter about her relationship with a certain German POW. He was fairly certain Phee had developed feelings for Sergeant Ebinger that went beyond a simple friendship. Those feelings could very well interfere with her relationship with her best friend now that her best friend's brother had been killed by Germans in Germany.

"My dear Phee," Frank said to himself as he drove home, "an unexpected dilemma is facing you tonight. God be with you."

27

SUNDAY 18 MAR. 1945

IT WAS JUST PAST midnight when Frank got home. The small lamp next to the phone in the hallway was on, but the rest of the house was dark. He removed his coat and hung it quietly in the closet, then checked the phone table for messages. There were none.

"Dad?" Phee called out softly from the living room. Wearing her nightgown and robe, she was curled up under a blanket on the couch. She rubbed her eyes. "What time is it?"

"It's after midnight," Frank whispered. "I drove Jack's car home from the Zetterholms'."

Phee sat up, stretched, then slowly stood. She looked at her dad with a sleepy, sad face. "Oh, Dad . . ."

Frank welcomed his daughter into his arms and held her without saying a word. Her blue chenille robe was warm, and her hair smelled like Drene.

"I'm too tired to cry," she said. "I've already had one good one today."

"I know, I know," Frank said, gently rubbing her back.

"I feel so awful, so . . . disappointed in myself. I wasn't here when Christa needed me."

Frank didn't necessarily want to change his daughter's mind because she needed to feel empathy for Christa and her parents. Feeling awful was not inappropriate. It was a reasonable reaction after getting bad news. Feeling disappointed in yourself was something else. Frank would try to quell that if he could. He led her out to the kitchen, and they sat at the table. Frank reached for a Red Delicious in the nearby bowl, but before he took a bite, he asked, "What time did you call Edith?"

Phee thought about this afternoon's events. "I guess it was a little after five. Rehearsal went long, and Roy didn't give me your message till then."

"So, let's say it was five o'clock when you got the news. Christa and I were over halfway to Sioux City by then. There wasn't time for you to be involved."

"But I should have—"

"No, you shouldn't have. You were obligated to finish your rehearsal, and you did. And now you can be there for Christa, after you get some sleep."

"I guess," she sighed, "but it's just so sad."

"It is, but we need to look ahead now, do whatever we can for the Rasmussens. First off, we need to get their car back before nine."

"I'll take it. I should stay with Christa. Can you tell Mrs. Lundeen I won't be in choir?"

"Sure. Will you need a ride home?"

"No, I can walk," she said, stifling a yawn. "I guess I should try to get back to sleep." They both stood, and before heading upstairs, Phee turned to her dad. "Thank you for being there for Christa and her folks today. I'm sure they were very grateful."

"They were."

She kissed his cheek. "Nighty-night."

"G'night, babe. I'll be up in a minute."

Frank finished his apple and tossed the core into the wastebasket under the sink, then trudged upstairs to the bathroom and to bed.

PHEE RETURNED THE RASMUSSENS' car to their driveway just before nine. She was a little nervous about seeing Christa and her parents, concerned about saying the right things. Surely, when she saw her best friend, she'd know exactly what to say.

As soon as she turned off the engine, the front door opened. Christa came out, and they embraced next to the car. The tears that were dormant last night were awake in Phee's eyes now. In fact, it was a flood.

"I'm . . . so . . . sorry," Phee said, her voice catching twice. There was no response from Christa, so Phee went on. "Oh, Christa, I'm so sorry about Danny. It's just the worst thing ever. I . . . I just can't believe it." Their embrace continued, but there were no tears from Christa. Phee was surprised she was so composed. And then, she finally spoke.

"I sure wish you'd been home yesterday and not out at the camp with those damn Nazis."

Phee pulled away. "What? Christa . . ."

"I needed you yesterday. I was such a mess. All I wanted was my best friend, and you weren't there."

Phee was dumbfounded. "But . . . I didn't know, Christa. I didn't find out from Mrs. Z until after you and Dad had left town."

Christa leaned back against the car, covered her face with her hands, and sighed. "I'm a wreck, Phee. I hardly slept last night. I kept imagining how Danny died, how he must have suffered. And then I imagined you, out there at the camp, laughing and having a gay old time with those German . . . bastards."

Phee was astonished. She'd never heard Christa use such language.

In a weak voice, Christa continued. "They killed my brother, Phee. They're horrible people, scum, every last one of 'em."

Phee was tempted to leave. Christa was obviously still in shock, consumed with anger and hatred. Phee knew nothing she'd say this morning would comfort her friend. "Christa, would it be better if I came back later, after you've had a chance—"

"What? To calm down? Get over it?!"

"No, of course not."

"You'd better come in. Mom wants to see you."

Phee followed Christa inside, remembering to hang the car key on the hook by the door. She took off her coat and laid it on a nearby chair just as Peggy came out from the kitchen. Christa hurried down the hallway to her bedroom but didn't close the door.

"Phee, we're so glad you're here. Come give Peggy a hug."

"Oh, Peggy, I'm so sorry."

"I know you are, dear."

"Is Jack here?"

"He walked down to the store early this morning."

"I'm sorry we didn't get the car back last night."

"Don't be. We didn't need it, and Jack needed the exercise. Why don't you come out to the kitchen and keep me company? Want some coffee?"

"No thanks."

Peggy poured herself a cup and brought it and a plate of muffins to the table. Nearby, there was a half-smoked cigarette smoldering in an ashtray full of butts.

"These look good," Phee said, reaching for a muffin.

"Help yourself. Hope you'll stay for lunch. Adam and his mom should be here soon. They're bringing soup. I'm sure there'll be plenty."

"I should have brought something."

"No, you shouldn't have. We'll see all sorts of food later today and all week, most likely."

"Especially after Dad makes the announcement this morning."

"Right, the announcement."

"Is Christa alright? I mean, I know she's not, she shouldn't be."

Peggy took a drag on her cigarette and blew the smoke out slowly. "She's taking this pretty hard. You know how close they were."

Hoping to distract Peggy from sad thoughts, Phee told her about Mollie's upcoming birthday party and about Bee and Nannie bringing the Engstroms. "I'm glad Helen's coming. It looks like she and Dad might be good friends."

"Do you think they could be more than friends?" Peggy asked.

"I don't know. Helen seems really nice. Mollie says Claire's her second-best friend after Charlotte."

Peggy smiled. "That's sweet. I think it would be wonderful if your dad found someone."

"Time will tell, as they say."

Peggy got up to pour herself another cup of coffee, and then, out of the blue, she asked, "So, how's your friend, Sergeant . . . Eslinger, is it?"

"It's Ebinger. Fine, I guess. We're not friends, per se. We had a rehearsal yesterday, for the concerts next weekend. Dad and the kids are invited to the first one on Saturday night, so—"

"We're thinking Danny's memorial service should be on Saturday," Peggy interrupted. "More people can come then. Some of Danny's friends will be home on spring break." Peggy's green eyes misted over as she thought about her son's friends. "Anyway," she continued, "we'll meet with Frank tomorrow to talk about it."

Just then, there was a knock at the front door.

"I'll get it!" Christa yelled, hurrying from her bedroom.

Adam and his mom, Hilda, walked in carrying a large enamel stock pot half full of vegetable beef soup, two loaves of homemade bread, and a cherry pie. Adam gave Peggy a hug, then Christa whisked him down the hall to her bedroom. Phee heard the door close, and she wondered if Christa's mom thought they should be alone in there with the door shut. And then she figured Peggy probably didn't care.

Jack walked in five minutes later, looking old and tired. Both Phee and Hilda gave him a hug before he excused himself and retreated to his workshop in the basement.

"Hilda, can you and Adam join us for lunch?" Peggy asked after turning on the stove under the soup. "You know we have plenty."

"Thanks for the offer, Peggy. I'm sure Adam will want to stay, but Vic's waiting at home. I really should be on my way. Don't worry about getting the pot back. I'll stop by later this week."

"Sure, and thanks again for everything. Jack will be thrilled to see that pie."

While Peggy walked with Hilda to the front door, Phee gazed out the kitchen window to the back yard where she and Christa spent hours playing when they were younger. The swing set and sandbox were still there, back behind the garage. She remembered Danny teasing them like crazy, but all in fun. He was a lot like Jamie, the best big brother in the world.

"Phee, can you do me a big favor?" Peggy asked when she returned to the kitchen.

"I'd be happy to."

She reached around the corner and grabbed an envelope from the buffet in the dining room. "I have a note for Mr. Campbell. I'd like for Christa to be excused from school this week. Could you drop it off at the office tomorrow morning?"

"Sure, I'll stop there first thing."

"I don't think she wants to miss the whole week, but I don't want her to be under any pressure."

"I'm sure it won't be a problem."

Just then, Christa and Adam walked in and joined them at the table. "We've decided to go to a movie this afternoon," Christa said.

"That's a great idea," her mom said. "What's playing?"

"*Here Come the Waves*," Adam said, "Bing Crosby and Betty Hutton. The ad in the paper said, 'they're saltwater crazy and full of romantic sizzle dizzle!'"

"Goodness!" Peggy said. "You certainly don't want to miss out on any romantic sizzle dizzle!"

Phee looked at Christa, hoping to see some peace, but she didn't. Any other time, she'd be invited to go with them to the movie. But not today; the invitation didn't come.

Suddenly, Phee began to feel a little queasy. The emotional toll from her encounter with Christa, along with the cigarette smoke and the cabbage in the soup simmering on the stove, were finally just too much. "Peggy, I'm starting to feel a little puny," she said, slowly standing. "I'd love to stay for lunch, but I should get home."

"I'm so sorry, Phee," Peggy said. "Did it come on all of a sudden?"

"Yeh, kinda. Nothing serious, I'm sure."

"Christa, you can drive Phee home."

Phee knew Christa would rather eat a handful of eight-penny nails than take her home right now.

"We'll both go," Adam volunteered. "I can drive."

"Certainly," Peggy said, standing to give Phee a hug. "Dear Phee, do take care of yourself. And thanks for coming over. We love you so much."

"I love you too." She took the note for Mr. Campbell, grabbed her coat, and followed Christa and Adam out to the car. On the short drive to the parsonage, Adam kept the conversation going as best he could. Neither Christa nor Phee was up to it, though.

"Thanks for the ride," Phee said when Adam pulled into the parsonage driveway. "See you soon." She slammed the door and hurried to the porch but didn't turn to wave as she usually did.

Frank and the kids were still at church, and Phee was glad to have some time to herself. She went to the kitchen and turned on the oven to heat up the leftovers she'd planned to serve last night. Her homework and practicing could wait. For now, she needed to lie down, close her eyes, and figure out how to salvage her relationship with her best friend. She never dreamed in a million years something like this could happen. She knew Christa's grief was driving this hatred for Horst and his comrades. Phee was devastated and wished she could be with Horst today. Somehow, she knew he'd make everything better.

Sun. Mar. 18, 1945

—Dear Daisy—

Sorry I didn't write last night. I was too tired and emotionally drained. I've not felt this sad since Mom died. Yesterday we found out Danny Rasmussen was killed in Germany earlier this month. Christa was home alone when the telegram was delivered. (How awful!) She came here hoping to see me, but I was at the camp for the dress rehearsal. Dad and Christa drove to Sioux City (in Doc Z's car) to get Jack and Peggy who were at a convention. I got the word about Danny from Mrs. Z after the rehearsal. I drove to their house and the kids and I had supper with them. (Note to Phee: don't forget to send a thank you note to Mrs. Z.) Dad got home around midnight. I took Jack's car back to their house this morning and hoped to spend some time comforting my best friend. Nope. Christa is mad at me for not being here when she came yesterday. She's mad at me for spending time with "those damn Nazis." She really said that! I couldn't believe it! Dad says she's in shock and she'll come around eventually. I sure hope so. I don't know what to do. I'm incredibly sad about Danny, and Christa's reaction makes it even worse. I understand as much as anyone that the passage of time helps diminish grief. I hope that's true for Christa, but in the meantime, I fear our friendship will be on the rocks for a good long while and I really hate that. Dad and I had a long talk about everything this afternoon. That helped a little. I worked on my history homework and I practiced. Mollie and Charlotte played in Mollie's room this afternoon. They laughed and laughed, and I was envious of their glee. Shame on me! Peggy gave me a note to give to Mr. Campbell tomorrow, in case Christa wants to miss school all week. I kinda hope she does. Shame on me again!

And life goes on. G'night.

PS—I almost forgot! Horst kissed me yesterday, or I kissed him, or maybe both. I loved it! (Sorry Christa, I did.)

28

SATURDAY 24 MAR. 1945

SEEING CHRISTA IN THE receiving line after Danny's memorial service this morning wasn't as bad as Phee had feared. When she whispered "love you so much, Christa" as they hugged, Christa didn't respond, but Phee thought she might have attempted a half smile or even a three-quarter smile. But Christa didn't seek her out at the luncheon after the service. Clearly, she needed more time.

As soon as they got home from church, Phee and Mollie went upstairs to Mollie's bedroom. Phee insisted her sister decide then and there what she'd wear to the concert at Camp Algona tonight.

"We are not going to repeat the December fiasco," Phee insisted. After staring in her closet at her limited wardrobe, Mollie finally chose the brown dress, the runner-up from December. On her way out, Phee said, "Mollie, I need to be at the camp, on the stage, at five thirty. Please be dressed and ready to go at five. Do you think you can manage?"

"Sure, but why don't you check on me right before, just in case?"

"Good idea."

After she practiced for an hour, Phee started a letter to Jamie. Should she mention she had feelings for Horst? No, not yet. Besides, someone else might read it. That wouldn't be good.

But she could tell her mom. Leaving a note for her dad who was napping in his chair, she grabbed her coat, and in less than five minutes, parked the car at the top of the hill on the east side of Riverview Cemetery.

The cemetery's grass was still dressed in winter brown, but spring had officially arrived in northern Iowa and today it felt like it. Visiting her mom's grave over the long winter had not been conducive to long conversations. Today, though, she'd have a nice long chat.

A few steps from Mary's grave was a small, curved marble bench, somewhat discolored from years of exposure to the elements. Engraved along the front edge of the seat were the words REST A WHILE. She appreciated the invitation and took a seat on the bench.

"Hi, Mom. Sorry it's been a while. I have a lot to tell you, so hold onto your hat." She began by telling Mary everything that had happened over the past month—the music program at school, making plans for Mollie's birthday party, practicing for her upcoming auditions in Sioux Falls and Mason City, and the long, sad, saga of Danny's death and Christa's anger and resentment.

"Oh Mom, I wish you were here. I know you could fix this with Christa and me. Dad's trying his best to sort it all out. I hope he can convince Christa she's being unreasonable, because she is, at least that's how I feel." She paused, listening for the still familiar sound of her mom's voice. "This weekend I'm accompanying the *Männerchor* again. They're singing German folk songs this time. Dad even remembers one from Augie. He and the kids will go with me tonight. Mollie's already picked out what she'll wear, thank God.

"So, I guess I'll tell you everything. Don't be shocked." After a big sigh, she said, "I think I'm in love with Horst. I know, it's completely ridiculous. I haven't told anyone, except Daisy. I probably won't tell Horst, but I might. I know he likes me, maybe a lot, but I'm not sure it's love. I hope it is. I really want him to love me . . ." She glanced at her watch. "Well, I'd better get home. Thanks for listening. I still miss you so much. Love you, Mom."

PHEE DROVE TO THE camp, and after dropping Frank and the kids off at Ed Mattson's office, she headed to the theater parking lot and pulled into "her spot." Inside the hall, she noted only about half of the choir members were on stage. Gerhard, the man Phee recognized at the rehearsal last weekend, walked over to the piano. "*Guten Abend,* Fräulein Swensson."

"*Guten Abend*, Gerhard."

"I have from our Herr *Direktor* a message."

"Is everything alright?"

"*Ja. Feldwebel* Ebinger will be delayed to the theater for a short time. He would like for you to help us make our voices warm."

She smiled. "Sure, I can lead the warm-up."

"*Wunderbar!*" I will call the others inside now." He hurried to the west stage door and shouted to his comrades who were outside smoking, and soon, all thirty-six men were in place on the risers.

Phee led the men through the routines Mrs. Goodwin used at school. They were quick learners, and when they finished, she received an enthusiastic round of applause just as Horst arrived at the stage door.

Phee blushed and Horst, smiling broadly, said, "I can see I am no longer needed."

The choir members laughed and a few shouted, "*Jawohl!*"

Horst winked at Phee, then waited off stage for the American audience to fill the hall. Just after six o'clock, he walked to the microphone at center stage. Following a short welcome, he spoke briefly about the pieces on the program. Phee loved watching him, noting his English had improved significantly since last summer.

"*Muss i denn,*" Frank's favorite, occurred about halfway through the program. Horst read the translation, then, unexpectedly, he said, "This song is a favorite of mine, and I have been told it is the same for someone in our audience. Our *Männerchor* would like to invite Pastor Frank Swensson of St. Peter's Church to sing with us. Pastor Swensson, please join me here on the stage."

Sitting with Mollie and the twins four rows back, Frank stood slowly amid enthusiastic applause. He looked at Phee who shrugged her shoulders and shook her head. When he reached center stage, he shook Horst's hand, then turned to the audience. "I'm not sure whose crazy idea this was, but it would be my honor to sing *'Muss i denn'* with this fine group. It's been at least twenty-five years, though, so I'd better have some music." A choir member stepped forward and offered his copy. "*Vielen dank*," Frank said. "Where should I stand?"

Frank joined the basses on the far side of the stage, and as soon as he was in place, Horst nodded at Phee who began the short introduction. At the end of the last verse, the choir received a standing ovation. Phee guessed Ed was probably in on this plan, but however it was arranged, she was proud of her dad and grateful that Horst had invited him.

At the end of the concert, Frank, Ed, and the kids came to the stage, and while they chatted with Phee, Horst joined them.

Mollie, standing next to Frank, chose to speak up this time. "I liked all the songs," she said to Horst, "especially the one Dad sang."

"We should say your father helped us to sound marvelous tonight, will you agree?

"He sure did! Can I shake your hand?"

Horst smiled and took her hand. "I hope you will come for another time, in a few months, perhaps."

"Well, we should be on our way," Frank said. "Sergeant, thank you again for the opportunity. I'll remember this for a long time."

"Goodbye, Sergeant," Mollie said with a big smile.

"*Auf Wiedersehen*, Fräulein."

AFTER THE SECOND CONCERT, Horst and Phee waited for the hall to clear before sitting together on the piano bench. Phee sighed, and Horst could tell she wasn't happy. "You are not pleased with our performance?" he asked.

"Oh, no, I'm very pleased. It was great, the best yet."

"So, what can be wrong?"

"I'm afraid I won't see you again for a while."

He reached for her hand. "I have also thought about it, and I might have a solution."

"Tell me."

"*Nein*, not yet. There must be a discussion. You will know when the decision has been made."

"I'm very curious."

"*Das ist gut*, to be curious. And I have just remembered your gift from the *Männerchor*. Wait here, *bitte*." He walked quickly across the stage to the storage room and returned with a box, a little larger than a book, wrapped in newsprint.

"This really isn't necessary, Horst."

"But it is. Please open it."

A small note card was attached to the box. "Thank you for our Fräulein Swensson," she read aloud. "You help us sound marvelous once again. Please make the arrangements to accompany us in future days. Yours very sincerely, the Camp Algona *Männerchor*." Inside the box she found a blue and white plaid cloth-covered book, about a half inch thick. She opened it. "Manuscript paper! Just what I needed!"

"We had hope for this reaction. You can use it for your next composition."

She flipped through the pages. "I've already been thinking about something but haven't written anything down yet. Now I can."

"For piano?"

"No, for mixed chorus, a Christmas song. I was thinking St. Pete's choir could sing it on Christmas Eve, if it's good enough, that is."

"The *Männerchor* will sing it, if we are celebrating the holiday in our camp."

"Oh, Horst, you have to be!"

He sat once more on the bench and kissed her cheek. "We should speak about the future, but not now, after such a fine evening."

"I guess you're right," she said, then looked at her watch. "I should go." And then, out of the blue, without planning or intending it, she asked, "Horst . . . how do you say, 'I love you' in German?"

Phee knew Horst did not expect that question tonight, probably not any night, but she asked it, and now he had to respond. She could say those three words in English, and he would understand. But tonight, she wanted to say them in German. "I want to know, Horst. It's really important."

"*Ja*, I can see it, but—"

"Please, tell me."

He reached for her hands. "If you say these words now, how will you think of it tomorrow?"

"Well . . . I'm quite sure it will make me smile."

He chuckled softly. "*Ja*, I suppose it will."

"And if I say it, how will *you* think of it tomorrow?"

He hesitated, and Phee worried she might have pushed a little too hard. "I have not heard these words before," he said, "only from my *Mutter*."

She lifted his hand, kissed it, and said with confidence, "So, maybe it's time for someone else to say them."

"*Ich liebe dich.*"

"What?"

"You can say it now. *Ich.*"

"Eeesh?"

"*Liebe.*"

"Lee-buh?"

"*Dich.*"

"Deesh. *Ich liebe dich,* Horst."

More than anything, Phee wanted Horst to say those words to her, but he didn't, and while she was a little disappointed, she knew she must be patient. It could happen someday. It probably would happen. In time, Phee was confident Horst would say, "*Ich liebe dich.*" And the next day, she'd smile.

29

THURSDAY 5 APR. 1945

HOPING TO ENCOURAGE PHEE and Christa to resolve their relationship dilemma, Frank arranged for the two girls and Christa's boyfriend Adam to meet with him in his office at four thirty this afternoon. Last week during Holy Week, Frank didn't see Christa in church until the eleven o'clock service on Easter morning when she sat with her parents near the back of the sanctuary. From what he could tell, there was no interaction between Phee and Christa that morning. Maybe today's meeting could help.

It was half past four, and Phee and Frank had been waiting in Frank's office for almost fifteen minutes. Phee was more nervous about this meeting than she was about her recitals last fall. She didn't have much faith it would go well.

They heard the back door open, and soon, Christa and Adam walked in. "Sorry we're late," Adam said. "I got hung up at school."

"You're not late at all," Frank said. "We were just talking about the Easter breakfast."

"I'm sorry I couldn't be there," Christa said, removing her coat and hanging it on the back of one of the chairs at the nearby table. "I just wasn't ready."

"We understand, Christa," Phee said, wanting to join the conversation. "We missed you, though."

"Let's have a seat, shall we?" Frank suggested. Christa sat across from Frank, either by accident or, more likely, Phee thought, by design. At least the two girls wouldn't have to stare at one another across the table.

"First off," Frank said after they were settled, "I'd like to start with a prayer." They all bowed their heads, and he began. "Gracious Father, thank you for this beautiful day and for the opportunity to speak to one another. Help us find the words that are in our hearts. Give us the gift of understanding and compassion, and help us find peace. In Christ's name we pray. Amen."

Christa smiled and nodded. "Thanks, Frank."

"So, Christa," Frank said, "and you too, Adam, Phee and I are glad you're here. We know you've given all this some thought, and we hope you'll share some of those thoughts with us, if you can."

No one commented. All eyes were on Frank, so he continued. "Now, I'm not here to convince anyone of anything. My role can be, not a referee, but, a moderator, let's say. I'm here to listen, and to counsel when needed, to keep the conversation focused. There shouldn't be any pressure for us to resolve anything today, necessarily. If we can, great. If not, we can try again in a week or two or however long you think it should be."

"It might be too soon," Christa admitted. "My emotions are still pretty raw."

"And if that's the case," Frank said, "just say the word and we'll call it a day."

"Let's give it a try," she said meekly.

"Okay, good. Thank you, Christa." He cleared his throat. "So, as you'd expect, Phee and I have talked about this, and I'm sure you've done the same with Adam and maybe others."

Christa looked at Adam and reached for his hand. "I've talked his ear off, poor guy."

Everyone chuckled, but the levity didn't last.

"Why don't you start, Christa," Frank proposed. "Give us your perspective, if you can."

"First off," she began, "you'd better get that tissue box over here 'cause I'm gonna need one, I can tell already."

"Oh sure," Frank said as he reached for the box on his desk.

Christa heaved a big sigh, then poured it all out. "Here's how I see it," she said, staring at the tissue box now sitting in the center of the table. "My dear, wonderful brother Danny, my only brother, was killed last month. He didn't just die, he was *killed*. It's the worst thing that has ever happened to me. I'm hurting, bad, and I have to live with my parents who are also devastated, and . . ." She took a deep breath. ". . . my best friend is spending so much time out at that camp with men who would have killed my brother given half a chance."

Phee winced. She expected it, but it was still hard to hear.

"For me," Christa continued, "knowing those men are living so close to town, well, to be honest, it was hard to stomach before Danny died, but it's so much harder now."

"You know, Christa," Frank interrupted, "I've counseled quite a few families who have lost loved ones in this war, and I've heard similar words from most all of them. Your feelings are not unusual or unfounded."

"But this is different, Frank. Those people don't have best friends who spend so much time out there, do they?"

"No, not to my knowledge, but—"

"They started this war," she said. "They should suffer for it. Instead, they're singing and playing games, and I bet they're eating better food than we do."

"Yes, that's mostly true," Frank admitted, "and there are a lot of reasons—"

"Well, I think it stinks. It's not fair."

"And you're resentful?" Phee asked softly.

Christa turned and stared at Phee. "You betcha I'm resentful! You would be too if you were in my shoes."

No one spoke, so Frank asked, "Phee, would you like to respond?"

She nodded, sighed, and began. "Christa, I hate it that Danny was killed. It's just the worst thing. I loved him, you know that. It breaks my heart."

"I know," Christa said, reaching for a tissue.

"It was so perfect. We both had an older brother we adored, and that alone meant so much. Both Jamie and Danny teased us all the time, but we loved every minute of it." Phee also reached for a tissue. "I'll miss that forever. Danny was a part of my life. It's just so hard to believe he's . . . that he'll not be around to tease me anymore."

Christa nodded and wiped her eyes.

"Please let me try to explain what performing with the *Männerchor* has meant to me, and why I hope it can continue."

"You can try," she said.

"You know I'm serious about continuing my music studies. Mrs. Z encourages me to play publicly whenever I can. I learn something new every time I perform. I have two auditions coming up, and I'm feeling very confident about them."

"But you play at school," Christa argued, "for Luther League, and you still take lessons."

"That's true, I do." Phee chose her words carefully. "Christa . . . the prisoners, the group I've come to know, they're here in Iowa because they were captured over there, somewhere. They were on the wrong side, the bad side. Early on, Chaplain Mattson told Dad he thought I could be a positive influence on those men, helping them forget all the bad stuff they were taught before the war. Maybe they'll think about all that when they go back to Germany in a few months or next year, after the war. Maybe—"

"I just think you should stop playing for the Krauts, that's all."

Phee took a moment, then said softly, "I'm sorry, Christa, I can't."

And at that moment, all four people sitting at the table understood the estrangement between two of them would most likely continue for some time.

Finally, Frank spoke. "It looks like we've hit an impasse, but I think this has been worthwhile. Let's give it some more time. Maybe we can agree to meet again, or—"

"Thanks for inviting us," Christa said as she pushed back her chair and stood. "I appreciate it, more than you know. I'd like to think about all of this. I'm still hurting, a lot, about everything."

"Of course," Frank said as he stood, "we understand."

Phee also stood, wiped her eyes, and nodded.

"Thank you, Pastor Swensson, for allowing me to sit in," Adam said.

"I'm glad you could be here, Adam," Frank said. "Feel free to come any time, both of you. My door is always open."

Christa reached for her coat. "See you later," she said, then walked out. Adam followed.

As they both sat once again at the table, Frank reached for Phee's hand. "Are you alright?"

She sighed. "No, not really, but I'm not surprised." And then, she asked the inevitable question. "Do you think I'm being unreasonable?"

Frank smiled. "I was wondering when you'd get around to asking me that."

"You don't, do you?"

"Phee, this is a difficult situation. Christa wants you to respect her feelings and end your association with all the Germans at the camp."

"She does."

"So, let's try this. Let's say . . . you agree to stop playing for the *Männerchor*. You get up from your chair, go to the phone on my desk, make a call to the Rasmussens, and you tell Christa, 'You're right.'"

"But—"

"You do that, and what have you accomplished? How would you feel?"

"I'd be resentful of her demands."

"Yes, you would. And Christa, while she might appreciate that you agreed to her demands, would still be grieving. She'd still be resentful of the prisoners. Her hatred for them will not bring Danny back. Your concession may not be the path to healing Christa thinks she needs."

"So, are you saying it wouldn't do any good for me to concede?"

"Probably not. We need to keep praying for Christa and her parents. God will intervene. He has the answers we're searching for." He squeezed her hand. "Phee, I honestly think, when the war's over, and Camp Algona is but a fleeting memory . . ."

It won't be fleeting for me!

". . . well, I'm confident your friendship with Christa will survive this."

"Then I won't need to stop playing at the camp," Phee said, feeling reassured.

"No, you won't. You've had your share of grief since your mom died. If playing at the camp makes you happy, then I'm all for it."

"Thanks Dad. That helps, it really does."

"Besides, Ed would have a fit if you stopped."

"Yeh, he probably would." *And so would Horst!*

Frank glanced at his watch. "Better get home and make sure those kids aren't burning the house down."

"Yeh, no kidding. I'll get supper started. Are you coming?"

"I've got a little work left on my sermon. I'll be home by six."

As Phee walked across the parking lot, the path she'd taken hundreds or even thousands of times, she was a little sad, but also relieved she wouldn't need to give in to Christa's demands to stay away from Camp Algona. *We'll just have to find another way to fix this, Christa.*

Sat. Apr. 7, 1945

—Dear Daisy—

Happy Birthday Sweet Pea! I can't believe my baby sister is 9 years (and 5 days) old! I remember Mom holding her in the rocking chair in their bedroom, trying to comfort her while she cried. (She was a very colicky baby.) Being a mom must be the hardest job in the world. Mollie's party was a big hit. Bee, Nannie, Helen, and Claire arrived at 10:30 and by 11 the party was in full swing. Helen brought their Bingo game and the girls loved it. I played for musical chairs and that was a riot. Mollie got a lot of nice gifts. I'll get her started on her thank yous tomorrow. But Daisy, here's THE BEST part of today—I got to see Horst! It was serendipitous (a recent Word of the Day, believe it or not). Bee told Dad he'd like to see the camp on their way home, so Dad called Ed who said we could all come out at 2. (The twins were at the Zetterholms' so they didn't get to go.) We took 2 cars. When we got to Ed's office, he was in a meeting with the German chaplains and the prisoner rep, Sergeant Somebody—and Horst! They were talking about the concerts planned for this summer. Ed invited me to join the meeting at the end while he took everyone around the camp. (They had decided earlier, among other things, that Horst and I would play a piano four hands piece on the concerts. Isn't that great?! It was Horst's idea.) The rest of the meeting didn't last long, and when everyone got up to leave, Horst said he'd stay behind so we could talk about our performance for the concerts. A guard was there, but he spent the whole time flirting with Julie who was at her desk. The door was open, but we could sit where they couldn't see us. We kissed—twice! I told Horst I could borrow music from Mrs. Z and I'd bring it the next time we meet at the theater. Now we have a reason to meet again! Yay! Everyone enjoyed the tour. Mollie and Claire were thrilled because they got to see Jupiter and Churchill (the baby horses). They're quite a pair, those girls. I'm glad they get along so well. I did some homework and practiced before supper. And tonight, we all played crazy eights. I'm bushed. A long but wonderful day.

And life goes on. G'night.

30

THURSDAY 12 APR. 1945

THIS AFTERNOON AT TWO thirty-five Iowa time, President Franklin Delano Roosevelt died. Some people heard about it on the radio, others got phone calls from family or friends. Secretaries interrupted meetings, nurses interrupted surgeries, and farmers' wives ran out to barns to give their husbands the bad news.

It didn't take long for the news to reach the pastor's office at St. Pete's. Frank had been there most of the day, working on Sunday's sermon. Just after three thirty, the phone rang, and Frank casually lifted the receiver. "St. Peter's, Frank Swensson speaking."

"Frank, it's Ed Mattson."

"Howdy-do, Ed. How's it going?"

Ed took a moment, then said, "Are you sitting down?"

Frank sat up straight. "Oh God, what is it?"

"We've just heard. President Roosevelt is dead."

Frank leaned back in his chair and closed his eyes. "When? Where?"

"We don't know too much yet. It happened about an hour ago. He's in Warm Springs, that's in Georgia. Been down there a couple of weeks."

"Heart attack?" Frank asked.

"No, they're saying a massive cerebral hemorrhage. Apparently, he went pretty fast."

"Well, shit. I mean, we all knew he wasn't a healthy man, but still . . ."

"I know. It's hard to believe."

"So, will you have a service out there?"

"Yes, and that's one reason I'm calling. I know it's short notice, but I'm hoping Phee might be available to play tonight, unless you need her there."

"I won't need her if Edith can play. Tell ya what. Let me call Edith. Phee should be home from school in about half an hour. Soon as I know what's going on, I'll call you right back."

"Sounds good. Thanks, Frank."

Edith had just heard about the president and was expecting Frank's call. She could play tonight, and they'd meet in Frank's office at seven fifteen to go over the service.

Frank shut his sermon notebook and prepared to walk home, but instead of turning right towards the back door, he turned left and strolled down the hall to the sanctuary. He took a seat in the front pew, bowed his head, and prayed for the president's family and the American people. He also prayed for Vice President Harry Truman who, if he hadn't already, would soon take the presidential oath of office. Frank figured Mr. Truman, the man whom almost no one knew, would need prayers more than just about anybody.

Before he left the sanctuary, Frank walked over to the piano. He did not consider himself a pianist by any stretch of the imagination, but he could plunk out a few familiar hymn tunes when he put his mind to it. "Nearer, My God, To Thee" was on his mind now because he remembered hearing a while back it was one of the president's favorite hymns. He'd include it in the service tonight.

WHILE FRANK WAS IN the kitchen listening to the radio, Mollie and the twins came in the front door. The boys were arguing about baseball, and apparently Mollie didn't have enough to eat for lunch. Frank suspected nothing was said about the president at school before they were dismissed, so he'd have to be the bearer of bad news now.

"Dad, can we eat early?" Mollie yelled. "I'm kinda hungry already."

Frank called out from the kitchen, "Sweet Pea, boys, come join me. We need to talk."

"Uh-oh, wha'd we do?" Tris asked. "Bet it was Mollie."

"Not me, I'm perfect!" she pouted.

"You're all perfect today," Frank said. "Sit. I'll treat you to some milk and cookies."

Frank turned off the radio, then poured their milk and reached for the Oreos on top of the ice box. "Does anyone have homework tonight?" he asked.

"I'm s'posed to memorize ten new vocabulary words," Mollie said. "I already have five, so it won't take me very long."

"Boys?"

"Nothing tonight," Gus said, reaching for another cookie. "Mrs. Wellman said we'd have some over the weekend, though."

"The reason I'm asking is because we'll be at church tonight for a memorial service for President Roosevelt."

"Why, is he sick?" Mollie asked.

"No, Sweet Pea, I'm afraid the president died today."

The kids were silent for a moment, then Gus asked, "Are we supposed to be sad?"

Frank smiled. "Well, Gus, I don't think you're supposed to be sad, but it would be perfectly fine if you were. A lot of people are sad or will be when they hear the news, mostly the adults, I guess. He's been president for a long time, you know."

"Was he killed in the war like Danny?" Mollie asked.

"No, he wasn't. They said it was . . . there was bleeding inside his head. It was very serious."

"I bet he worried too much about the war," Tris said after he took another sip of milk. "Do you think someone can die from worrying?"

"You know, Tris, I do think a person can die from worrying. We probably won't know if that's what caused the president's death, but he sure had an awful lot on his shoulders."

"Are you sad about President Roosevelt, Dad?" Gus asked.

"I am, in a way. It's not like when your mom died. But I admired the man, and he's led our country through some very difficult days. He was Commander in Chief of the Armed Services, so, I guess you could say he was Jamie's boss."

"Really?" Mollie said. "I didn't know that."

"He was pretty old, wasn't he?" Tris asked.

"If you mean older than your dad," Frank replied, "then yes, I guess he was."

"He was born in 1882," Gus remembered, "so that makes him . . . sixty-three. That's old."

Just then, Phee walked in the front door, and Mollie ran to greet her. "Did you hear? The president died."

"I did hear."

"Are you sad?" Mollie asked. "Dad is."

"I guess so, a little. He's been our president for as long as I can remember."

Frank walked out from the kitchen. "Are you alright?" he asked.

"Yeh, I'm fine. What a shock, though, huh?"

"Yes, it is. Phee, we need to talk about tonight and there's not much time. We're gonna have to eat fast. I'm planning a service at eight. Edith and I will meet at seven fifteen to map it all out."

"So, you don't need me to play."

"No, but Ed does. He called to tell me about the president and asked if you could play for their service tonight."

"I guess I could. Did he say what time?"

"No, but I said we'd get back to him as soon as you got home. Why don't you make the call and I'll get the soup on the stove?"

Phee got through to the Chaplain's office after two rings. "Phee, you're a life saver," Ed said after hearing Phee could play for their service. "I can't thank you enough. Can you be out here at seven?"

Phee thought about her algebra homework, and on top of that, she hadn't practiced yet today. "Sure. Should I wear anything special?"

"Whatever you wore to school will be just fine."

"Okay, I'll see you soon," she said, then walked to the kitchen. "Dad, they expect me out there at seven, and I need to look at the hymns and decide on the prelude and postlude. I know we're both under the gun. Can you get supper on the table?"

"Sure. I need to run over to the office, but I should be back in thirty minutes."

"I'll keep an eye on the stove."

"Tell the kids we'll eat at six," he yelled over his shoulder as he walked out the back door.

Just then, Phee had an idea. She called Roy Phillips who, luckily, was near the phone.

"Guard Barracks, Corporal Phillips speaking, sir."

Phee chuckled. "Hi, Roy, it's Phee Swensson."

"It sure is. What can I do for you, Phee?"

"Chaplain Mattson has asked me to play for the president's memorial service tonight."

"Great! I mean, that's nice. I hope to be there."

"Good, good. Uhm . . . the reason I'm calling . . ." *I should've thought this through before I called!* "I was wondering if you could arrange a meeting for me and Sergeant Ebinger tonight after the service. I know it's last minute, and it's fine if you can't. We need to talk about the concerts they're planning for this summer. Chaplain Mattson wants the Sergeant and me to play a piano duet."

"No kidding! With two pianos?"

"Well, not quite. Two people, one piano. Anyway, Mrs. Zetterholm loaned me some music and we need to decide what we're going to play."

"Far as I know that should work, but the Sergeant might have other plans. Tell you what. I'll try to get you a message right after the service so you'll know if he's coming."

"That would be great."

"I'll see you in a little while."

"Thanks, Roy."

Phee had just an hour to practice and get ready to go. She'd change into something a little nicer for the service, and for Horst, just in case.

THE MEMORIAL SERVICE IN the theater hall was well attended by army personnel and civilian staff. The stories offered by two soldiers about their personal encounters with President Roosevelt were touching and even a bit humorous. A few years ago, before the war, Colonel McNabb had met the president at a campaign rally in Omaha. Phee assumed the Colonel was a Democrat, but tonight, it didn't matter. Everyone in the hall was there to remember and pay their respects to a great man.

After the service, when the hall was almost empty, the west stage door opened, and Roy Phillips walked in.

"Hi, Roy." Phee said from the piano bench. "Is the Sergeant coming?"

"He is, but he's in the middle of a dance band rehearsal that'll go till nine. He said if you can wait, he'd come as soon as he could after his rehearsal."

"I can wait, no problem. I brought my homework along, just in case."

"Good. Oh, and I'll send a guard, Corporal Bickford if he's available."

Oh poo! Don't send a guard! "Thanks, Roy. I sure appreciate your help."

Phee spent about twenty minutes on her Algebra assignment, then had to stop because she was too anxious to focus on equations, factoring, and functions. She wandered over to the west stage door and opened it—no Horst. At ten past nine, she began to think he wasn't coming. *Maybe he couldn't get a pass to leave the compound. Maybe his rehearsal is going way overtime. Maybe he forgot.*

He didn't. The west stage door opened, and Horst hurried in. "I am sorry to come late for our meeting. I could not run because I would be shot for attempting to escape. Can you forgive me?"

Phee thought for a moment. "I guess so."

"We were very surprised to hear about the death of your president," he said, sitting next to her on the bench. "We think it should be Herr Hitler's turn."

"I'm so glad you feel that way."

"And now, we must decide on our music, *ja*?"

"We really should so we can start practicing our parts."

They spent some time looking at the pieces Phee had borrowed from her teacher. Horst was impressed with the samples from Edith's library and wanted very much to perform one or two of the Brahms dances on the concerts this summer. Phee, on the other hand, was more interested in Dvořák's *Slavonic Dances*.

"How will we choose?" he asked.

"We could flip a coin," she suggested.

"Flip a coin?"

"Yeh, like heads or tails?"

"*Ja, eine Münze werfen*. But I have no coin. Can you flip it for yourself?"

Phee reached in her pouch for her billfold. "I'm sure I have a nickel." She did. "You choose—heads or tails?"

"I would choose the head."

"And I get tails," she said while holding the nickel on the palm of her hand. "See, it's Thomas Jefferson on this side, and Monticello, his home in Virginia, on the other. If it lands with his face up, you win. If it lands with Monticello up, I win. Ready?"

"*Jawohl!*"

Phee walked to the center of the stage and tossed the nickel high in the air. When it landed, she bent over to look.

"And will it be my beloved Brahms?"

She stood up and smiled. "Nope!"

"Are you certain?" he asked, walking over to look for himself. When he got to Phee's side, he put his arm around her and kissed her cheek, then reached down to pick up the coin that had landed with Mr. Jefferson's lips kissing the floor.

"So tonight," he said, "we will begin to learn Herr Dvořák."

They struggled through the first of Antonin Dvořák's *Slavonic Dances*, Op. 46. Phee was so very happy, sitting next to Horst while they played beautiful music, or music that would eventually be beautiful. "That's enough for tonight," she said when they finished. "Oh, gosh, look at the time! You need to get back to your barracks! I don't want you to get in trouble."

"The Corporal knows about my meeting with Fräulein Swensson. He will speak for me."

"That reminds me," she said, looking across the hall to the lobby doors, "Roy said he'd send a guard over. I guess he forgot."

"I can walk with you to your car now." Before they stepped outside the stage door, Horst reached for Phee's arm. "I should kiss you now in case we have company outside the door."

Phee giggled, and they enjoyed a nice long kiss. Leaning against the stage door, she whispered, "Horst?"

"*Ja?*"

"*Ich liebe dich.*"

He kissed her again but didn't repeat the sentiment.

Oh well, you will someday.

31

FRIDAY 4 MAY 1945

LAST SUNDAY AFTERNOON WAS the spring music program at Algona High School. Before the mixed chorus performed, Phee was presented with the Most Accomplished Senior Music Student trophy and a crisp five-dollar bill. This honor had been bestowed on a senior student every spring for as long as anyone could remember, and four years ago, Jamie walked home with the trophy and cash. Christa found her after the concert to offer congratulations, and Phee hoped it was a sign of positive progress in their strained relationship.

Today was Phee's second piano audition. Last month, her audition with Dr. Judith Bowen at Augustana College went better than she thought it would. She liked Dr. Bowen, and Sioux Falls looked like a nice place to live. Mason City was their destination this morning. Edith drove again, this time traveling east on Highway 18. The audition was held in the sanctuary at Central Presbyterian Church. Both Phee and Edith were disappointed when they walked in and found Dr. George Ketterman sitting at an old upright piano instead of a baby grand. It had been tuned, though, and the tone was surprisingly good. Dr. Ketterman, one of two piano professors at the State University of Iowa in Iowa City, was an imposing figure—tall and thin, with a beard and handlebar moustache. He didn't care to hear the Chopin or the Debussy. Instead, he had Phee play the entire Bach "Prelude and Fugue No. 2 in C Minor" from the *Well-Tempered Clavier* Book No. 1 and the second and third movements of the Beethoven sonata she performed on her recital last fall.

Near the end of the audition, Dr. Ketterman brought out *Capriccio on Russian Themes*, a piece for piano four hands by Glinka, and asked Phee to play the treble part while he played the bass. Her sight-reading skills served her well, and Dr. Ketterman was impressed, or so it seemed.

After leaving the church, Edith and Phee found a diner and had a quick lunch before they drove back to Algona. On the way home, they had a serious conversation about Phee's future.

"Phee, I hope you're feeling positive about everything," Edith said. "These past two years, since your mom died, you've proven over and over you're a strong, very capable, extremely talented young woman. You can't waste it."

"You mean, by not going to college? I told you Dad and I have agreed I'll wait a year."

"Yes, you did, and I understand why. But I believe continuing your music studies is so important, and it doesn't matter where. Algona is a wonderful place to live, to grow up, but it will limit you if you stay. It will . . . hold you back."

"Do you think Algona has held you back?"

"Yes, I do, in some respects. From time to time, I've wondered, 'what if?' But I have a family I adore and music in my life almost every day, either with playing at St. Pete's or teaching. It's very satisfying. But you're better than I was at your age."

"I am?"

"You are."

"You mean it?"

Edith chuckled. "Yes, I mean it. You know I did very well at the university. I had two wonderful piano professors, learned to play the organ. And then, I moved to Algona and met Harold."

"The love of your life."

"Well, yes, he is. I'm blessed in so many ways. Finding a man like Harold is important, but so is having dreams and goals and discovering all the ways you can pursue them. In my view, a college environment is the most pragmatic way, if you will, to continue your musical journey. So, let's not even consider the possibility that you won't go to college next year—a year from this fall, I mean. You've just had two successful auditions. Let's build on those."

Phee was convinced, except she didn't want to think about college just now. Yes, it would happen, but, between now and when Camp Algona closed for good, she'd try to spend as much time as she could with the love of *her* life.

32

MONDAY 7 MAY 1945

ANTICIPATION SWIRLED AROUND ALGONA this morning. Adolf Hitler was dead; the end of the war in Europe was inevitable; and everyone within earshot of a radio was listening and waiting for the news. Surely it would come today.

And it did, except it wasn't official. Radio reports indicated that the word from Washington, DC would be forthcoming, but it didn't come. Nevertheless, the mayor and the Algona Retail Closing Uniformity Committee members met at the Chamber of Commerce and proceeded with the celebration. The siren at City Hall sounded at ten fifteen and continued blasting away for fifteen minutes. Hearing the signal for all businesses and schools to close, people rushed home or gathered in small groups downtown. Some school kids celebrated their early dismissal by riding their bikes up and down the streets, waving to passersby, giggling and shouting, "the war's over! the war's over!" There were big smiles on every face in town—or almost every face.

The twins and Mollie arrived home before Phee. She'd stayed at school to talk to Mrs. Goodwin about the program scheduled for one thirty in the high school auditorium. The mixed chorus and the band would perform, Mayor Kimball would speak, and Frank was asked to give the opening prayer and benediction. Tonight, most churches in town, including St. Pete's, would offer a short service of gratitude and remembrance.

Phee wasn't anxious to face her family, so she walked her bike home from school, occasionally waving to friends and acquaintances and even perfect strangers who shouted out or waved to her along the way. She was envious of those who were smiling and laughing, those who were overjoyed about the end of the war with Germany. *Lucky you.*

She leaned her bike against the house, then came around to the front door, heaving a big sigh before walking in. Mollie, who'd been watching from the living room window, ran to the door and gave her sister a hug. "Oh, Phee, it's wonderful! The war's over! Can't Jamie come home now?"

Phee forced a happy reply. "Well, the war in Europe seems to be over. And yes, I certainly hope Jamie can come home."

Frank walked out from the kitchen. "Glad you're home. Is everything alright?"

"Yeh, I stayed to talk to Mrs. Goodwin about the program."

"It seems the city fathers have jumped the gun. There's still no official announcement from Washington about the surrender."

"I'm sure the mayor's been planning this for weeks. Everyone is more than ready."

"Indeed, they are," he said. "Say, I'm planning a short service for tonight. Edith's a little under the weather so I need you to play. She said to tell you no lesson today."

Phee sat on the chair next to the phone, covered her face with her hands, but said nothing.

"What's going on?" Frank asked.

"Oh, nothing," she said with a sigh, "it's all just a little overwhelming."

"I know. It's hard to believe it's really happening. So, what about tonight?"

"I can do it. Just let me know what I need to know."

"I'll give you the hymn numbers. Will that suffice?"

"Sure. Better get upstairs and look at my homework. Can you get lunch going?"

"I think I can manage."

When she got to her bedroom, she gently closed the door, laid her books on the bed, walked to her closet, and stepped inside. Her bathrobe hung from a hook on the door. Burying her face in one of the sleeves, she cried her eyes out. When she was done crying, she had a thought: *I need to see Horst!*

DESPITE EVERYTHING ON HER agenda today, Phee managed to arrange a meeting with Horst. She had to leave a message for Roy Phillips in the guard barracks, and ten minutes later, he returned her call. She explained that she and Horst needed to rehearse the music they'd chosen for the summer concerts. Roy wasn't totally convinced, she thought, but said he'd look into it. Twenty minutes later, he called to say the meeting was set for four o'clock on the theater stage.

To provide evidence to anyone who might need to know their meeting was legitimate, Phee hoped she and Horst could agree on dates for their rehearsals over the next couple of months. The Burpee seed calendar, which she kept tacked to the wall in her bedroom, was in her music pouch. She also packed the Dvořák in case she recovered sufficiently enough from her miserableness to rehearse it.

Just as Phee pulled into the theater parking lot, an enlisted man with Sergeant stripes on his sleeve approached the car. He looked familiar, then she remembered he was in charge of the camp theater building.

"Miss Swensson?" he asked as she stepped out of the car.

"Yes?"

"I'm Ben Jackson. I believe we met last summer."

"Of course," she said, shaking his hand, "I remember."

"Corporal Phillips asked me to get the building open for you. He said you'd be here about an hour?"

"That's right. I'm here for a rehearsal."

"Let me unlock the door and get some lights on."

Phee followed Sergeant Jackson into the hall. "Just the stage lights will be enough," she said.

After the Sergeant flipped the appropriate switches, he said, "There ya go. When you're ready to leave, just exit through the lobby. I'll check back later to turn off the lights and lock up."

"Thank you, Sergeant."

She hoped Horst would be on time. They had a lot to talk about. The war with Germany was over, and she knew it meant their relationship would soon be over, too. It would take her some time to accept it. She wasn't close to accepting it this afternoon.

When Horst arrived, she reached for him and held him close. She wanted to be strong, but the tears flowed.

"We should not be sad with our time together," he said, wiping her cheeks with his thumbs.

She shook her head and tried to smile. "No, I guess we shouldn't."

"We should go to the piano. Our music will make you cheerful."

"I don't want to make music. I just want to hold you and kiss you."

"There will be time for that, but we should speak together now." He took her hand and led her to the chairs near one of the west windows. They sat face to face.

"Today is the absolute worst day of my life," Phee cried.

Horst smiled. "How can it be? We are together now. Today we learned your country and my country will end the fighting. Herr Hitler is dead, and the war with our countries is finished. How can that be sad?"

"Obviously, all that's good. In my head I understand, really I do."

"And your brother . . ."

"Jamie."

". . . the magnificent trumpeter. He should return to America soon, *ja?*"

"Yes, that's definitely wonderful."

"So, you can be happy today."

She reached for his hands. "We don't have much time. I know you have to be back for barracks check at five."

Horst sighed. "We must continue to prove we have not escaped from our camp."

"Let's go up to the stage," she said. "There is something we need to talk about."

When they got to the piano, Phee pulled the calendar and a pencil from her pouch. "Can we decide on rehearsal dates for the next few weeks? Graduation is on the twenty-fifth. I might be able to fit in one or two rehearsals before then. Sunday afternoons at three?" She circled the thirteenth and the twentieth, then checked the calendar for June and July. They decided most Sundays would work. She expected to be in town all summer except the first week of July when she'd be at the lake. "Can you have someone check the camp calendar to make sure the hall is free?"

"I will ask Sergeant Mueller, our enlisted leader, to arrange it. And Corporal Phillips will call to tell you."

"Good, that should work."

"We should visit Herr Dvořák while there is time," he suggested. They managed to play through the entire first dance, not without mistakes, not without stopping and starting several times. It was rough, but it would be better soon. But not too soon. They needed a reason to rehearse.

Phee felt much better. For the first time since she heard about Germany's surrender, she was almost happy. "Horst . . ."

"*Ja?*"

"I just had a thought. Don't be shocked." She took a deep breath. "I'd like to take you into town someday, just us."

Gathering his music, he stopped and turned to face her. "What can you mean? It is not possible, not without a guard."

"I know, but I don't want a guard to come with us. I know we could get in trouble."

"Serious trouble, *ja?*"

"Yes, probably. It might not work, but—"

"I can tell you a story about one of my comrades. He escaped some weeks ago. The authorities found him and returned him to our camp. He was made to live alone for two weeks with *Brot und Wasser* . . . bread to eat and water to drink and that is all. I spoke to him when he returned to us after his confinement."

"Did he say it was awful?" she asked.

"He had a smile. I think he might try again."

Phee chuckled. "Maybe he will."

"How can it happen, for us to leave without a guard, without others watching?

"Let me think about it this week. We could try next Sunday."

Holding hands, they walked down the steps and across the hall to the lobby door. Horst peeked through the small window, then turned to Phee and kissed her. "Today," he said, "when I heard the news about the end of the fighting, I had just one thought."

"What was it?" she asked.

"I thought, Sergeant Ebinger and Fräulein Swensson are not enemies now."

"That's true, we aren't. I don't have to pretend to hate you now." Horst was perplexed. "Oh, silly, I never hated you, not for one second. Not even in the beginning, last summer. I think I've admired you from the very first day we met."

"When our piano was new on the stage."

"And I heard you play Beethoven. I couldn't believe it because I was playing Beethoven then, too."

"A year ago, I arrived in Algona on the train from Nebraska. It was dark and raining very hard when we walked for three miles from the station. I was not happy to be here."

"And now?"

"And now, thank you for my friend Phee who has stopped me many times from being sad and angry."

They shared a tender kiss, then Horst turned to leave.

"See you next Sunday," she said.

Back on stage, Phee checked out the east side emergency door that had never been used, as far as she knew. It was locked, but she saw a key hanging from a hook to the right of the door jamb. She unlocked the door, opened it, and stepped out on the landing. Thankfully, there were no buildings on that side of the theater. All she could see was the camp cemetery in the distance. The driveway that came around from the parking lot ended near the steps.

"Maybe we can use this door next Sunday."

Sat. May 12, 1945

—Dear Daisy—

I'm a nervous wreck tonight. You already know it's because I'm planning to sneak Horst out of the camp tomorrow afternoon during our rehearsal time. He might say no to it in the end and that's OK. But tomorrow is Mother's Day, and I'm going to the cemetery to spend time with Mom. I really want Horst to be with me when I go. We'll only be gone a short time. I hope Private Mattingly's on duty tomorrow afternoon. That will help. Well, I'll see how I feel about this tomorrow. I can change my mind at the last minute. You'll know tomorrow night if I do or I don't. Wish me luck.

And life goes on. G'night.

33

SUNDAY 13 MAY 1945

IT WAS A BEAUTIFUL afternoon when Phee arrived at the Camp Algona guardhouse. Private Mattingly was on duty and was a little under the weather from a party the night before. When Phee got to the theater, she drove around to the far side and parked near the east stage door. Inside, she told Horst it was Mother's Day and she wanted him to "meet" her mom.

"I have thought about your idea this week," he said. "Perhaps we can do it for a short time, before we are missed." He understood it would mean a lot to Phee if he said "*ja.*" He got on the floor in the back seat of the car, and she covered him with a couple of old and smelly wool blankets. At the gate, Phee explained to Private Mattingly that she needed to run home for something and would be right back. He allowed her to keep the visitor pass on her dash for a quick return entry. Turning east onto Highway 18, the plan Phee had thought about all week was working perfectly.

The main entrance to Riverview Cemetery was near the north end of Cleveland Street, just a few blocks from the parsonage. Since it was mid-May, the daffodils had come and gone, but red and yellow and white tulips lined the entrance, offering visitors a preview of the beauty they'd see throughout the cemetery's rolling hills. Once she was through the gate, Phee turned east, then drove down one hill, curved to the right, and eventually reached the highest point of the next hill. She pulled off the gravel road, careful to avoid a nearby grave marker. When she turned off the engine, they remained still for a moment, listening. It was cool and breezy, and the oak trees near Mary's grave wore new spring leaves. Birds were everywhere, chattering musically back and forth. They always seemed to have something to say.

The afternoon sun caused shadows to spill eastward from each gravestone. Fresh flowers grew in pots at many nearby graves, and the lilies of the valley Phee and Mollie planted last year near their mom's stone were in full bloom.

"I think it's safe now," Phee whispered as she opened the back door. "Put on Dad's coat so the PW doesn't show." Seeing no one nearby, she took his hand and led him to Mary's stone which said, simply—

SWENSSON

MARY ANNE NELSON

JUL 14 1899 – DEC 7 1942

Sitting on the small marble bench, they held hands but remained still for a while. Then Phee began the conversation. "Hi, Mom, happy Mother's Day. It's the third one since you've been gone. I still miss you an awful lot. I do every day, but especially today." Horst squeezed her hand and she continued. "Mom, I want you to meet my friend Horst. We know he shouldn't be here, but I really wanted him to see where I come when I want to talk to you."

"It is an honor to meet you, Frau Swensson," Horst said respectfully.

Phee smiled. "I've already told you about him, so you know he's a very talented musician, and he's doing wonderful things with the music groups at the camp. I'm learning a lot from him."

"And I have learned much from your lovely daughter. You made a fine job raising your Fräulein. You can be very proud of her now."

Phee turned to Horst. "I thought you might think it's silly, talking to my mom as if she can hear me. You don't, though, do you?"

"She will always be your *Mutter*. There is no one else who knows you as she does. She watched you as you slept. She held you when you were sad or hurtful . . . hurting. She made you laugh, and perhaps she made you cry too, but not often." She wrapped her arm around his shoulders as he continued. "You must be . . . a reflection of your *Mutter*. How can I say it? You follow her ways, how she laughs, and listens, and loves, and the way she has respect for others. I can see that in you. I believe your *Mutter* was a good woman, and she wishes the same for her daughter."

"I do try to be a good person. It's not always easy. I'm sure people will say I'm a bad person for bringing you to the cemetery."

"But I am glad to be here. It has made a way for me to think of my *Mutter*. She is a generous and kind woman who is missing both of her sons. It should not be that way."

"Does your mother know about me?"

"She knows there is an American Fräulein who has performed with the *Männerchor*, but no more. In my next letter I will write about my friend Phee. There is more to say now."

Phee glanced over her shoulder once more and, seeing no one, kissed his cheek. "We'd better get back before someone misses us." She walked to the gravestone and gently touched the top. "Bye, Mom, I love you."

Just then, they heard a car's tires crunching the gravel lane just over the hill. Hand in hand, they ran to Phee's car. Horst jumped in the back while Phee got behind the wheel and started the engine. As soon as she pulled out, the approaching car appeared over the top of the ridge. Phee drove slowly down the hill in the opposite direction.

"WE'RE ALMOST AT THE turnoff," Phee said. "Better get under those blankets again."

As she approached the gatehouse, Phee held up the visitor pass. She expected Private Mattingly to step out and wave her through. "Uh-oh!" she whispered, "it's Corporal Phillips!" Thinking fast, she remembered her dad kept a copy of Walt Whitman's *Leaves of Grass* in the glovebox, so she reached over, grabbed it, and laid it on the seat next to her. With the window already rolled down, she pulled up slowly. Roy raised his hand and signaled her to stop. "Hi, Roy," she said, "what a nice surprise."

"Are you on your way to the theater?" he asked, not waiting for an answer. "Do you mind if I ride along?"

Oh, no, please don't! "Don't mind at all," she answered. "Hop in!"

While Roy walked around the front of the car, Phee whispered, "Don't make a sound!" He got in and slammed the door. "I promised Sergeant Ebinger I'd bring this book of poetry to him today," she explained. "I told Private Mattingly I'd be right back. He said to keep the visitor pass so I wouldn't need to stop to get another one."

"I guess that makes sense," Roy said. "I stopped by the theater to tell you and the Sergeant that your rehearsal dates had been approved. I was sure surprised when I got there and found the place empty."

"Sergeant Ebinger wasn't there?"

"Nope. I waited around for a little while, didn't see your car in the lot, so I figured you'd left."

"Maybe he went back to the barracks," she suggested.

When they arrived at the theater, Phee quickly concocted a reason for driving around to the east stage door. "I like to park on this side in the afternoons. It's shady, keeps the car cooler."

Roy smiled. "I suppose it does."

"I hope it's alright."

"It's fine by me."

"Would you like to come in while I wait for the Sergeant? I could play some of my audition music for you. Do you like Bach?"

Once inside, Phee hurried to the piano and got through the first two pages of the Bach before the lobby door opened, and Horst rushed in.

"I am sorry to be late!" he exclaimed, pretending to be out of breath. "I was stopped by two comrades who asked questions about our next rehearsal."

"Not a problem," Roy said. "Miss Swensson entertained me while we waited. It was beautiful, Phee."

"Thanks, Roy. I'm playing for the memorial service next month. Hope you'll be here."

"I'll sure try," he said. "Better head back. I'll see you two later."

As soon as they heard the lobby's outer door close, Phee cried, "Oh, golly, that was close! Do you think he knows?"

Horst joined her on the piano bench. "The Corporal is a curious man. We have had many conversations about interesting things. He told me he enjoys Shakespeare.

"But—"

"I can ask a question, or two questions. His answers might give us . . . how you say . . . the evidence that he knows or does not know."

"It might be best if you don't say anything at all. To be honest, I'd rather not know." She squeezed his hand. "Should we play through the Dvořák once?"

"Of course. It will make us calm, I think."

When they finished, Phee gathered her music. "It's been an exciting afternoon, hasn't it?"

"*Ja*, it was an adventure. I will always remember it."

She smiled. "Well, I should get home. See you next Sunday."

"Auf Wiedersehen, friend Phee."

"*Ich liebe dich,* friend Horst."

34

SUNDAY 27 MAY 1945

PHEE WAS IN A fine mood this afternoon as she drove to Camp Algona for her three o'clock meeting with Horst. On the way, her thoughts turned to last Thursday night's graduation ceremony and Mayor Ralph Kimball's address to the seventy-six members of the Algona High School Class of 1945. He told them that graduating from high school was a rite of passage, and he paid tribute to all the men and women who had served or were serving their country, including many AHS alumni. The band played for the processional and recessional, and the mixed chorus sang a stirring rendition of "God Bless America." Under her black graduation gown, Phee wore her new yellow and white polka-dot dress, a gift from her dad. "I'm tired of seein' you wear all those old dresses," Frank said as he handed her two crisp five dollar bills a couple of weeks ago. The next day, she and Mollie went shopping at Crystal's. When Phee walked out from the dressing room, Mollie exclaimed, "You look like sunshine!"

At the front gate, there was a message from Roy Phillips asking Phee to meet him in the lobby of the headquarters building. After parking the car, she grabbed her music pouch and hurried to the front door.

"Hi, Phee," Roy said as he held the door open, "thanks for meeting me."

"What's going on, Roy?"

"Let's have a seat over here." He led her to a small corner reception area.

Phee was very worried. Something had to be seriously wrong. "Why am I not at the theater rehearsing with Sergeant Ebinger?" she asked.

"You're not rehearsing with the Sergeant because he's required to watch some films. All the prisoners have to watch them today. He couldn't get out of it. I tried to call you, but the line was busy."

"Oh dear, somebody must've left it off the hook. So, what is it they're watching?"

"I haven't seen them, and I don't know many details, but they've got something to do with the concentration camps over there, you know, in Germany and other places."

"There was an article about that in the paper this week."

"Yeh, horrible, sickening stuff the Nazis have been doing for years, I guess."

"Did you talk to the Sergeant?"

"I did. He was concerned about your rehearsal being cancelled."

"We can reschedule, or just meet again at our time next Sunday."

"That's what he said. Oh, and he wanted me to give you something, said it was a gift for your graduation." Roy reached inside the leather satchel he'd laid nearby, found a large brown envelope, and handed it to Phee. "I'll let him know it was delivered as promised."

"Please do. And tell him I'll see him next Sunday at three."

"You got it," he said. "Well, I need to get back."

"Thank you, Roy. I must admit I was a little worried."

"Sure, I understand. The Sergeant's fine, but he'll probably be in a foul mood for a while after seeing those films."

"No doubt."

Roy walked down the hall to his office while Phee stayed in her seat. She was disappointed she wouldn't see Horst today, but at least she knew he wasn't sick or injured, or worse. After dropping the envelope in her pouch, she walked to the car, then decided to stop at the old Lover's Lane on her way back to town. When she got there, she found a shady spot and turned off the engine, then looked inside the envelope and found three items: two white envelopes and a small, almost flat package wrapped in

Christmas paper. She laid each item on the seat next to her, then chose to open one of the envelopes first. It was a card, signed by all the members of the *Männerchor*, congratulating Phee on her graduation from Algona High. She recognized most names, those she could decipher at any rate.

Inside the second envelope, she found a letter from Horst. Before reading it, she considered how her life had become so much more complicated since last summer when they first met. Over time, while falling in love with him, she continued to live her life without her mom and kept her family as whole as she possibly could, day after day. She managed to keep up with all her studies and church obligations and her efforts to be a better pianist. She missed her brother Jamie, and, like everyone else in Algona, she survived rationing and recycling and war bond drives and constant war news and worry. Her best friend's brother was killed in the war, and her relationship with Christa continued to be strained because of that horrible event. And yet, Phee had never been happier than she was right this minute, sitting in her dad's car on the old Lover's Lane, holding a letter from Horst in her hand. With no one nearby, she read it out loud.

Dear Friend Phee,

Please receive my apology for this fast written letter. You will hear from Corporal Phillips that I am unable to meet today. My plan for surprising you with this envelope will happen without our being together on the stage. It cannot be helped, for later in the day we are made to watch films that should make an impression about the leaders in our homeland, to provide an evidence of their foolish and unlawful ways. We do not know what to expect but we have been told it will make us serious and angry. Without the benefit of seeing them up to now I am unable to make comments. We should wait to have this discussion at another day. If you have not found everything in the envelope you should look now for I will continue to write about it. —And now you have seen everything, ja?

Phee reached for the small package, removed the paper, and found a white piece of cloth folded around a very small object. Slowly, she unfolded the cloth and found—a necklace. A delicate silver chain was attached to something silver. It was round, or almost round, about an inch in diameter or a bit smaller. On one side, she saw four letters engraved—P S H E. "It's our initials!" She turned it over and saw three more letters. "I L D. What's that?"

Hoping Horst explained the "code" in his letter, she continued to read.

With help from my comrade Fritz Dresher I have made a jewelry piece for your graduation day. He was a Silberschmied before the war and can make many beautiful things. On one side you will see the letters for our names and on the reverse you will see I L D which you will know if you think about it with much strength. I will keep it a mystery in case you cannot find it in your mind. We can look at it together next week. For now, I will send my best wishes for a successful departure from the Algona high school. And I have one more gift for you, but it will remain with me until next week. Until then—auf Wiedersehen from Your Friend Horst

"Oh, Horst, you silly man, you didn't tell me."

Choosing to leave the necklace wrapped in the cloth, Phee put everything back in the envelope and started the engine. On her way home, she thought about how blessed she was in so many ways. At last, she was a high school graduate. The wicked war in Europe that had hovered over everyone for years had ended. The despicable Adolf Hitler was dead. Jamie would soon be home, she hoped. But best of all, she'd fallen in love with Horst. She loved everything about him, and she hoped he'd soon feel the same about her.

35

SUNDAY 3 JUNE 1945

IT HAD BEEN TWO weeks since Phee and Horst had practiced the Dvořák and two weeks since they'd kissed. That was about thirteen days too many for Phee, at least the kissing part. Today she would thank Horst in person for her necklace and tell him she was thrilled—no, overjoyed—when, last Sunday night, she figured out the meaning of I L D—*ich liebe dich*.

She arrived at the camp theater about ten minutes early so was surprised to hear Horst playing the piano when she got to the lobby. As she stepped inside, she decided to wait a moment to listen. The music was both familiar and unfamiliar, and she wondered about the composer. And then she knew. It was Horst Ebinger!

"It's your piece! Have you finally finished it?"

He continued to play, completely focused on the music and not on Phee as she came up the steps to the stage and waited. *"Ja*, do you like it?" he answered at last.

"I do."

Horst placed the music in a large envelope and handed it to Phee. "It is good you like it because it is for you."

She was overwhelmed but managed to say, "Oh Horst, gosh, thank you. It must be the nicest gift I've ever received!"

He chuckled. "Perhaps it is true, but your friend Horst disagrees. I believe Americans receive many nice gifts at regular times."

"I can think of another very nice gift I received just a week ago." She unbuttoned the top button of her blouse to reveal the necklace. She smiled, then wrapped her arms around him. "I L D . . . *ich liebe dich*. You *do* love me!" she whispered before she kissed him.

Horst pulled away, smiling while touching her hair, her cheek, her lips. His fingers brushed her skin as he reached for the necklace, and she softly gasped.

"*Ja, wunderschönen* Phee. *Ich liebe dich.*" Then he explained why it took so long to tell her he loved her. "I was . . . concerned, to make your life so . . . complicated, it seemed wrong. Can you understand?"

"No, I can't, because I know how I feel about you, and I wanted more than anything for you to feel the same."

"So, it will remain only with us, *ja*?"

"I won't tell a soul."

"Perhaps we should visit Herr Dvořák," he said, sitting again on the bench.

"We should, but . . . I wanted to ask you something first. You don't have to talk about it, what you saw last Sunday. I just thought you'd want to—or need to." She joined him on the bench.

After a big sigh, he said, "It has been one week since we were witnessing the horrors of our countrymen. Do you know about it?"

"A little. There was an article in the newspaper."

"There are comrades who do not believe it to be true. It causes them to be . . . sick. Those of us from the Afrika Korps saw nothing of it. The Volkssturm, the young men and the old men who were forced to fight in the last months of the war, they might have seen something, but they are silent."

Horst stood and walked to the edge of the stage. Phee almost regretted she brought it up, but she really did want to know what Horst believed to be true.

"I do not want to believe my countrymen could do these things," he said, "but when I saw it with my own eyes, on the screen in the dark room, I must think the British and American soldiers who made the films could not have—"

"Lied about it?"

"*Ja*. In the films we saw concentration camps in Dachau, in Buchenwald, Bergen-Belsen, Auschwitz-Birkenau."

"Have you been near any of those places?"

"I have been to Dachau some years ago. It is a peaceful village near München . . . Munich."

"So, you believe the films?"

Horst nodded. "I must. I am . . . disgusted and angry. I have tried to speak to my comrades. Some, perhaps most, believe it is true, but they do not want to talk about it. For me, I must find ways, with my life . . . to make . . . I do not know the word."

"Amends?"

"Or, to compensate in any ways that I can."

"I know you'll find a way, Horst. Our concerts in July and August will help. Dad and Chaplain Mattson are calling it 'A Concert for Reconciliation.'"

"Recon . . .?"

"Reconciliation. I looked it up in the dictionary. It means understanding, coming together. There's one meaning I especially like: bring into harmony."

Horst smiled. "I like it too."

"I suppose we should run through our piece while there's still time."

They did, and progress was made. In fact, if they had to perform it tomorrow, they'd do a fine job. But they'd not let on to anyone that the Dvořák was almost ready. They wanted and needed their weekly rehearsals to continue.

When it was time to leave, Phee reached for the envelope from Horst and pulled out the manuscript pages. At the top of the first page she saw:

Lieder für Freunde
von Horst Ebinger
Camp Algona, Iowa U.S.A.
03 Juni 1945
Gewidmet Phee Swensson

"*Lieder*," she said. "I know it means song, and *für* is . . . for?"

"*Ja*, it is Songs for . . ."

"What's *Freunde?*"

"It is us, friends."

"Songs for Friends. Perfect."

"I thought you would like it," he said.

"And *gewidmet?*"

"It means . . . dedication."

"You dedicated this to me?"

"It could be no one else."

"Oh, Horst, thank you so much! This means the world to me."

"And so, can we meet again in one week?" he asked.

"We should be on the calendar for Sundays through June. You might want to double check." Phee finished gathering her music and the envelope. "Walk me to my car?"

Before they left the lobby, he grabbed her arm, pulled her close, and kissed her. "*Ich liebe dich,* Phee," he whispered.

She smiled. "Oh, how I love hearing you say that! *Ich liebe dich,* Horst, so very much."

Fri. Jun. 15, 1945

—Dear Daisy—

Jamie's home!! Or at least he's back in the good ol' USA. This has been The Best Day*! It all started at breakfast when Dad spilled the beans that Jamie was flying from France to Washington, DC today. Dad had known since Wednesday but kept it to himself 'til this morning. The kids were so excited. I took a bunch of Jamie's letters out to the front porch and read 'em for the umpteenth time. No more censored V-Mail letters (I hope!). It was hard to concentrate on anything today, but I managed to get an hour of practicing in. Tonight at supper Dad let Mollie pick the Word of the Day. No surprise—she picked "Jamie." Ed called after supper and we talked about the memorial service coming up on the 24th. Dad said he'd make sure Jack and Peggy knew they were invited. Christa too, of course, but I doubt she'll go and that would be a shame. We played cards at the dining room table tonight, waiting for Jamie's call. When it looked like it wouldn't come, we all got ready for bed, and while I was brushing my teeth, the phone rang. Gus got there first, and yes, it was Jamie! We all took turns. I went last. Oh, Daisy, it was SO wonderful to hear his voice. I cried—couldn't help it. He sounded tired but happy. He isn't sure when he'll be able to come home. They've got a lot of stuff coming up, he said. But it sure feels good tonight, knowing he's sleeping on American soil for the first time in* two long years. *Dad thinks it could be Thanksgiving before he can get leave to come home. That's just too long. Please God, let it be sooner than that. I can't wait to tell Horst! Oh, I so wish they could meet. I just know they'd get along—they're about the same age—they're both so talented—and they both love me! Ha!*

And life goes on. G'night, Jamie.

36

TUESDAY 3 JULY 1945

"Hot diggity dog!"

Gus's glee summed up the mood in the parsonage this morning as the Swenssons prepared for the twins' annual birthday celebration at Bee's Bungalows on West Lake Okoboji. During the summer season, there were six cabins available for weekly rental at Bee and Nannie's resort. The small, pale green, two-bedroom cabins were located about half a block west of Arnolds Park, an amusement park that had its beginnings in 1889 when Wesley Arnold built a sixty-foot toboggan-style waterslide on the property. Over the years, with the addition of more rides and concessions and a dance hall, the park became the most popular tourist attraction in northwest Iowa.

Mollie was especially excited about this lake visit because she'd invited her friend Claire Engstrom from nearby Spirit Lake to join them on Thursday. After getting the green light from Nannie, Frank invited Claire's mom Helen to stay for supper Thursday evening, and she'd also join them for breakfast Saturday morning when she came to pick up Claire.

By ten o'clock, they got the car packed and hit the road. As usual, the conversation on the drive centered around everyone's expectations for their four-day visit. There would be daily trips to Arnolds Park, and when they weren't at the park, they'd be in or on the lake. The twins expected to go fishing with Bee tomorrow morning, and Mollie couldn't wait to see Claire. Phee was happy she could relax and let someone else do the cooking for a change. Frank didn't say much about his hopes, but Phee figured he was glad to be without church obligations for a few days, and spending time with Helen would be nice, too.

It was just past one o'clock when Frank turned down Sandy Road and pulled into the short driveway behind Cabin 4. The kids piled out and made a beeline for the picnic table next to Bee and Nannie's cabin where Nannie was putting out a quick lunch.

"Oh, it's so good to see you all again!' she cried. "Welcome, welcome!'

"I'll help Frank with the suitcases," Bee said. "You kids stay here and take a load off."

"Bee, tell Frank to leave everything in the car," Nannie said. "We'll get them settled later. We're ready to eat."

"Are we in number six again?" Tris asked, helping himself to a Bing cherry from the large bowl on the table.

"You are," Nannie answered, "and Phee, we're putting you and Mollie and Claire in Cabin 4."

"Sounds good," she said. "I brought homemade rye bread and coffee cake."

"Wonderful! I'm afraid our sugar ration kept me from baking much, but there will be cake tomorrow."

"Hope it's lemon," Gus said.

"It'll be lemon when I bake it in the morning," she replied.

While they ate, the sounds from nearby Arnolds Park drifted across the well-manicured lawns between the cabins and the park. It was a cheerful sound, with adults and children alike enjoying the rides and other attractions that made the park so inviting every summer.

"We got a nice card from Jamie the other day," Nannie said. "He sure wishes he could get home before we close up in September, but he doesn't think it'll work out."

"Yeh, I wouldn't count on it," Frank said as he reached for his beer. "We're just glad he's not thousands of miles away now."

"It's a little over a thousand miles from Algona to Arlington," Gus remembered. "I checked it out on the map in our classroom right after Jamie moved to Virginia."

"It's probably four times that to Paris," Phee said.

"I'd love to see Paris," Mollie said, "the Eiffel Tower, Notre Dame. What's that famous museum?"

"The Louvre?" Tris suggested.

"Yeh, the Louvre. I wonder if everybody in Paris has a poodle. I saw a picture in a magazine where a lady was walking five poodles under the Eiffel Tower."

"That's about five poodles too many for me," Bee admitted.

The conversation eventually turned towards tomorrow's birthday celebration. Bee and the twins would go fishing early, no later than six, he said. Nannie hoped to fry up some "catch of the day" for the big birthday meal at noon, with cake and presents to follow.

After lunch, everyone got settled in their cabins, then Bee and Frank took the kids to the park while Nannie and Phee stayed behind to clean up.

"So," Nannie began, "you're a high school graduate. Now what?"

"'Now what' is right. I seem to be pretty busy this summer. You know about the big concerts coming up."

"Only that they're happening, and you're involved."

"They asked for volunteers from all the church choirs in town, so that'll be a nice big group, hopefully. Rehearsals start next week. I think most of us from St. Pete's will sing—Dad too—and I'm playing a duet with Sergeant Ebinger."

"Isn't he the fellow whose brother was killed last winter?"

"That's right. Dad and the kids were up here when I called to tell him."

"So, what's it like, playing with a POW?"

It's wonderful! "Oh, I don't know. It was kinda strange at first, I guess. But he's nice enough, and very talented."

"What do you know about him?"

"Not too much. He's from Potsdam, that's near Berlin. His mom and sister are in Wittenberg with his aunt. It was supposed to be safer there during the bombings. His father's an attorney. I guess he's a Nazi."

"Aren't they all Nazis, or whatever they're calling themselves now?"

"I thought so, at first. I guess some were 'die-hard Nazis' and some were just soldiers."

"Is your Sergeant . . ."

"Ebinger, Horst."

"Is your Horst a die-hard?"

"Oh no, not at all. He was in a band in North Africa. Can you believe it? Same as Jamie, sort of, only he played percussion."

"It's curious, isn't it? Those men, the prisoners, have so many privileges while they're here. I suppose some people resent it."

"Yeh, some do. I guess I haven't told you about Christa."

"I know about her brother. Is there something else?"

Phee sighed. "Oh, gosh, where to start?" Phee explained the sad situation to her grandmother as honestly as she could. "She thinks I should stop playing for the *Männerchor*."

"And?"

"Truthfully, I think she's being unreasonable. Mrs. Z thinks I should keep doing it. And it's not like the camp will be there forever. We don't know when it will close, but it's bound to be soon."

"Well, Christa just needs time. She's had a big shock. This will work itself out. You two are best friends, after all."

"That's what Dad said. She didn't come to the memorial service at the camp last month. Her parents, Jack and Peggy, were there, and Christa should have been since they honored Danny, among others."

"Well, we should pray for the family. In the meantime, you're here and we're so glad. I noticed Frank has a fresh haircut. Is it because he's seeing Helen this week?"

"Probably."

"He looks very handsome. I hope he and Helen enjoy their time together."

"I'm sure they will. I like her. I think they make a nice couple."

"You know, Phee, I wondered how long it would take me to feel comfortable with Frank finding someone new. I think I'm ready now."

"Let's figure out how to get them together without Dad feeling so self-conscious about it."

"That's a good idea," Nannie said as she drained the dish water. "Let's go out to the table and put our heads together."

While the two women sat at the picnic table plotting their cupid plays, Frank, Bee, and the kids rode the Giant Dips roller coaster for the third time today. Everyone but Mollie had enjoyed this ride for years, but today she found the courage to ride it for the first time, and she loved it.

The day ended with everyone sitting around the fire pit on the beach, singing songs while Frank played his ukulele. After a rousing rendition of "John Jacob Jingleheimer Schmidt," Frank grabbed a stick and poked the burning logs, causing embers to float above the pit like fireflies. The lake air had cooled after the heat of the day, and the warmth from the flames was welcomed. Tree frogs and crickets sang their nightly duets while an almost full moon shined brightly overhead.

"I don't know about the rest of you," Frank said as he stood and stretched his long arms skyward, "but I'm ready for bed. Nannie and Phee, thanks for a wonderful supper."

"You're welcome, Frank," Nannie said. "Hope you all sleep well tonight."

"I always do," Phee said. "Nothing better than Okoboji air for a good night's sleep."

"You kids go on," Bee said. "I'll take care of the fire."

Frank, Phee and the kids walked barefooted across the cool grass to their cabins.

"You can sleep in a little if you want," Phee said as she stuck her head in Mollie's room. "I'll make sure you're up in time for breakfast."

"Thanks," Mollie said. "Phee?"

"Yeh, Sweet Pea?"

"I'm so glad I rode the roller coaster today. It was marvelous!"

"I'm glad too. It *is* marvelous."

"G'night."

"Sweet dreams."

Before she turned out the light, Phee wrote to Daisy, then laid in the dark, conjuring up a perfect scenario for sneaking Horst up to the lake sometime later this summer. Obviously, they couldn't take her dad's car, so they'd ride the bus. Horst would wear Jamie's old clothes and a cap and sunglasses. When they got there, they'd walk down Sandy Road past Bee's Bungalows but wouldn't stop. Most of their time would be spent at the park. They'd ride the Giant Dips at least five or six times, and it would be marvelous.

37

WEDNESDAY 4 JULY 1945 - PART 1

PHEE WAS IN BED, dreaming. She was on a boat out on the lake, except this boat was more like a yacht, much too big and opulent for West Okoboji. It was moored away from the shore, but she could see Arnold's Park and Bee's Bungalows off in the distance. The boat had two decks and a kitchen just like the galley kitchen in Cabin 4. On the upper deck, a small linen-covered table with two place settings of fine china, silverware, and crystal goblets awaited an elegant meal. Champagne chilled in an ice bucket nearby, and a small plate with caviar-laden Ritz Crackers sat in the center of the table.

In her dream, Phee wore her royal blue velvet recital dress, and Horst, wearing a tuxedo, stood next to her. A radio played soothing music, and they began to dance cheek to cheek on the deck. Suddenly, there was a news flash on the radio, but the reporter spoke not in English but in German. She peered over his shoulder and saw a Nazi flag flying from a pole on the stern. And then, across the lake, she saw planes dropping bombs on the shore, causing huge explosions, fire, and destruction. Phee tried to scream but she couldn't. Horst turned and walked away, and when she pitifully called out to him, he stopped and turned back. But it wasn't Horst—it was Adolf Hitler!

Phee gasped, opened her eyes, and stared at the knotty pine ceiling over her bed. Cobwebs hanging in the corner near the small window glistened in the morning sun. She heard Mollie stirring next door. Glancing at her alarm clock, she discovered it was almost eight thirty. Since she wanted to swim this morning, she skipped a shower and put on her bathing suit under her red shorts and white sleeveless blouse. Stopping at Mollie's bedroom door on her way out, she said with a full voice, "Hey, Sweet Pea, better get up or you'll miss breakfast."

Mollie moaned and pulled the sheet over her head.

"C'mon, kiddo, up and at 'em. Big day ahead."

Phee walked to the picnic table where the rest of the family was gathered.

"Good morning, sleepy head," Frank said. "Where's your sister?"

"I told her to get up, but you know Mollie," Phee answered, stopping to kiss the twins before she sat. "Happy birthday, boys."

"Yeh," Gus said, "we'll see her for lunch if we're lucky."

"I'll go," Nannie said. "Phee, help yourself to some breakfast."

"We caught a bunch o' fish this morning," Tris said proudly, "walleye and catfish, mostly. I caught a pike!"

"Good for you—good for us," Phee said while reaching for a piece of coffee cake.

"We'll clean 'em after breakfast," Tris said.

"I'm more than happy to leave the fish cleaning to you fellows," Phee said. "I'm going in for a swim in a little bit." She could tell it was going to be a hot, hazy, humid day—perfect for spending time in the water or lying on the beach.

While Bee and the twins got the fish presentable for Nannie's fry pan, Frank lounged in one of the white Adirondack chairs at the top of the beach. He was still reading Phee's copy of *Berlin Diary* and hoped to finish it this week.

The lake water temperature was perfect, cool enough to be refreshing, warm enough to be comfortable even at first dip. Phee dove off the dock, then swam out about thirty feet. Before turning back, she looked across the water to the opposite shore where all those bombs exploded earlier this morning. She was relieved it was only a dream.

After a refreshing twenty-minute swim, Phee returned to the beach and laid on the colorful beach towel she'd brought down earlier. The sand, unshaded for the past couple of hours, was soft and warm under the towel. Laying on her stomach with her head turned away from the park sounds, she closed her eyes but didn't sleep.

THE TWINS' BIRTHDAY LUNCH was full of laughter and yummy fried fish and steamed fresh vegetables from the Nelsons' garden. Nannie's lemon cake was a hit with everyone, even Mollie who swore she wouldn't like it. After a harmoniously enthusiastic rendition of "Happy Birthday," the twenty-two candles adorning the cake were swiftly extinguished by the birthday boys. Concluding the celebration, they opened gifts from everyone and seemed pleased with their loot. Fishing poles from Bee and Nannie were by far the biggest hit. The boys were keen on giving them a test drive right away.

"Can we, please?" Gus pleaded.

"Better not go back out today," Bee said. "Let's try again in the morning when those fish'll be lookin' for those early worms."

"Aw, shucks," Tris lamented.

"I thought you might like to go back to the park this afternoon," Bee suggested. "Free admission on your birthday, don't forget."

"I think we should go tonight," Gus said. "It's so hot today, I'd rather go swimming."

"I'll join you," Frank said, "*after* my nap, that is."

"I'm gonna read my book after we get the dishes done," Phee said. "I'll go back in later."

While Frank and the kids retreated to their rooms for either a nap or a wardrobe change, Phee and Nannie cleared up the dishes and had a nice chat about Mary's sister Millie who lived near Brainerd in central Minnesota. Millie and her husband Bart owned cabins on Gull Lake very similar to Bee's Bungalows except there were just four rentals plus the larger cabin they lived in year-round. They purchased the property four years ago, and the cabins were full most summers despite the war and its restrictions.

"I got the nicest card from Millie and Bart for graduation," Phee said. "She wants me to come up and stay with them sometime."

"Oh, I hope you can."

"I can't believe we haven't met Bart yet," Phee said, pouring herself a glass of iced tea.

"Oh, he's a nice fellow. Loves teaching those junior high kids. He sure was a good catch. I wasn't sure it would ever happen for our Millie."

"Better late than never, huh?"

Nannie chuckled. "Absolutely."

Phee hung the dish towel on the nearby rack. "I think we're done here. Guess I'll go read for a while."

"You enjoy, dear."

Phee kissed her grandmother on the cheek, then walked to Cabin 4 to grab *A Tree Grows in Brooklyn*, her birthday gift from Mollie last August. She finally had time to read it this summer and was almost done. With her glass of tea, she settled on one of the Adirondack chairs on the grass east of the cabin. The ice melted quickly, and the condensation trickled down the sides of the glass like an icicle melting in the sun. The chilled water dripped on her blouse each time she took a sip, and she enjoyed the brief cool respite on her breast as it soaked through.

After giving herself permission to take a short snooze, Phee closed her book and laid it on the chair's wide armrest. Through her half-closed eyes, she became aware of someone walking down Sandy Road from the east. It was a man, and he was far enough away she couldn't tell anything about him except he was carrying an object over his shoulder, like a bag or something. He looked like he was in uniform. *Lucky guy, a soldier home on leave.* As she closed her eyes again, she heard the soldier whistling, and there was something familiar about that whistle.

Sitting up on the edge of her chair, Phee rubbed her eyes, hoping to gain a clearer look at the whistling man in uniform with a duffle bag slung over his shoulder. And then, as he got even closer, she knew. *Jamie!!*

Knocking her tea glass off the armrest as she stood, Phee ran across the gravel driveway in her bare feet. "Ow! Ow! Ow!" she cried out. When he saw her, Jamie stopped and dropped his bag to the ground.

"Oh my gosh, oh my gosh!" she cried as she jumped into his arms. "What in the world are you doing here?! Why didn't you tell us?!" She pulled away, held his face in her hands, gave him a kiss, then hugged him again. Tears rolled down her cheeks as she realized her dear brother Jamie was really and truly home from the war.

"Okay, okay, enough already!" Jamie cried. "I'll explain everything when we're all together."

"This is the most incredible surprise! Everybody'll be so shocked! I just . . . wait . . . I know. I'll sneak you in! They'll go nuts! How should we do it?" She took his hand and pulled him back up the road so they could plan the surprise. "I know," she said, "Dad's car needs gas. You walk back to the corner, and I'll pick you up there. We'll go get gas and then drive back for the big surprise."

"Okay, that'll be fun," he said, walking back to grab his bag.

While Jamie retraced his steps, Phee returned to her chair and grabbed her sandals. After she told Bee she was taking the car to get gas, she picked Jamie up at the corner, then drove on to the gas station about a mile up the road.

"So, how did you get here?" Phee asked on their way back to the cabins.

"I left Arlington Monday morning. Got to Chicago and changed trains. Pulled into Algona late last night and walked up to the house. I thought about catching the bus this morning, but then decided to hitchhike so I could sleep in a little."

Phee pulled in behind Cabin 4 and whispered, "Stay here, I'll be right back." She first stopped in her dad's room to wake him and tell him to come out to the table. Then she ran to her grandparents' cabin. "Nannie, c'mon out. I've got something I want to tell everyone. It'll take just a minute." She ran down to the beach and got everyone's attention. "Bee! Boys! I need you to come up here by Nannie. Where's Mollie? Oh, there you are. C'mere, Sweet Pea, just for a minute."

The kids were not at all anxious to hear Phee's news, but they grabbed their towels and walked slowly up the beach, kicking sand along the way while Frank sauntered out of Cabin 6. Phee had everyone's attention, but just barely. *Good! They're not the least bit interested.*

"So, here's my news. I just drove the car over to the Standard station to fill it up and on my way back, I ran into someone from home. I thought you'd like to say hello. He's getting something from the car. I'll bring him around."

The kids grumbled, Bee rubbed his chin, Nannie looked at her watch, and Frank yawned, a big one.

Phee ran back to the car and motioned for Jamie to follow her. When they got to the corner of the cabin, she whispered, "They're all there. Go!"

Everyone was facing the lake except Frank. He saw Jamie first, stood, saluted, and called out, "James Edward Swensson! Welcome home, Sergeant!"

Everyone turned and all hell broke loose. Mollie screamed, and the twins yelled "Jamie!!" Nannie covered her mouth with her hands and began to cry, and Bee shouted, "Well, I'll be damned, if it isn't our handsome soldier boy, home at last!"

38

WEDNESDAY 4 JULY 1945 - PART 2

BY NATURE, THE SWENSSONS and the Nelsons were an affectionate lot, always had been. So, there was lots of hugging and kissing and a few happy tears streaming down cheeks this afternoon.

"Good golly, Miss Mollie, how you've grown!" Jamie hollered amidst the chaos. "I guess you boys have too, now that I look at ya."

"I imagine you're starving," Nannie said. "You sit and I'll fix you something quick."

"Thanks, Nannie. I didn't have much for breakfast, so that'll be great."

As they all settled at the table, Mollie asked, "Did you get to have a cake on your birthday, Jamie?"

"No, but some of the boys in the band would usually help you celebrate your day. Sometimes we'd go out for dinner, get away from that army chow. I guess it depended on how busy we were."

"I believe you were in North Africa for your twenty-first," Frank remembered.

"That's right, in Algiers."

"Did you see any camels?" Tris wanted to know.

"I did, actually, quite a few. They're fascinating animals."

"Where were you on your birthday this year?" Phee asked.

"We were in Paris in January, just moved into new quarters at the University. It was about the nicest place we stayed over there—modern and clean, and plenty of heat, finally."

"You know we're gonna want to know everything you did while you were over there," Bee said. "Better start now 'cause you'll probably need a few days."

"Let 'im eat, Bee," Nannie said as she brought out a tray.

"How long can you stay?" Phee asked, knowing it wouldn't be nearly long enough.

Jamie took a swig of his Schlitz. "Not long, I'm 'fraid. I have to be back at Fort Myer Sunday night. I'll need to be on the Friday afternoon train to Chicago. I can catch the bus to Algona Friday morning."

"You'll do no such thing," Frank said. "We'll just head home a day earlier than we'd planned."

The kids moaned but they knew there was no arguing. Then Mollie realized there was a problem. "But what about Claire? She's coming tomorrow afternoon."

Phee had an idea. "Maybe Helen could bring her down today and stay for supper tonight."

"That's perfectly fine with me," Nannie said. "All the food's here. Frank, why don't you give Helen a call and see if they can change their plans." He did. They could.

After Jamie got settled in Cabin 3, he joined Frank and Phee and the kids for a swim. Nannie got busy in the kitchen, and Bee worked on the fire pit so it would be ready for tonight.

It was just after five when the Engstroms arrived. Mollie ran to the car, grabbed Claire's hand, and led her straight to the picnic table so she could meet Jamie first thing. Helen followed closely behind, and Frank made the introductions.

"It's great to meet you, Helen," Jamie said as he stood to shake her hand. "Say . . . we've got a Dan Engstrom in the band, a clarinet fellow. I don't suppose he's a relative."

"Not as far as I know," Helen said. "Could be a cousin."

"And Claire," Jamie continued, "it's sure nice to meet you, too."

Claire smiled, and Mollie grabbed her hand again. "I wanna show you our cabin," she said. "You're gonna love it!"

"Phee, why don't you come help me in the kitchen," Nannie suggested.

"I'll come too," Helen offered.

Nannie shook her head. "No, ma'am, you stay put. You're our guest. I'm sure the men will keep you entertained."

DURING SUPPER, JAMIE ENJOYED sharing stories about all the different places the band played overseas, who they performed with and for, and what it was like flying across the Atlantic Ocean. He admitted he couldn't have survived without the Red Cross—the decent food they served, first run movies, a place to relax or read the *Stars and Stripes*. Whenever the mail was delayed, and it often was, the Red Cross was a great source of news from the home front.

"What was your most favorite place?" Gus wanted to know.

"Hmm, that's a tough one," Jamie said.

"Mine would be Paris," Mollie interrupted.

"Paris was very nice, especially on V-E Day, but I think my favorite city has to be Edinburgh, up in Scotland."

"Why's that?" Frank asked, reaching for another slice of Phee's Swedish rye bread.

"Well, for one thing, it wasn't bombed like London was. We took a tour of the city, and our guide was quite a character. There's a castle up on a hill we got to visit, and the cathedral, St. Giles, is right in the middle of town."

"The Scottish church is Presbyterian, you know," Frank added.

"That's right," Jamie said. "The thing is, everything over there is so old, and we saw places we'd learned about in school. Too bad there was a war on."

"Did you see any Germans?" Tris asked. "We have a camp full of 'em in Algona."

"We did see some marching along the road in Algeria, Italians too. I suppose some of those Germans could be in Iowa now."

"Well," Bee said, "I don't know about the rest of you, but I'm ready for some Giant Dips. Who's with me?"

Turned out, everyone sitting at the table wanted to go to the park tonight. Nannie insisted on leaving the dishes for later so they could all enjoy their outing together. When they got to the front of the line at the Giant Dips, the entire party got to ride together—Gus and Tris in the very front car, followed by Frank and Helen, then Mollie and Claire, Phee and Jamie, and lastly, Bee and Nannie.

Before they returned to the cabins, Jamie and Phee checked out the Roof Garden's entertainment for tomorrow night. They learned that Creezy and the Coasters out of Fort Dodge would be on stage in the park's big dance hall from eight to midnight.

"Would you like to go?" Jamie asked.

"Sure! Maybe Dad and Helen would like to come, too."

"Let's ask 'em," he said. "Better get back. Don't want to miss the pit."

The sun hadn't quite set, but its rays were blocked by the tall pine trees west of the cabins. The temperature had dropped some and there was a nice breeze coming off the lake, a perfect night for singing around the fire. Frank and Helen sat together, and Phee noticed they weren't quite touching but almost, and smiling, often laughing.

As Frank strummed a few opening chords on his ukulele, Bee said, "You know, being here with all of you—forgetting about the war, even for just a little while—it's balm for the soul."

"What's 'balm'?" Mollie asked.

"It's like . . . a salve," Bee answered. "You know, when you fall down and scrape your knee and you need somethin' to help it heal. Welcoming Jamie home today, celebrating your birthday, riding the coaster, watching the fireworks here in a little while—it's all balm for the soul."

"Well, I love being at the lake," Mollie said. "It's just swell!"

Laughter filled the evening air as Frank continued strumming. "What shall we sing?" he asked. "Let's let the birthday boys pick first."

Gus and Tris looked at each other, nodded, and both shouted out, "Jeepers Creepers!"

"Good choice!" Frank said as he strummed the wrong chords. "Hang on, I'll get it. Yeh, that's better." Everyone joined in on the first verse and Frank sang solo on the second because no one else knew the words.

"Who's next?" he asked. "Jamie, give it a shot."

"Let's do 'Side by Side,'" he said, putting his arm around Phee.

Nannie's choice was "Let Me Call You Sweetheart," and she gave Bee a smooch at the end.

After the fireworks, spectacular as always, Frank ordered the kids to bed. The twins went reluctantly until Bee reminded them they had an early morning date with the fishies. Mollie and Claire were sweetly agreeable, but Phee suspected she'd hear plenty of giggling from their bedroom when she finally turned in for the night.

While the fire in the pit died down, the six adults remained to enjoy the final embers.

"This has been quite a day," Bee said. "Think I'll turn in myself."

Helen looked at her watch. "I should be going."

"I'll walk you to your car," Frank said.

"Nannie, you and I can get those dishes washed up in a hurry," Phee said.

"I'll help," Jamie offered. "Oh, and Dad, Phee and I are going to the Roof Garden tomorrow night. Would you and Helen like to join us?"

"Sounds like fun. Whadaya think, Helen?"

"Well, it's been a long time, but I'd love to."

"Great!" Frank said, clearly pleased. "I'll pick you up at, say, seven thirty?"

"I'll be ready," she said. "Nannie, thanks for a wonderful meal, and especially for letting Claire spend time with your family."

"We love having her, Helen," Nannie said. "We'll see you tomorrow night."

While Jamie and Nannie got started on the dishes, Phee momentarily excused herself. In a loud whisper, she said, "I wanna spy on Dad and Helen. Be right back."

Nannie disapproved. "Now, Phee . . ." But then, she smiled. "Just don't let them see you."

Thanks to the dim streetlight across from the short driveway, Phee could see the silhouette of her dad and Helen talking near the car. As Helen reached to open the door, Frank took her in his arms and kissed her. Then she got in and drove away. Frank stayed and watched her car disappear around the corner while Phee hurried back to the kitchen.

"They kissed!" she said, again in a loud whisper.

Jamie and Nannie smiled. Phee grabbed a dish towel and a wet glass, and while she slowly dried the sides and bottom and inside, she thought about her mom, hoping she approved of her dad and Helen because it seemed inevitable now.

39

THURSDAY 5 JULY 1945

PHEE WANTED TO TALK to Jamie about Horst. Her older brother was the only person she trusted to keep her secret. If it was going to happen, it would have to be tonight.

While they waited for their dad and Helen to arrive, Jamie, looking very handsome in his uniform, and Phee, wearing her yellow graduation dress, sat in the chairs at the top of the beach and talked about her auditions last spring.

"I had Dr. Ketterman for music theory my second year," Jamie said. "He was a tough teacher, but fair."

"He was kind of intimidating," Phee said, "but I think I did alright."

"His piano students are top notch. You'd do well at Iowa, Phee. I hope it's high on your list."

"Will you come back to finish?"

"I haven't decided. I'll definitely finish my degree, but I'm not sure it'll happen in Iowa City."

Frank honked when he pulled up behind Cabin 4, and before long, the two couples followed the sidewalk past the Giant Dips, the Fun House, and on to the Roof Garden. The line at the ticket window was long, so Jamie and Frank joined it while Helen and Phee walked out on the pier to enjoy the view across the smooth-as-glass lake.

The Roof Garden had been around for over twenty years, and was, according to a sign on the wall near the ticket window, the second largest dance floor in America. Some big-name bands had played there over the years—Louie Armstrong, Tommy Dorsey, Glenn Miller. It was a popular spot for dancers and music lovers of all ages.

Tickets in hand, the men found Helen and Phee, and the four of them climbed the stairs to the dance hall level. Inside it was loud and crowded, and Phee noticed there were quite a few men in uniform in the hall. She wondered if she'd see anyone she knew.

During the band's first break, Phee and Jamie sought out some fresh air on the veranda. After a couple of minutes, Phee looked over the railing to the street below and saw Roy Phillips smoking a cigarette while talking to two soldiers she didn't know. She waved and shouted, "Roy! Hi! Up here!" He looked up, smiled, and waved back. Phee took Jamie's hand and led him down to the sidewalk and through the crowd to the street.

"Fancy meeting you here," she said. "Look who surprised us yesterday. Roy, this is my brother, Jamie. Jamie, this is Roy Phillips from the camp." The two men shook hands, and Phee continued. "I think I've told you Jamie's in The Army Band at Fort Myer."

"Yes, ma'am, you have. Welcome home, Sergeant Swensson. That was quite a long deployment you fellows had."

"Two years to the day," Jamie said.

"I'd like to talk to you about that sometime. Gotta be more exciting than Camp Algona."

"Yes, well, sometimes there was more excitement than we wanted."

"Jamie has to catch the train to Chicago tomorrow afternoon," Phee said, "so we're heading home in the morning."

"It's a shame it's such a short visit," Roy said, "but I bet you're making the most of it."

"We sure are," Jamie replied as he put his arm around Phee's shoulders. "Sounds like the band's back on stage. Shall we go up?"

"I'll go with you," Roy said. "Phee, may I have the next dance?"

She smiled. "Sure, I'd like that."

Back inside, Roy led Phee to the middle of the floor, while Jamie wandered around the edge until he found a girl who looked lonely and asked her to dance. Her two companions were wide-eyed and giggly as they watched their friend swaying in the arms of the handsome soldier.

While they danced cheek to cheek to "Embraceable You," Phee was reminded that Roy was quite a good dancer. And then, out of the blue, he asked, "Won't Sergeant Ebinger be envious when I tell him I got to dance with the fair Fräulein Swensson tonight?"

Phee took a step back. "I doubt it."

"I don't," he said as they continued dancing. "There's no doubt the Sergeant is crazy about you. And it's pretty obvious that you—"

Phee pulled away again. "Oh gosh, is it really!?"

"Then I am right!"

After a moment's hesitation, Phee grabbed Roy's hand and led him to the nearest exit, out onto the veranda, and back down the steps. She hoped Jamie was having a good time inside because it looked like she was about to have a long and serious discussion with Roy about Horst. While butterflies danced in her stomach, she spied an unoccupied bench across the street.

"Phee, I think you're great," Roy began as they sat, "probably the nicest girl I've ever met. And I've been watching you—"

Phee gasped. "What?"

"No, not like a stalker, nothing like that. I just mean, I like you, a lot."

Phee was stunned. How could she not know? "I like you too, Roy," she admitted. "It's nice to have a friend at the camp who . . ."

". . . can accommodate your friendship with Sergeant Ebinger?"

"Well, no, I mean, yes . . . sort of."

"Phee, I need to ask you a question, and I'd like an honest answer."

Oh no, please don't ask! "Sure, ask away."

Roy cleared his throat. "Have you been taking Sergeant Ebinger outside the camp?"

That's it, he knows. "Well . . ."

"I want the truth, Phee."

"It sounds like you already know the answer."

Roy pulled out a pack of Camels, lit one, then sat back on the bench and blew a single smoke ring in the air. "That day I met you at the front gate—Mother's Day, wasn't it? He was in the car then, wasn't he."

Phee took a deep breath. "Yes, he was."

"Is that the only time?"

"It was, honest to God. You're right, it was Mother's Day. We just went to the cemetery to visit my mom's grave. We were only gone a short time."

"You broke all the rules, you know."

"All of them?"

"Enough of them, certainly, and there could be repercussions. There *should* be—"

"Oh, Roy, you won't tell on us, will you?"

"This is serious, Phee. You've put me in a difficult position. I've waited too long to report this, but I still could."

"It was my idea, Roy. I'm to blame. He didn't want to do it. He did it for me."

"It doesn't matter whose idea it was, Phee. It was still wrong."

"What will happen to Horst?"

"Well, for one thing, he could be transferred to another camp."

She had not considered that possibility, and the sound of it made her nauseous. "Oh God, no. Roy, you can't report us. Please, I'm begging you. It would ruin *everything*."

Roy knew she was right. Reporting this incident to his superiors would indeed ruin everything, including his friendship with Phee. The war with Germany had been over for almost two months, and Camp Algona would be closing, possibly by year's end. In a few months, Sergeant Ebinger would no longer be a part of Phee's life. "I won't report you," he decided, "even though I could get in a lot of trouble if someone finds out. But Phee, you know it can never happen again."

She touched his arm. "Never again, I promise."

"So, do you want to tell the Sergeant about our conversation, or do you want me to tell him?"

"I will. We have a rehearsal Sunday afternoon. You can stop by and check on us."

Roy grinned. "I don't think that'll be necessary. I trust you."

Phee was somewhat relieved. "I can't thank you enough, Roy. You are such a wonderful friend."

"I hope this is the only conversation we need to have about this." He dropped his cigarette on the ground and stepped on it.

"Absolutely," she agreed.

"Should we go back in?"

"Yeh, let's do."

IT WAS A WARM night, and even with all the windows open and a nice breeze coming through, it was hot inside the dance hall. And the band, while top notch and easy to dance to, was loud. By ten o'clock, Frank and Helen had had enough fun and decided to call it a night. They found Phee and Jamie to let them know they were leaving.

"We'll walk you out," Jamie said, almost shouting.

When they got to the street level, they said their goodbyes. "I'm so happy for Dad," Phee admitted as they watched Frank and Helen walk away arm in arm. "It's still a little strange, though, seeing them together."

"But it's time," Jamie said. "It doesn't mean he's stopped loving Mom. He just needs someone else to love. I like Helen."

"Me, too. Truth is, there should be a pastor's wife in the parsonage again. I really need to get on with my life next year."

"Yes, you do. Wanna to go back up?"

"Nah, I'd rather go sit on the dock."

"That sounds great. Let's go."

"GREAT BAND TONIGHT," JAMIE said. "It reminded me of some of the dance jobs we played overseas."

With her sandals parked next to her on the dock, Phee dangled her bare feet in the cool lake water. "It's wonderful you could play for the troops. I bet it really helped the soldiers who were homesick or recovering, or both."

"Oh sure. As I've said, we played for the big wigs too, but the most satisfying jobs were for the troops and the locals. They sure ate it up."

"You haven't talked about any of the bad things you saw. Surely you couldn't escape all of it. When was the first time you were really scared, assuming you were?"

"Scared? I guess it was when we were in Algiers. One afternoon we were in our quarters when there was a huge explosion. It shook the building, broke windows, knocked plaster off the wall. There was a lot of smoke down at the wharf, at least a mile away. We heard later that three of our ships had sunk. A lot of our men died that day."

"What about air raids?"

"Oh yeh, we heard 'em constantly in London. Had to go to the shelter with our gas masks and helmets, no matter what time of day or night. They said we'd be court-martialed if we didn't."

"That sounds awful!"

"Yeh, but the absolute worst were the buzz bombs. We called 'em 'doodlebugs.' One night, one flew right over our camp and landed about a hundred yards away. I think I was more scared that night than any other time the whole two years."

"Did you see a lot of bomb damage?"

"When we toured England, we did. It was almost like we were watching a movie—very surreal."

"What was Italy like?"

"Ugh! Don't remind me. We spent two weeks in Sicily, and I was sick the whole time. I won't give you the gory details, but a bunch of us got dysentery. I lost almost twenty pounds on that trip. Not one of my fondest memories."

"But our prayers were answered that you'd come home safe and sound when so many didn't."

"Like Danny Rasmussen. How are things with Christa?"

Phee sighed. "Not great. I've hardly seen her since graduation. I've talked to her folks at church a few times this summer, and I took a loaf of Swedish rye bread over to their house on Monday. They're doing pretty good, considering."

"Christa's going to Ames in the fall, right?"

"Far as I know, she and Adam will go down in September."

"And how's your German friend, the Sergeant?"

Phee hesitated—*I guess this is it*—then turned to face her brother. "It's Ebinger, Horst, and he's fine, wonderful, actually."

"Wonderful?"

"Please don't be disappointed, Jamie. We've grown . . . close, very close. In fact . . . I love him, a lot, and he loves me. We're crazy about each other."

In the darkness, Phee couldn't quite make out Jamie's expression, but she figured he was shocked, or puzzled, probably bewildered, and most likely concerned.

"Oh, Phee . . ."

"It's fine, really it is. We know it's only for now. He'll have to go back to Germany by the end of the year or even sooner."

Jamie sat very still, staring at the lights across the lake. "I'm trying to understand how this could have happened. It's not like you're ever alone with the guy."

"That's true, sort of. At first, there was a guard there every time we rehearsed, but they've been lenient about that these past few months."

"Does anyone else know?"

"Funny you should ask. I had a conversation with Roy Phillips earlier, about Horst. He told me he suspected, and I had to be honest."

"So, what did Corporal Phillips have to say about all this?"

Phee cringed, then decided to be honest with Jamie, too. "He wanted to know if I'd been sneaking Horst out of the camp."

"Good God, Phee, you haven't been, have you?!"

"Shhh!" she whispered. "You'll wake everybody up!"

"Please tell me you haven't been sneaking a prisoner of war out of Camp Algona."

"I did, but just once."

Jamie got up and began to pace back and forth across the wide end of the dock. Mumbling incomprehensibly, he rubbed the top of this head, continued pacing, then returned to Phee's side.

"Phee, you took a huge risk," he finally said.

"I know. Roy put the fear of God in me tonight when he said Horst could be transferred to another camp if we try it again. I promised we wouldn't."

"So, where'd you go, if you don't mind my asking?"

Phee chuckled. "You'll love this. We went to see Mom."

"Mom?! You went to the cemetery?!"

"It was Mother's Day. We sat on that little marble bench and we both talked to her. It was so nice."

"That's not a particularly romantic destination."

"I know, but it was wonderful."

"I guess you've kept Dad in the dark about all this."

"Of course. He'd have a cow if he knew. I'd never be allowed to set foot out there again. So, obviously, this is between you and me and Roy, and Daisy, and Mom."

"Obviously."

"I'm so glad I told you, Jamie. It's been hard, keeping it to myself."

"Yeh, I get that. But Phee, be careful."

"I will."

"Guess we should head in," he said. "Wonder if Dad's back?"

"Let's go see if the car's here."

"I kinda hope it's not," he said as he helped Phee to her feet.

It wasn't.

40

SUNDAY 8 JULY 1945

DURING CHURCH THIS MORNING, Frank got a little choked up when he told the congregation about Jamie's surprise appearance at the lake. Once again, he thanked them for their support and their prayers for all the men and women who had served or were serving their country. He announced there would eventually be a plaque with the names of those who had served in this war displayed in a prominent place in the church.

Phee was a little anxious during the service. Not because she was bored; she wasn't. Not because it wasn't one of her dad's better sermons; it was. And not because she was hungry or had a headache. She was anxious because she was seeing Horst this afternoon, and she was planning to tell him about her conversation with Roy outside the Roof Garden last Thursday night.

When she arrived at the camp's front gate a little before three, Phee was pleased to see Private Mattingly on duty. "Hello, Private," she said, "long time no see."

As usual, Private Mattingly was pleasant and cordial. "Yes ma'am, it's been a while. I had to go home for my granddad's funeral."

"Oh, I'm so sorry. Where's home?"

"Norman, Oklahoma."

"No kidding. I don't think I've ever known anyone from Oklahoma. You'll have to tell me all about it someday."

"And I'd be more than happy to," he said while handing her the visitor pass. "Have a nice afternoon."

When she got to the stage, she reached into her pouch and pulled out a gift she found in one of the shops below the Roof Garden last week. It was a small wooden sailboat painted a light shade of blue with a white sail, with WEST OKOBOJI hand-painted in black on one side and ARNOLDS PARK on the other. A totally useless gift, she knew, but she hoped it would remind Horst of her when he returned home to Germany.

"Greetings, friend Phee," Horst said as he came through the lobby door.

"And greetings to you, too, friend Horst," she said, returning the little boat to her pouch.

He hurried to the stage, took Phee in his arms, and kissed her like he hadn't seen her for weeks.

"I've missed you so much!" she moaned. "Are you alright?"

"*Ja,*" he said as he held her face in his hands, "I am alright, now that we are together."

"It's so good to be back. I have a lot to tell you."

"I can see you have been in the sunshine."

"I have! I just spent three glorious days at the lake." Phee's enthusiasm was on display as she told Horst about Jamie's surprise visit. And then, there was Roy. "I saw someone else up there—Corporal Phillips."

"I knew he was to go for some hours in the last week."

"Jamie and I and Dad and Helen went dancing at the Roof Garden, that's a dance hall at Arnolds Park, near where we stay with Bee and Nannie."

"Your *Grosseltern* . . . grandparents."

"That's right. Anyway, we ran into Roy at the Roof Garden, and he and I had a chance to talk." She sighed. "He knows I took you to the cemetery."

"Perhaps I should be surprised, but I am not. What will he do?"

"He said he'd keep quiet if I promised it wouldn't happen again."

"And you promised?"

"I had to, Horst. Roy said you might be transferred to another camp. I couldn't bear that. We're still friends, thankfully."

"And we should remain friends with the Corporal until the end, I think."

"Oh, yes, absolutely, friends to the end."

They sat at the piano and played through the Dvořák without stopping, first time. It was in the bag.

"I have something for you," he said when they finished.

"I have something for you, too."

"I have brought the program for our concerts coming soon."

"Good! I really wanted to see it."

"And what can you give your friend Horst?"

"Something I found at the lake." She reached inside her pouch and pulled out the small sailboat.

He smiled. "It reminds me of my childhood with our *Segelboot* . . . sailing boat, on the Wannsee."

"How nice. I'm so glad."

"The boat is large enough for all of us to ride across the lake. I like to remember it. We were happy then, for the most."

She picked up the program Horst brought. "I see we're second on the program. I'm glad we're early."

"*Ja*, so you can relax after Herr Dvořák. But for me, it is a busy time for conducting my *Männerchor* and my dance band and my orchestra."

"Do you need me to play for the Tchesnokov?"

He shook his head. "*Nein*, but you should plan to accompany the *Männerchor* in some months, for one time at least and perhaps more, if we are still here."

"Have you heard anything?"

"Colonel McNabb makes it possible for my comrades to continue building the nativity scene. If we are in the camp until the end of the year, the *Männerchor* will perform with it."

"I'm working on my Christmas song. It's almost done."

"Bring it to me when you are finished. I will decide if my men can sing it."

Phee looked at her watch. "Oh, gosh, it's getting late. You need to get back."

They gathered their music, and Horst placed the small sailboat in his breast pocket. While they walked to the lobby, Phee remembered to tell him about the bizarre dream she had last week. He found her story quite amusing and laughed harder than she'd ever heard him laugh.

"My dear friend Phee," he said, catching his breath, "such an . . . *empörend* . . . outrageous story you have told. I must tell my comrades."

"Oh, no, you can't! You'll give us away!"

"That is true. Perhaps I will say I saw it in a magazine."

"Just be careful."

"No one will know Fräulein Swensson has made a dream about dancing with Herr Hitler."

On her way home, Phee decided, at least for now, she'd forget about sneaking Horst out of the camp again. "It's not worth the risk, Phee."

41

SUNDAY 29 JULY 1945

AT LAST, ONE OF the most anticipated days of the summer for many Algonans had arrived. Frank and Phee were on their way to the high school for this afternoon's concert that would feature the city band, singers from several church choirs, and Horst's ensembles. Frank and Phee were both singing in the massed choir and needed to be in the gymnasium for the dress rehearsal at two thirty.

The logistics for this event were somewhat daunting. Because so many POWs were performing today, security was extremely tight. By now, Colonel McNabb and his staff weren't concerned about escape attempts, nor were they worried about prisoners behaving badly. For the most part, the men who were involved in the musical groups at Camp Algona had been model prisoners.

The tight security was mostly for the benefit of those who might be apprehensive about attending today's concert. In the past couple of weeks, there had been two articles in the newspaper about it. According to the police chief, all available officers would be on duty at the school, and army guards not needed at the camp would accompany the prisoners on the buses. The bleacher section to the left of the stage was reserved for all the POWs, and the guards would sit between the prisoners and the public. Still, a number of people would not attend today's concert on principle even though the war with Germany had ended almost three months ago. For some, these men were still the enemy.

The buses from the camp arrived early so all the prisoners and their equipment could be unloaded and moved inside before the civilian participants arrived. All the music for Horst's groups—the dance band, the orchestra, and the *Männerchor*—was in a box under the piano, a nice Lester baby grand borrowed from the choral rehearsal room.

On the short drive to the high school, Frank and Phee talked about the weather. There'd been severe storms in Oklahoma and Kansas the past two days, and the weather prognosticators on the radio indicated those storms could potentially move towards northwest Iowa. For today, the heat and humidity would make for "gallons of sweat in the gym," as Frank put it.

"I hope they've got the big fans going," Phee said. "That'll help a little."

As they neared the school, Frank said, "I'll drop you off and go park. Oh, and I told Edith to take the kids home after the concert, so we won't need to look for them."

"Alright, see you inside." Phee grabbed her music pouch and hurried through the heavy double doors. She was greeted by at least four hundred chairs set in rows on the canvas-covered gym floor. A large temporary stage was constructed at the south end of the gym, with risers for the singers placed behind the chairs and music stands for the musicians. They'd managed to devise a workable placement for everything so changes between performing groups could be swift. With the heat in the gym, the audience members shouldn't be given too many opportunities to get antsy.

The PTA mothers had set up a table with glasses of water for the performers. Phee took a glass with her up to the stage. When she got to the piano, Horst turned and smiled. "Fräulein Swensson," he said, "it is good to see you. You look lovely today."

"Thank you, Sergeant," she said, almost but not quite blushing. "Have you played the piano yet?"

"*Ja*, it is a good instrument."

"Would it be alright if I warmed up?"

"Certainly."

Phee played a few chords, a couple scales, then the first dozen or so measures of the Dvořák. Despite the heat, the piano was still in tune. "That should do it," she said. "Don't want to give anything away."

Promptly at two thirty, Mrs. Goodwin, the high school choral teacher, approached the microphone on the stage and invited all the singers to find their places on the risers. They began each number, then she asked Horst and his orchestra to quickly take the stage to rehearse the final piece on the program. Since there wasn't room for the *Männerchor* on the risers, they would sing from their seats in the nearby bleachers.

While she stood on the back riser in the alto section, Phee watched Horst as he spoke to his musicians. She wondered what he'd be doing in five or ten years. Would he lead an orchestra or a choir or both in Germany? Would he choose something else entirely, like the law, or politics, or business? She hoped it would be music. How could it not be music?

The ushers, volunteers from the high school faculty, opened the doors at three thirty and for the next half hour, people filed in, filling all the chairs before they were directed to the bleachers. Phee and Horst waited off to the side while the municipal band members found their seats on stage. Phee looked for Christa in the French horn section but didn't see her and wasn't surprised. She wondered if Jack and Peggy were in the audience, then decided they probably weren't there, either.

At five past four, Mayor Kimball walked to the microphone to begin a brief welcome that included an apology for the heat. Following the mayor's remarks, Colonel McNabb briefly explained how the concert was conceived and implemented. He said, as far as he knew, today's concert was unique in the history of prisoner of war camps in the United States. By the time he finished, the gym was almost completely full. Phee was pleased so many people had come out on this hot and humid afternoon, as it showed the prisoners how much the good people of Algona appreciated and enjoyed fine music.

Before the concert began, a color guard from the camp entered from the back carrying the American flag. Everyone, including members of the band and the POWs, stood as three soldiers marched single file down the center aisle. After the band played the "Star Spangled Banner," the program continued with a transcription of German composer Richard Wagner's "Pilgrim's Chorus" from his opera *Tannhäuser*. From their nods and smiles, it was obvious the prisoners appreciated the selection.

After the band finished and left the stage, Phee and Horst climbed the steps and walked to the piano. Horst raised the lid, then joined Phee on the bench. At that moment, Phee realized they hadn't practiced bowing. She leaned over and whispered in his ear, "We forgot to practice our bow."

Horst turned and whispered, "Follow me."

It took just over four minutes to perform the "Dance No. 1" from Dvořák's *Slavonic Dances*. When they finished, applause erupted. Horst stood immediately, stepped back from the piano, and held out his hand. Phee hesitated, then reached for it. They bowed once, then left the stage as the POW string quartet prepared to play Brahms. The dance band followed with two Glenn Miller pieces, the *Männerchor* performed a song by Tchesnokov as well as two Negro spirituals, and the orchestra played Beethoven.

The sixty-eight members of the massed church choir did a fine job with Barber's "Sure on This Shining Night" and a medley of songs from the Broadway musical *Oklahoma!* Then, while the orchestra members returned to the stage for the final number, Mrs. Goodwin walked to the microphone.

"We're calling today's event 'A Concert for Reconciliation,'" she began, "not *of* reconciliation, but *for* reconciliation. There is a difference. I looked up 'reconcile' in the dictionary." She looked at her notes. "The first meaning is 'to make friendly again or win over to a friendly attitude.' Another meaning involves settling a quarrel. But here's my favorite: 'to bring into harmony.

"Before we finish our program today, I'd like to acknowledge one person in particular who has worked tremendously hard to make this concert a success. You've seen him on stage a number of times today, as a performer and a conductor. His talent, including his talent as an arranger, seems to know no bounds. Sergeant Ebinger, please come up and take a bow."

He did, and she continued. "As you may know, the hymn we're about to sing is based on 'Ode to Joy' from Beethoven's Ninth Symphony. Verse three is particularly significant." She checked her notes again. "You'll hear 'thou art giving and forgiving, ever blessing ever blest' and 'teach us how to love each other, lift us to the joy divine.' Ladies and gentlemen, thank you so much for coming today. We hope you enjoy our final piece, 'Joyful, Joyful We Adore Thee.'"

As the hymn concluded, the audience members stood almost immediately with the ovation lasting a good two minutes. Mayor Kimball and Colonel McNabb, who were sitting in the front row with their wives and other dignitaries, came to the stage to shake hands with some of the performers. Phee looked for Horst and found him at the water table chatting with one of the PTA mothers who was obviously enthralled.

"It went well, don't you think?" Phee asked after he returned to the stage.

"I believe it did," he said, "but we can . . . how you say . . . find a room to improve it when we perform at our camp next week."

"Find room for improvement," she said, smiling.

"You should go now to have a celebration with your family."

"Wish you could join us."

Horst smiled and said very softly, "I will be in your heart, will I not?"

"Always," she whispered.

42

MONDAY 30 JULY 1945

FRANK WAS HOME TAKING it easy after yesterday's big event at the high school. He was also recovering from Vacation Bible School which had kept him and Phee and the kids busy each morning last week.

After lunch, Mollie went next door to play with Charlotte, and the boys got on their bikes and pedaled over to the Zetterholms for an afternoon of fun and games with Paul. Phee's piano lesson was at four, so she and the twins planned to ride home together after her lesson.

The weather yesterday was uncomfortable, but today was worse. The weatherman on WHO had been warning everyone that a thunderstorm would most likely develop to the south and west of Algona later this afternoon. Just before five o'clock, Frank stepped out the back door and looked up at the sky to see if anything was brewing. The taller neighborhood trees obscured his view to the west, but overhead he saw nothing but fluffy cumulus clouds. And then, he heard distant thunder.

Frank turned up the volume on the kitchen radio when he walked by, and he was glad he did. Regular programming was interrupted to announce the sighting of a tornado in the clouds about thirty-five miles southwest of Algona, just east of Pocahontas. Frank thought it was a little too close for comfort, so he went to the phone to call next door to the Coopers.

"Dorothy? Hi, it's Frank. Do you have the radio on . . . I just heard on WHO, they've spotted a tornado due east of Pocahontas . . . well, send Mollie home, and you and Charlotte come, too. I'd feel better if you two were here, in case we need to go to the basement . . . right, see you in a minute. 'Bye."

Next, he called the Zetterholms. It was two minutes past five. "Sure hope those kids haven't left yet." It took five rings before Edith answered. "Edith, it's Frank. Have the kids left . . . how long ago . . . there's a tornado east of Pocahontas, and I don't know for sure . . . no, that's fine. I'll get in the car and try to catch up with 'em . . . no, everything'll be fine."

Just then, the house got very dark, and just as suddenly, the wind picked up dramatically, bending trees back and forth as if giant hands were shaking the life out of them.

"Edith, gotta go. You and Paul get to the basement . . . right, I'll be in touch. 'Bye."

Frank grabbed the car key and ran out the front door. The wind had gathered strength, with leaves and dust and, of all things, a tumbleweed, rolling up the street in front of the parsonage. The sky was a very dark gray, almost green, and Frank was scared for the first time in a long while. As he got to the car, Mollie, Charlotte, and Dorothy ran across the yard to the porch. "Get inside!" he yelled. "Go straight to the basement! I've got to find Phee and the boys!"

"I wanna go with you!" Mollie screamed.

"No, you stay here! I'll be right back!"

He headed north on Cleveland, then turned west onto Hayes. Leaves and debris slammed into the side of the car, and just as huge raindrops began to splatter on the windshield, Frank caught a glimpse of his three children about a block away, pedaling as fast as they could. He laid on the horn to get their attention. As soon as they met in the middle of the block, he opened the driver's door, got out, and yelled, "Leave your bikes! Get in, quick!"

Phee climbed into the front seat, the twins jumped in the back, and Frank sped back to the parsonage.

"Oh my gosh!" Phee cried, almost out of breath. "I'm so glad you found us!"

"Yeh, Dad," Tris said, "way to go!"

"I really thought we could make it home," she said. "It didn't look that bad when we left."

"They spotted a tornado east of Pocahontas," Frank said. "It could be here any minute."

"Wow!" Gus shouted. "I've never seen a tornado!"

"And you're not going to see one today either," Frank said. "We'll run to the basement as soon as we get home. Charlotte and her mom are down there with Mollie."

As Frank pulled into the driveway, it was raining harder, and quarter inch hail pinged on the roof and hood of the car. They all got out and ran to the porch.

"I'm gonna run up and get some towels," Phee said as she opened the front door.

"Skip the towels!" Frank yelled. "Downstairs—now!"

All the windows in the house were closed, thanks to Dorothy and the girls. When they got to the bottom of the basement steps, Mollie ran to her dad. "It sure is loud," she said. "Will our house blow away?"

"No, it won't," Frank said. "I'm sure we're not in the path."

Dorothy, managing a feeble smile, sat on an old kitchen chair near the fruit cellar. She held Charlotte on her lap.

"Oh poo!" Phee said, remembering she didn't get the clothes off the clothesline before her lesson. "Guess I should've brought the clothes in earlier."

"They probably weren't dry anyway," Dorothy said, "the humidity's so bad today."

Just then, the two dim light bulbs hanging from the ceiling flickered twice and went out. Darkness enveloped the damp basement as inch-sized hail began to fill the two nearby window wells. Mollie, with her arms wrapped around her dad, held on tight.

"Everyone just stay where you are," Frank ordered.

"Frank, maybe a prayer would help," Dorothy suggested.

"I was just going to . . ."

But, at that moment, comforting words of hope and yearnings for safety and stillness remained unspoken, interrupted by a loud noise outside. All seven people in the basement gasped. Phee grabbed the twins, Dorothy covered Charlotte's head with her arms, and Mollie screamed.

For the next six minutes and twenty-eight seconds, no one in the darkened basement moved or said a word as they listened to Mother Nature have her way with their town. Phee kept her arms around the boys while she tried to imagine what was happening outside the parsonage, in their neighborhood, at the fairgrounds, downtown, at the camp. *The camp! Oh no!*

Her dad said the tornado was coming up from the southwest. Camp Algona sat about a mile west of the city limits, and as far as Phee knew, all the buildings were wooden structures with no basements. She didn't remember Ed pointing out storm shelters during their tour last summer. It seemed unlikely there would be shelters for that many people at an installation that was temporary by design. If a tornado struck the camp, there would be casualties, probably many. She suddenly felt very weak and sat down on the floor, taking the twins with her.

"You okay, babe?" Frank asked. No answer. "Phee?"

"Yeh, I'm fine. Just felt like sitting."

By now, the sky had lightened some, so it was almost possible to see everything and everyone in the basement. It was still raining, but not as hard; it was still windy, but considerably less. The hail had ceased, thankfully.

"I'm going upstairs to have a look," Frank said.

"Can we go too?" Tris asked.

"No, everyone stay down here till I know the coast is clear."

"Don't go!" Mollie cried, clinging to her dad. "I'm scared!"

Phee stood and reached out to her sister. "Come here, Sweet Pea. Dad'll be right back."

Frank started up the steps. "I'll stay inside. I just want to see what it looks like out there." When he got to the landing, he looked out the back-door window towards St. Pete's. "Church looks fine from here," he said loudly so all could hear, hoping his initial positive assessment would relieve at least some of their anxieties. While he walked through the kitchen, dining room, living room, and hallway, they heard the floor creaking under his feet. The creaking ended when he got to the second floor.

Before long, Frank returned to the basement. "Phee, I've got good news. You don't need to worry about bringing in the clothes."

"Oh no, are they gone?" she asked.

"'Fraid so."

"Oh, poo! Some of us are gonna have to buy some new underwear."

"What else did you see?" Gus wondered.

"It's not as bad as I expected. There are a few trees down, lots of branches and other debris. And it looks like the car is dented some from the hail."

"What about our house?" Dorothy asked.

"It's fine, from what I can tell."

"Is it safe to walk home now? I'd like to go check on it."

"Sure," Frank said, "the sky's starting to clear in the west. We should be able to get outside now. But I want you kids to stay in."

"Da-ad," Gus whined, "I wanna see the trees!"

"Later, Gus. Dorothy, I'll walk you two over, then I need to check on the church."

"I can start supper," Phee volunteered. "Dorothy and Charlotte, you're welcome to come back and eat with us."

"That's real nice of you, Phee. We'd be happy to. What time?"

"How 'bout seven? It'll be something quick and easy."

"I made bread this morning," she said. "I can bring it if you want to make sandwiches."

"That would be perfect. Why don't you give a loaf to Dad? He can drop it off on his way to church."

While Frank escorted Dorothy and Charlotte out the front door, the kids ran from window to window in hopes of getting a glimpse of any storm damage. At that point, no one knew for sure if a tornado did or did not touch down in Algona or the camp today. But Phee could not feel relief until she knew for sure it didn't.

43

WEDNESDAY 1 AUG. 1945

THANKFULLY, THE STORM THAT whirled through Algona two days ago was not a tornado. But the winds were strong enough to cause some damage to property both in town and at Camp Algona. Trees were down, blocking several streets and roads, and two short sections of railroad tracks had to be cleared.

Yesterday, as soon as the phone lines were restored, Phee tried calling Roy Phillips, but the line was busy for almost an hour. When she finally reached him, he told her there were a few injuries on both the prisoner and American sides of the camp, but none were life-threatening. There was enough damage, though, that the repeat concert scheduled for next weekend at the camp was postponed indefinitely. Phee asked Roy to find Horst and have him call her. He said he'd try.

Frank phoned Bee and Nannie from his office yesterday afternoon, letting them know the family was fine and they needn't worry anymore. Then he tried Helen, three times, but there was no answer.

By Wednesday, things were getting back to normal. After supper, the twins did the dishes, then they ran out the back door and grabbed their bikes which they'd rescued from Hayes Street yesterday morning. Phee and Frank remained at the kitchen table, and just as their conversation turned to Wagner's *Ring Cycle* which was playing at a reasonable volume on the Victrola in the dining room, the phone rang.

"I'll get it," Phee said, hoping it might be Roy, but it wasn't. Phee called to her dad. "It's Helen." Their conversation was brief, and when Frank returned to the kitchen, he was smiling.

"She sounded so worried," Phee said.

"She's fine now," Frank said as he sat in his chair at the end of the table. "Phee, there's something . . ." The phone rang again. "I'll get it," he said with a smile.

Phee stayed at the table in case it wasn't for her, then heard her dad say, "Sure, hold on, I'll get her." It was Phee's turn to hurry to the phone, and as she reached for the receiver, Frank whispered, "It's Roy Phillips," and returned to the kitchen.

"Hi, Roy. Were you able to find Horst?"

"Yes ma'am, he's right here."

"Hello, Fräulein Swensson. This is your friend, Sergeant Ebinger, speaking to you from the guard barracks that was not damaged too much from the storm."

"It's so good to hear your voice. Are you alright?"

"*Ja*, I can say I am a survivor. Hiding under a bed mattress when the wind blows too strong can save a man from injury."

"I was so worried about you. Will there still be a concert at the camp?"

"The decision has not been made," he said, "but we must be confident."

"I guess I won't be allowed to come out there for a while," she lamented.

"We are told no civilians until our camp is put together again. It will be finished soon, I think, with many of us working to repair the damage."

"Did the theater survive?"

"I have heard the buildings in that space were not damaged. I believe our piano is safe."

"Thank God! We'll need to practice there again."

"And we will," he said, "I have confidence about it."

"Please tell Corporal Phillips to let me know as soon as I'm allowed back out there."

"He will call when it is time."

"Good."

"It seems this telephone is needed by others, so I will say auf Wiedersehen, Fräulein Swensson."

"Alright. Horst?"

"*Ja?*"

"*Ich liebe dich,*" she whispered.

"*Ja*, and from me the same."

Frank had made a pot of coffee. He offered a cup to Phee when she returned to the table. "Better not," she said, "it's a little late."

"Was that your friend Horst on the line?"

"Uh-huh. He's fine, and Roy is, too."

"I should call Ed tonight, get the scoop from him."

"Dad?"

"Yes?" he said, stifling a yawn.

"Did you want to talk to me about something?"

Frank blew on his hot coffee. "Yeh."

"Is it about Helen?"

He smiled and nodded. "Good guess." He told her he thought—he wasn't one hundred percent sure, but more than likely—he cared very deeply for Helen.

"That's wonderful, Dad. I really like Helen, and Mollie and Claire—"

"They're quite a pair, aren't they?" Frank said with a chuckle. "Almost another set of twins."

"I thought the same thing!"

"Helen's ten years younger than me. I guess that doesn't matter all that much."

"So, you're robbing the cradle. I don't think anyone will mind."

"I prefer you not mention this to anyone. I'm still sorting it all out, and I don't want to get anyone's hopes up, or disappoint anyone, the kids especially. I'm not sure how they'll react."

"Well, we know Mollie will be over the moon. The boys? Yeh, it could be a problem. I can tell you Jamie will be thrilled to pieces. We did talk about it at the lake."

"Oh, you did, huh? You didn't say anything to Bee or Nannie, did you?"

"Dad, they both want you to find someone to love again. They're very fond of Helen and Claire."

"That's a relief. I do want Mary's folks—"

"Don't you worry about Bee and Nannie. They love you and they want you to be happy. We all do. I don't know Helen very well, but I think she's about as genuine as they come."

"That she is," he said, reaching for her hand. "I love you, Phyllis Anne."

"I love you too, Dad."

Frank finished his coffee, then steered the conversation in a slightly different direction. "So, is there anyone you want to tell me about, someone with a heavy German accent, maybe?"

Phee smiled. "I was wondering when you were going to ask me about that. There's not much to say. He's my friend, we've gotten to know each other pretty well over the past year, and I enjoy performing with him."

"Is it just the music, then?"

Don't tell him, Phee. "Remember the conversation we had last year on the front porch, when I wasn't sure about meeting with him that first time?"

Frank nodded. "I remember."

"We thought I could be a positive influence, somehow."

"Do you think it's working?"

"It could be. He's getting it from other places, too—Roy Phillips, probably some of the guards, movies, magazines. I think the concert on Sunday really opened the eyes of some or even most of those prisoners."

"Now I will agree with you about that."

"That's why I hope we can do the concert again at the camp, so more of the prisoners can see the collaboration, I guess you could say."

"Well, I'm not sure we sorted everything out about your friendship with the Sergeant, but it sounds like you're comfortable with your relationship and everything's under control."

"I am—it is," she agreed. "He's a good friend, and I'll miss him when he's gone, for a while anyway. But life goes on. I tell Daisy that every night."

"Every night?"

"Almost."

"Guess I'll go call Ed. What do you think, should I invite him to supper soon?"

"Sure, that's a great idea." Phee poured herself a glass of water and gazed out the window over the sink, watching Mollie and Charlotte playing on the swing set in the Coopers' back yard. There were three swings, and tonight the middle one was empty. Maybe one day soon, she'd see three girls playing on the Coopers' swing set—Mollie, Charlotte, and Claire. *Oh, golly! Triplets!*

44

TUESDAY 14 AUG. 1945

SINCE THE "STORM OF the Decade" blew through Algona, it had been an extraordinary couple of weeks. The weather had cooperated, as if Mother Nature was making up for her wrath on the last Monday of July. It was sunny and warm but not hot or humid. Most Algonans had gone about their business, avoiding fallen trees and branches that hadn't yet felt the blade of a saw. It would take at least another week to get everything cleared from streets and sidewalks, but they were making progress. A few small groups of guarded prisoners from the camp were enlisted to help with the clearing up, and Phee was delighted to find Horst on one of the work details in their neighborhood. As an NCO—non-commissioned officer—he wasn't required to work, but he relished the opportunity to get away from the camp, help his neighbors, and maybe serendipitously see someone he knew. And he did!

But perhaps the most significant events of the past two weeks occurred on the other side of the world, and they led, at long last, to the unconditional surrender of Japan to the Allied forces. On the sixth of August a powerful new weapon, an atomic bomb, was dropped on the Japanese city of Hiroshima by an American B-29 bomber. The resulting death and destruction should have convinced Japanese Emperor Hirohito and his government that their aggression on all fronts must end immediately, but it didn't. So, another bomb, more powerful than the first, was dropped on Nagasaki three days later. Finally, the Emperor was persuaded, and at six o'clock Iowa time, President Truman made the announcement the whole world had been waiting for—the war with Japan was over.

Officially, V-J Day wouldn't be declared until the surrender document was signed by the Allies and Japanese sometime later. But that didn't stop the almost spontaneous celebration in the streets of Algona tonight. The Chamber of Commerce instructed all stores and businesses to lock their doors just after the six o'clock whistle blew. Kids on bikes, soldiers from Camp Algona, regular folks from all walks of life, joined in the jubilation. But it was bittersweet for countless families—across Algona, across Iowa, across America—for so many lives were lost pursuing the peace being celebrated tonight.

Before supper, Mollie and the twins insisted on heading downtown for the festivities, so Frank walked with them so they could join the impromptu parade that was underway on Main Street. Phee chose to stay home to get supper started, but also to reflect on the events of the past couple of weeks—a storm like no other she'd witnessed, her dad's admission he had feelings for Helen, and the massive death and destruction that was purportedly needed to end the war. For Phee, it was all a bit much.

But tomorrow, she'd finally get to see Horst. Roy Phillips called yesterday to let her know civilians were being allowed access to Camp Algona once again. Horst asked if Phee could come to the theater at three o'clock for a meeting/rehearsal, and his request was approved.

At just past seven thirty, Frank and the kids returned from the parade. "I'm starving!" Tris yelled.

"You kids run upstairs to wash up," Frank said. "Is everything ready?"

"Just about," Phee yelled from the kitchen, "give me five minutes."

Tonight, it was Spam and baked beans and a lime Jell-O fruit cocktail salad. Phee tried to limit their Spam meals to once a week, but sometimes she was at a loss for meal ideas and Spam seemed to fit the bill just about every time it was served. The kids liked baked beans, and Jell-O was pretty much everyone's favorite. While they ate, Phee asked about the parade.

"It was even bigger than the last one," Tris said, "in May, I mean, when the Germans surrendered."

"And there were hundreds of soldiers," Mollie added.

"I don't think there were 'hundreds,'" Frank said, "but there were quite a few."

"It's still going on," Gus said. "Can we go back down after supper?"

Frank glanced at his watch. "It's a little late. By the time we get the dishes done, it'll be almost dark."

"Why don't we stay home and play some cards while we listen to the radio?" Phee suggested. "There might be more news about the surrender."

"And that's exactly what we'll do," Frank said as he took his dishes to the sink. "Any objections?"

The kids were a little disappointed, then decided it was a reasonable Plan B.

Mollie, always the last to finish her meal, took a bite of Jell-O and said, "We haven't decided on the Word of the Day. I vote for surrender."

"Perfect!" Frank said. "Sweet Pea, can you give us the definition?"

"Well, I don't know what the dictionary says, but I'd say it probably means . . . give up, put down your guns, raise your arms, and stop fighting!"

"I think she cheated," Phee said. "I bet that's exactly what it says in the dictionary."

"Good job, kiddo," Frank said. "You can add it to the list. I'll find a deck o' cards. We'll play in the dining room for a change."

There was more news about the surrender on the radio tonight, but they didn't break into regular programming, waiting instead for the usual top of the hour news reports. So, while a hot game of hearts was enjoyed in the parsonage dining room, *Fibber McGee and Molly* and *The Bob Hope Show* played in the background. For Phee, it was a wonderful evening with her family. Tomorrow, she'd drive to Camp Algona for the first time in over three weeks. Inside her music pouch would be the piece for choir she'd worked on all summer. She hoped Horst would like it, because she really wanted the *Männerchor* to perform it on their Christmas program, *if* there was a Christmas program, *if* there were any singers left in the camp in December, *if* the camp still existed in December.

45

WEDNESDAY 15 AUG. 1945

PRIVATE MATTINGLY WAS ON duty at the Camp Algona gatehouse when Phee pulled up this afternoon. When she saw his smiling face, she couldn't help herself. She turned off the engine, hopped out of the car, and gave him a big hug. "I'm so glad you're alright!" she said. "Were you here when the storm hit?"

It took the Private a moment to recover from Phee's unexpected demonstration of affection, but he was obviously pleased. "No, ma'am. I was over there in the guard house, gettin' ready to come on duty."

"Were you scared?"

The Private laughed. "Yeh, I kinda thought . . . this is it! Nobody was hurt bad, though, and that's a miracle."

Shading her eyes from the bright afternoon sun, she looked around and said, "It does look a little different out here."

"Pro'bly 'cause some of the trees are down."

"Gosh, I guess you're right."

"I don't think they'll bother replacing 'em. We'll not be here much longer."

Phee didn't want to know, but she was curious. "Have you heard when they'll close the camp?"

"Only rumors."

"Well, I'll sure miss you when you're gone."

Handing her the visitor pass, he said, "Have a nice afternoon."

"I will. Thank you, Private."

When she got to the theater lobby, she heard Horst playing his piece. He ignored her as she dropped her music pouch on the floor near the piano and moved to stand behind him. When he finally stopped, he swiveled around on the bench, stood, and smiled. "*Hallo*, friend Phee."

"Hello."

He glanced out to the lobby, then pulled her close and quickly kissed her.

"I've missed you," she whispered, then moaned as his hands caressed her back. She very much enjoyed his touch. They sat together on the piano bench, and Horst returned to his music. She followed along, and when he reached the bottom of the page, she turned it for him.

"*Danke*," he said and continued. When he finished, they sat quietly. Phee felt a level of contentment she'd not felt in a while, and then Horst changed all that. "So," he said, "the war is over, *ja*?"

Phee laid her head on his shoulder and sighed. "It's wonderful news, I guess."

"But it is such a long war, with so much death and sadness. It should be ending before now."

"Of course, you're right."

"The American soldiers will come home, and the German soldiers—"

"Don't say it! It's too awful to think about. I don't want you to leave. I can't live without you!"

He laughed and hugged her gently. "Oh, my dear Phee. Your friend Horst is . . . how you say . . . impressed with your words. He loves you for saying it, but you can live a good life, perhaps a very good life, without a German soldier always nearby."

"No, I can't."

"We must find a way to make a smile for you. What should it be?"

Phee stood and walked to the edge of the stage. "I want us to figure out how we can spend as much time as possible together until—"

"Until we cannot?"

"That's right, until we cannot. It could be months and months, couldn't it? "There *will* be another *Männerchor* concert, I hope, and we can work on another piano four hands. And—"

"And there is more?"

"Yes. I brought my Christmas song. I finished it, and I'd like you to look at it."

"*Wunderbar!* Show it to me, *bitte*."

Phee found the blue and white plaid book of manuscript paper in her pouch, then played and sang her song while Horst sat next to her on the bench. It was written for mixed choir, but she wanted him to arrange it for the *Männerchor* in case they could perform it in December. "You could translate it, if your men will sing it, I mean."

"*Ja*, I can do it. It will not be difficult. And do you have a name for your lovely song?"

"I do. It sounds like a lullaby, so I thought 'Christ Child's Lullaby' might work."

"'*Wiegenlied des Christkindes*.' It will be my next project. When I have finished and can give it to the choir, you will come to hear it."

"That will be wonderful! Do you think you'll still be here in December?"

"I have spoken with Sergeant Mueller. We agree I will remain close to the end because I lead the music groups. Some of my men will be in the first groups to leave. They have been here for the longest."

"But couldn't you ask for them to stay longer, too?"

"Perhaps, but I believe it is too soon to worry. For today, we should visit Herr Dvořák, *ja*?"

"Good idea."

The notes were familiar, but since it had been over two weeks, they played it twice. It had a happy ending, and it usually brought laughter from the performers. Today was no exception.

"We should find another piece to work on," Phee suggested.

"And it would be my turn to choose, would it not?"

"I suppose so. Brahms?"

"Do you think I have changed my mind since before?"

"I doubt it."

"Today I would choose *Liebeslieder Waltzes*."

"I think those are in one of the books I got from Mrs. Z. I'll check." Reluctantly, she decided it was time to leave. "Thank you for looking at my piece. It will mean a lot if your choir can sing it."

"It will be possible," he said.

"Oh, Horst, you are so wonderful."

"*Das ist gut.* A man should be wonderful for another person, especially a beautiful woman."

Phee smiled while she packed her pouch. *Beautiful woman . . .*

They walked to the lobby together, but before they left the building, Horst took Phee in his arms for one last kiss.

"I will stay to practice my music," he said. "Auf Wiedersehen, friend Phee."

"*Ich liebe dich,*" she whispered.

"*Und ich liebe dich,*" he replied.

While Phee drove back to town, she heard on the radio that gas rationing would end today. *What great news!*

Sat. Aug. 25, 1945

—Dear Daisy—

Happy Birthday to me!! I'm FINALLY 18! I thought it would never get here. Not that it means all that much, I guess. I still can't vote, and I can't drink beer yet but that's OK. I've tried it. Yech! Today was a good day, overall. The <u>best</u> thing was getting a birthday card from Christa! I was <u>so</u> surprised! She just signed her name, nothing more, but it made my day. Dorothy volunteered to make me an angel food cake, so we had that for dessert tonight. It was delish! Bee and Nannie sent money and Dad did too. Well, he didn't send it, it was in a card. I'm sure I'll find ways to spend all that at the end-of-summer sales next week. Mollie made me a cute card (with Charlotte's help, she said) and offered to make my bed for an entire week! How sweet (especially since she almost never makes her own)! The boys gave me a box of assorted candy from Polly's. How could I not absolutely love that?! A telegram from Jamie arrived this afternoon. He said his card will be late. He probably hasn't bought it yet! Ha! I'll see Horst tomorrow afternoon, but I don't think he'll remember today is my birthday. I didn't remind him last weekend. Oh well. Just being with him will be the only gift I need. I love him <u>so</u> <u>much</u>!

And life goes on. G'night.

46

TUESDAY 4 SEPT. 1945

"I CAN'T BELIEVE IT's time for school again," Phee said as she turned off the stove under the coffee pot. It was a little past eight thirty, and Phee and Frank had just finished breakfast. They'd already walked the kids and Charlotte to school. Gus and Tris moaned about having to get up early, but uncharacteristically, Mollie was up at the crack of dawn, ready to greet the new school year with a smile and enthusiasm her new teacher would surely notice.

"Yep," Frank said, "and here you are, hangin' out with your old man on a school day. How's it feel?"

The fact that she was not starting college this week had not totally escaped Phee's consciousness. Circumstances being different, she'd be in Sioux Falls or Iowa City or St. Peter or Decorah, joining all the other freshmen who were finding their way around an unfamiliar campus. "It feels great," she answered, "and it'll feel even better after you go to your office. I think I'll write some letters this morning and mail 'em at the p. o. I might stay downtown a while, try to spend some of that birthday money."

"Be sure to let me know what I gave you."

She tugged his beard and said, "I certainly will."

After cleaning up in the kitchen, Phee went to the basement to wash the sheets and pillowcases. As she hung them outside on the clothesline, she was thankful for the warmer than normal weather today. It wouldn't be long before she'd be hanging everything in the basement again.

Back inside, she sat at the kitchen table and wrote a letter to Jamie about her birthday and their fair outing three days later. The Swenssons tried something different this year, enjoying the sights and sounds of the Kossuth County Fair after supper. It was cooler and the lights were splendid. The lines at all the rides were longer, though.

She found out from Horst on Sunday that the repeat concert, postponed because of storm damage at the camp, had been rescheduled for this coming Sunday afternoon at four. And they both learned from Roy Phillips about the initial plans to deactivate Camp Algona. It would take several months, and some POWs would be moved to other camps where labor was still needed. Roy said the last prisoners would leave Algona early in the new year. So, if it was true that Horst would remain at the camp until the end, he and Phee still had time. But time for what?

After she returned from her walk downtown, Phee drove to Cal's to get what she'd need for tonight's supper and a few items for the rest of the week. As soon as she got home with her groceries, she made Apple Brown Betty, a sugarless dessert she hadn't made in ages.

"Somethin' sure smells good in here!" Gus yelled as he and Tris came in after school. "That better be dessert I smell."

Phee wiped her hands on her apron and called out from the kitchen, "Just out of the oven."

"What else are we havin'?" Tris asked as he poured himself a glass of water.

"Can it be a surprise?"

"I s'pose."

"Do we have time to ride our bikes?" Gus asked.

"Sure, just don't ride all the way to Fort Dodge. Be back by six."

At half past five, Frank walked in the back door carrying tonight's newspaper. "Did you find anything downtown?" he asked.

"Sure did," she said, "two blouses at Crystal's, on sale, and a book at Carlyn's. Thanks, Dad. You picked good."

"Did we get any mail?"

"We did. There's a letter from Helen for you and one from Claire for Mollie. She's next door. The boys are out riding."

While Frank walked to the front hall to get the letter, Phee sat at the table and opened the paper to check the grocery ads. "What does Helen have to say?" she asked when Frank returned to the kitchen with the letter.

"Her in-laws are throwing her a big birthday party next month on the sixth. She's invited me up for it."

"That's nice. I hope you'll go."

"She thought we could all come up the night before, stay with Bee and Nannie, like we did last winter. I'll check my calendar tomorrow. Far as I know, we don't have anything major or minor happening that weekend."

"Except Sunday."

"I could call in sick."

"I'd love to see you try," she said, getting up to check the potatoes. "Why don't you go next door and encourage Mollie to join us in about fifteen minutes?"

While Phee poured the boiling water from the potatoes into the sink, Frank wandered next door, whistling all the way. Phee was glad her dad and Helen might soon spend time together, might plan for their future. All their lives could be changing, maybe soon.

47

FRIDAY 5 OCT. 1945

SOMETIMES, BEING A PREACHER'S kid—a PK—was hard. Kids who were PKs knew they were PKs from a very early age. Their friends knew they were preachers' kids and probably didn't think much about it. But there were expectations about preachers' kids that other kids didn't have to worry about. Their dads were "men of the cloth," chosen by God, some thought, and the children of those men were, in some respects, reflections of their dads' profession. So, at the very least, they were expected to be well-behaved, rule followers, and certainly good Christians.

Phee didn't often think about being a PK, but she thought about it when she woke up this morning. Today, she would lie to people she cared about and loved. She was certain she'd suffer grave consequences as a result, but she didn't care. She loved Horst and he loved her. Yes, she promised Roy last July she would not do this. Yes, her dad planned to take the whole family to Bee and Nannie's in Spirit Lake after the kids got home from school today. But two weeks ago, she and Horst came up with a plan, and later tonight, after his ten o'clock bed check, she would aid and abet his escape from Camp Algona. Phee was confident their plan would work. It just had to.

Phee's lie number one: "Dad, I feel like crap. My temperature's almost a hundred. I don't think I should go to Spirit Lake with you and the kids today. Give my love to Bee and Nannie and have a great time at Helen's party."

Phee's lie number two: "Hi, Mrs. Z, I have a huge favor to ask. Dad and the kids just left for Spirit Lake, and I just found out I have a rehearsal at the camp tonight. Could I please borrow your car? I'll get it back to you in the morning first thing."

Phee's lie number three: "Hi, Roy, it's Phee. I have big favor to ask. Would it be possible for Sergeant Ebinger and me to rehearse for about an hour at the theater tonight? Sure, before they set up for movie night would be just fine. Six to seven would work for me. Call me back and let know if it's approved. Thanks a bunch."

Roy did call back to say their rehearsal time had been approved and it was on the calendar. When Phee got to the camp just before six, he greeted her at the gate. "Hi, Roy," she said, "didn't think I'd see you here."

"I see you're driving a new car tonight."

"Yeh, it's Mrs. Z's. Dad and the kids are out of town, so she let me borrow it for tonight."

"Do you mind if I ride over to the theater with you?"

"Don't mind at all. I'd love the company."

He handed her the visitor pass, then walked around to the passenger door and got in after glancing in the back seat.

"So, how've you been?" he asked. "Haven't seen you since the concert last month."

"I'm fine, keeping busy. How are things in the Chaplain's office?"

"Funny you should ask. Things are winding down a little. I found out today I'll be back on guard duty for the last few weeks."

"Back on guard duty?"

"Yeh, I guess you don't know I came here last year as part of the guard contingent. When they found out I could speak some German, they placed me with Chaplain Mattson."

"So, how do you feel about guard duty?"

"Oh, it's alright. There's not much to worry about at this point."

"I s'pose not." *Except later tonight!*

Phee pulled into the parking lot and turned off the engine. "It was good to see you, Roy. Thanks for riding along."

"My pleasure. I'll probably see you when you leave. Have a good rehearsal."

"We will. See you later."

Horst was already on the stage when Phee got to the hall. "I just had an interesting conversation with Corporal Phillips," she said as she hurried across the freshly polished floor.

"And what did you learn from the Corporal?" he asked.

"He's back on guard duty."

"I must be very careful," he whispered. "Our friend might be watching as I make my escape."

"I'm starting to get a little nervous," she said. "I'm not sure I'll be able to practice the Brahms."

"But we should try. It will be . . . a distraction for us."

For the remainder of their hour, they played and talked and kissed and talked and played. They were distracted, just enough.

"I should be on my way," she said. "Do we need to talk about later, one more time?"

"I will find you. I have the Lover's Lane map you made. It is not far for me."

"And if you're not there by eleven thirty, I'll drive home."

"I will be there," he said with confidence.

When Phee got to the gate, Roy was there to bid her farewell. As she handed him the visitor pass, he made an obvious attempt to look in the back seat, then waved her on.

HORST'S PLAN FOR ESCAPING from Camp Algona was not his own. Three weeks ago, he had an interesting conversation with Manfred Winkler, a comrade from the Afrika Korps. A year ago, Manfred had found a way to leave and return to the camp without being detected. Horst decided if it worked for Manfred it could work for him, too.

The plan was risky. The eight watchtowers that were strategically positioned around the three prisoner compounds were manned by guards with machine guns twenty-four hours a day. Horst was aware of that, but he also knew the guards were, by now, not expecting to see anything unusual within their sights. Over the past year and a half, there had been only three successful escape attempts from Camp Algona, and all prisoners involved had returned to the camp voluntarily, or with help from the authorities, after a short outing. The war had ended, and most of the POWs understood they'd been treated well by the Americans at their camp. There was no logical reason to leave Camp Algona without permission unless a prisoner wanted to spend a few days in solitary confinement.

Running under the tall perimeter fences on the south side of Compound 1 was a large rainwater culvert. The culvert's opening was about twenty yards from the nearest watchtower, and at night, the floodlights from the tower illuminated the ground near the opening. However, there were small pockets of darkness on either side where a man could remain undetected. The steel grate that covered the culvert's opening was loose, and Horst's twice daily stroll this past week offered him opportunities to give it a few quick kicks to loosen it even more.

Manfred Winkler's description of his journey to freedom through the culvert told Horst he could end up a muddy mess when he got to the other side. It hadn't rained for over two weeks, though, so Horst was hopeful his prison garb would remain relatively unsoiled. But just in case, Phee said she'd bring along a couple of towels and some of Jamie's old clothes and shoes.

Phee pulled into the otherwise unoccupied old Lover's Lane at precisely ten thirty. Even if everything went smoothly, she knew Horst wouldn't be able to join her there until at least eleven o'clock. She turned on the radio but kept the volume low. Laying her head on the seat back with her eyes closed, she hummed along with Perry Como's big hit, "Till the End of Time." It was a mellow song, but Phee thought all of Perry's songs were mellow. Just as Helen O'Connell and Tommy Dorsey's band began their rendition of "Tangerine," Phee opened her eyes and saw someone running up the road to her left. *He made it!*

"Stay down," Phee whispered as she parked as close as she could to the parsonage back door. "Wait here till I get the door open."

Earlier, before she left the house, Phee closed all the curtains and turned on most of the lights so everything would be ready for their tour. She glanced over to the Coopers' back yard before motioning for Horst to join her inside. He hurried past her, and she quietly closed the door.

"Do you want something to drink?" she offered.

"A glass of *Liebfraumilch* would be very nice," he said with a wink.

"Huh?"

"You will not have this wine in your home. Perhaps no one in Algona—"

"We have beer in the icebox."

"I will be fine without it. May I have a kiss instead?"

"Not yet," she teased. "I'd like to show you around the house."

"I can see we are in the *Küche*, where my friend Phee cooks wonderful food for her family."

"I'm not sure it's wonderful, but they eat it, usually."

"And your *Mutter* spent much time here, *ja*?"

"Yeh, she was a great cook." Phee gently massaged the back of the kitchen chair where her mom always sat, lost in thought for a moment. "Shall we continue?"

He followed her through the dining room, stopping to look at the collage of family photos on the wall over the buffet. "Here is your *Mutter*," he said, looking at the portrait from her parents' wedding day in 1918, "a beautiful woman. I can see her lovely daughter in this photo."

"I do sort of look like my mom," she said, walking back to have a look. "I've got her nose, for sure."

"And her smile," he added.

They stopped at the piano in the living room, and Horst took a seat on the bench. He reached for the book of English Folk Songs, her birthday gift from Tris last year.

"It was my mom's," Phee said, pointing to Mary's name at the top of the cover. "Some of the songs are quite beautiful."

"I can play while you sing."

"Uhm, why don't we continue the tour upstairs?"

Horst stood and reached for Phee's hand. She led him to the hallway. At the bottom of the staircase, she took the first step up, then turned back and smiled.

"It is our next adventure," he said, "but we can say no to it."

Phee had no intention of saying no. She'd thought about it for weeks, months, actually. In her fantastical dreams, she'd already experienced what was about to happen upstairs in her bedroom. She knew tonight would be her only chance. She would not change her mind.

"AND THIS IS MY room," Phee said, leading Horst through the open doorway. The bedroom was dimly lit by one small lamp on the dressing table. He walked slowly through the room, noticing the pictures and posters on the wall, touching some of the books on the bookcase. The closet door was open, and when he saw her blue chenille robe hanging on a hook, he said, "I would like very much to see you wearing this now."

"Really? It's just my bathrobe."

"Just this, nothing else."

"Oh . . . alright . . . sure."

"While you do it, I will watch the beautiful outside world, a world without the tall fences and barbed wires and guards." He moved to the window near her nightstand and slowly pulled the curtains aside. The window faced a darkened St. Pete's so there was little to no chance someone would see them.

While Horst undressed on the other side of the bed, Phee went to the closet, reached for her robe, and draped it across the small bench in front of the dressing table. She sat to remove her shoes and socks, then stood and slowly pulled her sweater over her head. After unzipping her slacks, she let them fall to the floor and stepped away. *Just this, nothing else.*

She unhooked her brassiere, laid it on the dressing table next to her hairbrush, and reached for the bathrobe, still slightly damp from her bath earlier this afternoon. *Just this, nothing else.*

Before she closed the front of the robe and tied the belt around her waist, she removed her panties and left them on the floor next to her slacks. "I'm ready," she whispered.

Horst turned from the window and stared at Phee for the longest time, or so it seemed.

"Is everything alright?" she asked.

"I am standing here, seeing such beauty. Please allow me to enjoy it for a moment."

Phee smiled. She was nervous, but not too.

"Come sit with me here," he said softly.

Phee closed the bedroom door, then walked around the end of the bed and joined him. He took her hand and kissed it. "Phee, I want to make love with you, but you can say no, and we will stop now. I have much respect for you, I hope you know it."

"I do, Horst," she said, turning towards him and gently touching his face. "I love you with all my heart. I want this so much."

As he leaned to kiss her, he reached inside her robe and touched her breast. She gasped, and then—

Time stopped for Phee as she at last understood true love and intimacy. Horst was gentle, tender, passionate. Phee was overwhelmed with indescribable waves of pleasure, unlike anything she could possibly have imagined before this moment. They didn't speak. Only the sounds of their shared passion filled the small room. Her flesh upon his, his upon hers—touching—stroking—kissing—holding—loving.

When it was over, they lay in each other's arms, listening to each other's breaths and beating hearts. At last, he whispered, "Are you alright?"

Phee moaned softly, then kissed him. "I'm perfect, absolutely perfect."

"I wanted to be gentle—"

"You were perfect," she interrupted, "absolutely perfect."

They both chuckled, then Phee yawned. "Oh, gosh, I'm so tired. Can I please fall asleep in your arms?"

Horst kissed her forehead, her nose, her lips. "I would like it very much."

They both drifted into a satisfying slumber, a shared peace that was disrupted all too soon by a distant train whistle. Phee raised her head to look at the clock and moaned. It was almost three thirty.

"Horst, wake up," she said as she wrapped her robe around her shoulders. "We need to get dressed."

He opened his eyes, stretched his arms towards the ceiling, then sat on the edge of the bed. "We should return to camp now, before the sun comes."

"Horst?"

"*Ja?*"

"Thank you for loving me," she whispered while touching, then kissing his cheek. She reached for her clothes and rushed across the landing to the bathroom. In five minutes, they were both dressed and ready to leave.

Algona was still asleep as Phee and Horst drove back to the old Lover's Lane. When she stopped the car, he kissed her, opened the door, and he was gone.

Sat. Oct. 6, 1945

—Dear Daisy—

I slept in 'til almost 9:00 this morning, and then I laid here for a while, remembering what happened in my bed hours earlier. I think I was still glowing! I decided to drive to the cemetery to talk to Mom about everything before I returned Mrs. Z's car. I just had to tell someone. This afternoon I got caught up on the ironing, made a grocery list, and hoovered the floor downstairs. (Upstairs crud will have to wait.) I practiced, too. Dad and the kids got home a little later than they expected tonight. I had supper ready when they came in. Dad said Helen's party was a lot of fun. She really liked her sweater. I'm glad. After supper, I asked Dad if he popped the question. He said no, but they did talk about it. They'll come for Thanksgiving, probably with Bee and Nannie. That should be wild! I bet they announce their engagement when we're all together. Well, better sign off. I'll turn out the light now and hopefully dream about Horst. So glad I'll see him tomorrow.

And life goes on. G'night.

48

SUNDAY 28 OCT. 1945

OH GOD ... I'm so tired ... I can't do this.

It was concert day at Camp Algona. After lunch, Phee sat at the dressing table in her bedroom with her eyes closed, refusing to look in the mirror. When her eyes were open, all she saw was a young woman with undeniable symptoms. She so hoped they were imagined, but for the past week, she'd experienced mild nausea, tender breasts, and most of all, fatigue. She was just plain tired much of the time now. Phee had never been a napper, but lately, each afternoon after her dad returned to his office, she slowly climbed the stairs to her bedroom, plopped down on the bed, and was out like a light in seconds.

Phee knew why this was happening, these changes in her body. Two days ago, when she was home alone, she pulled the *Encyclopedia of Health* off the bookcase in the living room and turned to page three sixty-six. Her heart sank as she read the words under "Pregnancy, early signs of." She recognized almost every symptom listed. And her period was a week late. She was never, ever late.

But today, she must try to put all that aside and prepare her mind and body for the two concerts at the camp theater this afternoon. The Swenssons and the Zetterholms were invited to the three o'clock performance, and Phee was glad her teacher would get to hear the

Brahms. Yesterday's dress rehearsal went well, but Phee could tell the members of the *Männerchor* were somewhat less enthusiastic about this one. Some of them would be leaving the camp soon, and all were uncertain of what they would find when they returned to their homeland.

As promised, Horst led his choir through Phee's Christmas song, "Christ Child's Lullaby," at the dress rehearsal. She was enthralled as she listened to the *Männerchor* sing her "*Wiegenlied des Christkindes.*" Horst hinted they would probably perform it during Advent if enough of his singers were still in the camp.

The Swenssons arrived at the theater in time for Phee and Horst to run through the first part of their duet. Just after three o'clock, Colonel McNabb walked to the microphone at center stage, welcomed everyone, then introduced Horst who gave a brief overview of the pieces on the program. After the strings finished Mozart, Horst returned to the microphone and began to introduce the Brahms. It was not at all what Phee expected to hear.

"Johannes Brahms, as I am sure some of you will know, was a German composer. He was an excellent pianist, and, as you may guess, or maybe not, a Lutheran."

"Good for him!" Frank shouted from the third row. The audience laughed.

Horst continued. "Herr Brahms was born in Hamburg in Germany, but he lived many years in Vienna, a lovely city so full of music you cannot escape it, even in the public toilets." More laughter. "When people think of German composers, they remember Bach and Beethoven. Of course, these men were geniuses. But, for me, Brahms has so much emotion in his music, in all of it, from his symphonies, his piano sonatas, his variations, his rhapsodies, and his waltzes. Fräulein Swensson and I will perform sixteen short waltzes for you today. We hope you will hear our emotion as we play."

Horst looked at Phee who was sitting in the front row. "Fräulein Swensson, please join me on the stage. Ladies and gentlemen, I will tell you something about the Fräulein. We met over one year ago. I was in our camp for some weeks up to then when she and her father came for a visit. We were . . . how you say . . . shy with one another at the first. But over some time, we found we share a love for music, especially the piano. When we were asked to perform at the summer concert in the high school, we had to find music we both enjoyed. We each had a favorite, so she threw a coin with Thomas Jefferson into the air to see the winner. It was Fräulein Swensson's choice, the Dvořák *Slavonic Dances*. I was disappointed, but I made a smile so she would be happy."

Phee, waiting off to the side, smiled and shook her head.

"And then it was time to prepare for our concert today, and as you would expect, I was the winner, to play my beloved Brahms. The Fräulein made a big smile so I would be happy." More laughter from the audience. "We hope you enjoy our music."

As soon as they began to play, Phee forgot her concerns, her fatigue, her sadness about these being the final concerts at the camp. She wasn't aware of her family or her teacher, nor did she hear a baby's muffled cry in the back of the hall. The notes on the pages became more than Brahms's detailed instructions for where her fingers should land and how long they should remain there. They formed a unique connection with Horst, and the result was powerfully emotional.

The men of the *Männerchor*, the final group on the program, rose to the occasion, and the audience was mesmerized. At the end of the concert, Horst acknowledged the soloists and Phee, their accompanist, and after the applause ended, she left the stage to greet her family and the Zetterholms.

"Oh, Phee, it was marvelous!" Mollie cried. "I think you're the star!"

"Thanks, Sweet Pea, but I'm not a star. I just played the piano."

"And you played beautifully," Edith said. "I think it's the best I've heard from you in all these years."

"Thanks, Mrs. Z. We practiced hard."

"It certainly showed today," Harold said. "Congratulations, Phee."

"And we get to play it again in about an hour," Phee said just as Horst walked across the stage and down the nearby steps.

"Sergeant Ebinger, wonderful concert," Frank said.

"*Danke Ihnen*, sir," Horst replied while shaking Frank's hand. "Your daughter is a big help for us."

Phee smiled and shook her head. Then dear, sweet, precocious Mollie asked, "When are you going back to Germany? I bet Phee would like it if you stayed here."

Phee was mortified. Of course, she wanted him to stay! But no one knew she felt that way except Horst and Roy and Jamie and probably her dad.

"It is Mollie, *ja*?" Horst asked.

"Uh-huh."

"Mollie, I have not been told about the day I will leave our camp. For me, it will be too soon. There is much to consider, to make plans."

"Do you think there'll be another concert, Sergeant?" Frank asked.

"There is nothing on our calendar, but we should wait until December to know the answer. There might be music then."

"Well, we'd better saddle up," Frank said. "Good luck on the next concert."

Horst returned to the stage to help set up for the second performance while Phee decided to walk to the headquarters building where she knew there was a water fountain. When she got to the theater lobby, she saw Roy Phillips talking to another soldier.

"Hello, Phee, wonderful concert," Roy said. "You were great!"

Phee gave him a hug. "Thanks, Roy. Can you walk with me over to the headquarters building? I could use some water."

"Sure thing. I'll find a glass you can bring back."

On the short walk across the street, they talked about the camp Halloween dance coming up Wednesday night. Roy mentioned that Horst's dance band would provide the music. "Would you like to go to the dance?" he asked after handing her a glass of water from the staff lounge.

"Uhm, sure, I'd love to," Phee said as they started back to the theater.

"It's from seven to ten. I can pick you up at quarter to seven."

"That should be fine," she said. "Roy, I do have a favor to ask."

"Sure, what is it?"

"Do you think you could help us, Horst and me, schedule some rehearsals between now and . . . the end?"

"You mean when the Sergeant leaves the camp?"

"I don't know if we'll have any more performances. We'd just like to get together and play."

"And play music, you mean?"

"Of course, silly."

"So, you want me to get some rehearsals on the calendar?"

"Could you? Sundays at three seems to work."

"I'll see what I can do."

"Thanks, Roy, you're the best!" She gave him a peck on the cheek, then walked backwards towards the lobby door. "See you soon," she said as she waved.

THE SECOND CONCERT WENT better than the first, Phee thought, but she knew it was the last time she and Horst would perform together. When they were finally alone on stage, she walked around the piano and stood next to him.

"Thank you, Horst, for everything," she said as she put her arm around his waist. "I mean it. I'm so lucky. I've had the most wonderful experiences here at the camp, and it's all because of you. But I am a little sad today."

"Because we will not prepare for another performance?"

"Yes, but maybe this will help. I asked Corporal Phillips earlier if he could get some rehearsal times for us on the calendar. I said Sunday afternoons at three. Does that sound alright?"

"*Ja, das ist gut.* We will have many more days to make music."

"I sure hope so. Oh, and one more thing. Roy invited me to the Halloween dance. He said your band will be playing."

"We are preparing with fewer comrades, but it is enough for dancing."

"That's good. Well, I'd better go. Walk me to my car?" She grabbed her pouch, and they walked out into the crisp night air. The sun had set, but the cloudless southwestern sky was still aglow. "See you Wednesday night," she said, blowing him a kiss.

Wed. Oct. 31, 1945

—Dear Daisy—

Happy Halloween! What a night! I got to dance with Horst! More on that in a minute. Dad took the kids downtown for the big Halloween bash at 5. Gus was a hobo, Tris was a ghost, and Mollie wore my black cat costume from 8 years ago—it just barely fit her. I wore it the first time Christa and I went trick-or-treating together. She was a pink and white fairy—we were quite a pair! I managed to get a nap in before Roy picked me up tonight. It was the first time I'd seen him in civilian clothes. I told him I was a goldfinch since I wore black (pants) and yellow (sweater). Ha! There was lots of food on tables set up in the theater lobby, and everything was yummy. The place was packed, and I almost got overheated. Roy and I danced some, but we sat out at least half the time. He didn't seem to mind. We shared a table with Seth Poole, one of the guards, and Joyce Randall from town who was in Jamie's class. Seth and Joyce are an item (good for them) and wonderful dancers. It was fun catching Joyce up on all of Jamie's news. Horst's band sounded wonderful! They're short three or four players (they've left the camp for good), but you wouldn't know it. Before the last dance of the night, Roy spoke to Horst, and when he came back to the table, he said Horst wanted to dance with me! Roy said it was alright with him, bless his heart. We danced to "I'm in the Mood for Love." Perfect! Before we left, Roy found a sack and filled it with candy for the kids. He's such a sweetheart. When we got home, he walked me to the door and asked if he could kiss me good night. I was a little surprised, but I said "okay," and it was nice. If it wasn't for Horst—well—

And life goes on. G'night.

49

SUNDAY 11 NOV. 1945

TODAY WAS ARMISTICE DAY, so it didn't surprise Phee too much when she got a call from Roy Phillips this morning. He told her there would be a ceremony in the theater this afternoon at the time she and Horst were to meet for their regular rehearsal. Roy said they could move the rehearsal to seven tonight, and she said that would be fine.

The Swenssons ate supper a little early because of Phee's meeting at the camp. Their conversation centered around their Thanksgiving Day plans. With Bee and Nannie and Helen and Claire coming down from Spirit Lake, there would be a houseful. Ed Mattson and Dorothy and Charlotte Cooper would also join them for the big meal. Recently, Frank had been having twice-weekly phone conversations with Helen, but he hadn't yet shared any nuptial news with Phee.

Next week, Bee and Nannie and Claire would stay at the parsonage both Wednesday and Thursday nights, and Helen was invited to stay next door with the Coopers. To Phee's delight, everyone would bring food including pumpkin pies for dessert, so all she would need to worry about was the turkey and beverages.

On her way to the camp, Phee considered telling Horst she might be pregnant. *If he knew about the baby, maybe he'd stay or come back to Iowa as soon as he could find a way. Wasn't telling him the right thing to do?* Phee would have at least a partial answer to that question within the hour.

When she arrived at the theater, she found Horst alone on the stage standing next to the piano. "Am I late?" she asked.

"*Nein*, I am early," he said with a serious look on his face. "We have much to talk about."

"Is something wrong?"

"Today I had a meeting with my *Männerchor*. Some of them will leave the camp in the next week. They will not return."

"Oh gosh, really? How many?"

"Almost half. We must perform with fewer singers in the next month, perhaps . . . sixteen will remain."

Phee walked to the piano and sat on the bench. Horst did not join her.

"I have more to say," he said. After a big sigh, he continued. "I have a letter from my *Mutter*, from Wittenberg, with much . . . despair. She has not heard from my father for more than one year. I was very worried about that. He is not there to protect them, and neither is her son, her only son now."

"What do you mean, 'protect'?"

"She did not write many words, but I believe there have been problems with the Russians in Wittenberg, and many other places in Deutschland where they have made it . . . their land, their homes. Some of my comrades have heard it from their families who have written more about it. I am concerned for my mother and my sister, even more than before."

"Oh, Horst, I'm so sorry. Do you think your father has been arrested? It doesn't seem reasonable he can't reach your mother for a whole year."

"My mother cannot contact his colleagues, where he was working before, in Berlin, where there is so much destruction. She wants to go there to look for him, but my Aunt Gerda is keeping her in Wittenberg for a longer time."

"Oh, my dear Horst, this is all such a mess." She rose from the bench and went to him. "How can I make it better?" And then she remembered. "I brought that book of English Folk Songs I showed you at the house last month."

He smiled. "To remind us of our night together."

"I'll pick one," she suggested. "You play, I'll sing." She chose "I Love My Love" by Gustav Holst. It was a good choice.

"What time do you need to be back at the barracks?" Phee asked when they finished the song.

"We still have our check at ten o'clock. But I should return now. I would like to write a letter to my *Mutter*."

"We can meet again next week. We won't have many more chances. Oh dear, now *I'm* sad."

"I do not want my friend Phee to have sadness in her heart," he said. "We will always be happy together, will we not?"

"We will," Phee replied as she kissed his cheek, "always."

They grabbed their coats and walked together to the dimly lit parking lot. Phee opened the car door, tossed her music pouch on the seat, and got in. "I'll see you next week," she said, then closed the door.

Horst motioned for her to lower the window. He bent down, reached for her chin, and kissed her. "*Ich liebe dich*, Phee," he whispered.

"*Und Ich liebe dich,* Horst."

While she drove back to town, Phee thought about Horst's mother and sister and the concern he had for them. She finally understood why he couldn't stay in Iowa. He had to return to Germany to take care of his family, and it broke her heart.

50

THURSDAY 22 NOV. 1945 - PART 1

THANKSGIVING DAY

IT WAS EARLY, AND Phee was still in bed, but awake. She heard voices downstairs and thought she should get up and help with breakfast, but she was confident Nannie and Helen would do a fine job without her. So, she stayed, comfortable where she was, remembering last Thanksgiving at the Rasmussens. Everyone was happy, everyone got along, everything was just about perfect. It was so different now. The war was over, Danny was dead, Christa and Phee were still estranged, and Phee was in love with Horst and most likely pregnant. And on top of all that, Frank and Helen—

Someone knocked on her bedroom door. "Phee, are you up?" It was her dad.

"Almost."

"Can we talk?"

"Sure, come on in." She sat up, leaned against the headboard, and patted the bed, inviting him to sit next to her. "What's up?"

Frank closed the door and sat. He was holding the picture of her mom he'd taken on their honeymoon. The framed photo had set on the dresser in their bedroom for as long as Phee could remember. "I've always loved that picture," she said. "Mom looks so happy."

"She was," he said as he stared at the photo. "I was wondering . . . would you like to keep it in here . . . now?"

At first, Phee was surprised at his question, but then she understood. "Sure, I'd love to have it in here." He smiled and nodded. "So, do you have something you want to tell me?" she asked.

"I do," he said.

"About Helen?"

Frank laid the picture on the nightstand. "We've decided we're gonna get married."

Phee grinned. "Oh, Dad, I'm so happy for you, and not a bit surprised."

"We plan to tell everyone at breakfast and I'm nervous as all get out." He walked around the bed to the window and looked out at St. Pete's.

"I understand why you're nervous," Phee said, "but you love Helen, right?"

"I do. I wasn't sure until a couple of weeks ago, but I am now."

"And she loves you . . ."

"She says she does."

". . . and that's what's most important.

"I guess so. She knows it won't be an easy life, being a pastor's wife and mother to all of you."

"I'll be here to help, at least till next fall. Have you picked a date?"

"Not yet, but we want Ed to do it, so it'll be sometime before the camp closes. We talked about New Year's Eve or New Year's Day, for sure no later than mid-January."

"I like New Year's Eve, maybe late in the afternoon, then we can have a big party in the fellowship hall. Or will it be in Spirit Lake?"

"No, Helen wants it to be here."

"Has she talked to Claire?"

"Last week, she said. It's kind of a lot for Claire to take in. She thinks the boys are a little intimidating. But Claire's crazy about Mollie, and that'll help a lot."

"I'm sure it will." Phee looked at her alarm clock. "I should get dressed and get downstairs. I bet breakfast is almost ready."

"I believe it is." Frank reached for Phee's hand, pulled her up, and gave her a hug and a kiss. "Thank you, Phyllis Anne."

"Everything's going to be just fine," she said.

"Hope you're right. See you downstairs."

As expected, breakfast was lively. They managed to squeeze nine chairs around a table more suitable for eight. With three more people coming in for the afternoon meal, the kids' table would be set up in the living room for Mollie, Charlotte, and Claire.

"Who needs more coffee?" Helen asked. "I can make more."

"I think we could use a fresh pot," Frank said.

When Helen returned from the kitchen, Frank stood and cleared his throat to get everyone's attention. It worked fine except for Mollie and Claire who were chatting away at the opposite end of the table.

"Sweet Pea, Claire, can I have a moment of your time?"

"Sure, Dad," Mollie answered, "what's up?"

Frank looked at Helen and smiled, then almost began what he hoped would be a meaningful and heartfelt conversation with his family. He'd played it over and over in his mind, but before he could utter one word, Gus and Tris looked at each other, grinned, and shouted in unison with great authority, "You're getting married!"

There was silence, then gasps, and everyone except the grinning twins—and Phee—were wide-eyed and stunned.

Finally, Frank sat, reached for Helen's hand, and said, "Well . . . yeh."

There was lots of hugging and kissing in the dining room this morning. By all accounts, it was unanimous: Frank and Helen had everyone's blessings.

Then Mollie asked, "Can we be flower girls?"

And Nannie asked, "Have you picked a date?"

And Bee asked, "Where will the nuptials take place?"

And Phee asked, "Have you talked about the honeymoon?"

And Tris lamented, "I s'pose we'll have to be acolytes."

And Nannie asked, "Do your parents know, Helen?"

And Phee wondered, "What about music?"

And Claire asked, "What will you wear, Mom?"

And finally, Gus asked, "Can we throw rice?"

When the ruckus finally died down, Mollie asked the question that caught everyone's attention. "Will Helen be my mom?"

Because he knew his youngest child better than anyone, Frank had anticipated this question and had an answer for her, at least he thought he did. "That's a very good question, Sweet Pea. Technically, Helen will be your stepmother."

"Like in Cinderella?" she asked.

Suppressing a grin, he answered, "I can assure you, Helen will be nothing at all like Cinderella's stepmother."

"Mollie, I promise I will love you with all my heart," Helen added. "That goes for all of you."

"So, this means Claire will be our stepsister, right?" Tris asked, then continued sarcastically. "Great, another girl in the house."

"Tris, be nice," Phee admonished.

"Just kidding," he said, looking at Gus for support.

"Don't look at me," Gus said. "I still wanna know about the rice."

And then Mollie asked, "Do we have to call you 'Mom'?"

It was another Mollie question Frank had anticipated. "Sweet Pea, Helen and I have talked about this. She's happy to be called Mom or Helen. It's up to you."

"Your dad's right, Mollie," Helen added. "If you're more comfortable with Helen, then please—"

"Helen Swensson," Bee mused. "Sounds nice, doesn't it?"

"It sure does," Frank said, once again reaching for Helen's hand.

"We should get the kitchen cleaned up so we can start round two in a little bit," Phee said. "You kids are off dish duty today. Don't want you breaking the good china." On her way to the kitchen with her dishes, she asked her dad, "Are we calling Jamie or is he calling us?"

"He said last week he'd call at six tonight, our time."

"I don't think he'll be surprised about your news."

"I'd like him to be my best man, so I sure hope he can be here."

"You'd better decide on a date right away. Might be hard for him to get leave."

Nannie and Helen carried in the last stacks of dishes from the dining room. "Frank and Bee and I will do up these dishes, Phee," Nannie volunteered. "You and Helen go on out to the living room and talk about the wedding."

"Are you sure?" Phee asked.

"Yes, dear, now scoot."

Helen and Phee retired to the living room with their coffee and made themselves comfortable on both ends of the couch.

"I guess you'll give notice at your high school next week," Phee said.

Helen nodded. "First thing Monday. I dread it, in a way. I love working in the office. That job has kept me sane since Blake died. Mr. Ferguson is a wonderful boss, and I'll sure miss the kids.

"Maybe you can find something here, after you and Claire get settled."

"We'll see."

Phee changed the subject. "So, the wedding . . ."

"I like New Year's Eve," Helen said. "I know it doesn't give us much time, though."

"Helen, I hope you know you can count on me for anything."

"I appreciate that, Phee. There is one thing." She took a sip of her coffee, then asked, "Would you consider being my maid of honor?"

Phee had not expected that question from Helen this morning. "Oh, gosh! What about your sister—Harriet, isn't it?"

"She's in California with the rest of the family. I talked to her last week. She said she can't make it to the wedding."

"Gee, I'm sorry. You must be disappointed." Phee glanced at the family pictures hanging on the wall over the buffet in the dining room. Her mom and dad's wedding picture was still there. Would it end up in her bedroom, too? "Helen, I'd be honored to be your maid of honor."

"Oh, Phee, I'm so pleased! Thank you so much."

Suddenly, Phee felt like a nap. "I think I'll go upstairs to rest a bit before I have to think about that turkey. Why don't you go break the news to Dad."

"Sure, you go on up," Helen said. "Everything's under control down here, or it will be as soon as I get out to the kitchen." She reached for Phee's hand. "You are such a dear, Phee. We're so blessed to be joining this family."

"I'm glad you feel that way. I'm so happy for you and Dad."

As Phee slowly climbed the stairs up to her bedroom, she had an overwhelming desire to talk to her mom. After she got Tom Turkey in the oven, she'd drive to the cemetery. She set her alarm clock, giving herself just thirty minutes to snooze, laid her head on the pillow, and was asleep in seconds.

51

THURSDAY 22 NOV. 1945 - PART 2

AT TWO-THIRTY, DOROTHY AND Charlotte walked over from next door carrying a relish tray, homemade rolls, and a pumpkin pie. Ed Mattson drove up a few minutes later. Frank had insisted he not bring anything, but he walked in with a box of goodies from the officers' mess and a six pack of Schlitz. The turkey was done by three-thirty, and by serving time, Frank had carved up a good portion of it.

Before everyone was seated, Frank gave what Phee felt was one of his best blessing efforts in a good long while. There was plenty to be thankful for this year, and he didn't leave anything out—food, family, friends, the end of the war, Jamie's safe homecoming, and lastly, he thanked God for Helen and Claire.

When they finished the main course, Frank suggested they delay dessert for an hour so everyone had a chance to digest their dinner. While Bee, Nannie and Dorothy started the dishes, and the kids headed either to the basement or upstairs, Frank, Helen, Ed and Phee remained at the dining room table to discuss wedding plans.

"So, Ed, what do you think about December thirty-first, mid-afternoon?" Frank asked. "That would give us time for the reception before the Luther League kids need to get ready for their party."

"I'll get it on my calendar," Ed replied.

Frank drummed the table with his hands and said, "Okay then, what's next?"

"Better talk about the ceremony," Helen suggested.

Phee grabbed a hymnal from the bookcase in the living room, and they went over "The Solemnization of Marriage" Order of Service which Frank had almost memorized. He'd talk with Edith about the music. Flowers? Just Helen's and Phee's bouquets and Frank's and Jamie's boutonnieres, plus rose petals for Mollie and Claire and a corsage for Edith. The sanctuary would still be festive with Christmas decorations so nothing more would be needed.

"The simpler, the better," Frank suggested more than once during the discussion.

They decided to put their honeymoon plans on hold until spring or summer when traveling by train to visit Helen's family in San Francisco would be easier. In the meantime, the Warden Hotel in Fort Dodge would suffice for their wedding night if they weren't already booked up for New Year's Eve. Frank said he'd call down tomorrow to check.

During dessert, Ed told everyone about the camp's impressive nativity scene a few of the prisoners had worked on since last January. He said the public would be invited to see it on weekends in December, and the *Männerchor* would provide music for thirty minutes each Sunday afternoon. "Phee, I understand from Sergeant Ebinger they'll perform a song you've written for them."

"That's right. I wrote it last summer."

"Oh, Phee, how wonderful!" Helen said. "Claire and I will have to come down so we can hear it."

"I hope you can," Phee said. "Ed, do you think there will be enough prisoners left to sing next month? It seems like they're leaving pretty regularly now."

"It depends on who gets placed on which list. They'll all be gone by mid-February, that I do know."

"An end of an era," Frank admitted.

"Well, I should be on my way," Ed said as he pushed his chair back. "Thanks again for having me. Everything was delicious. I won't need to eat for a week."

"So glad you could join us, Ed," Nannie said, "and what good timing, with the wedding coming up and all."

"I'll walk you out," Frank offered.

When he returned to the dining room, Frank found Phee and Helen in the middle of a serious conversation involving wedding attire. Helen said she hoped Phee wouldn't feel obligated to buy something new. Phee said she'd take advantage of the situation and would find the perfect dress.

"Helen," Frank said, "I think it's time you and Claire got a tour of this place."

"Mollie gave Claire the grand tour earlier," Helen said, "but you're right. I should get a look at all the nooks and crannies before we move in."

AT FIVE PAST SIX, the phone rang.

"It's prob'ly Jamie," Frank said, rising from his chair in the living room. "I'll get it."

Usually, long distance phone calls were kept short, but not tonight. After Frank, after Helen, after Mollie, after Claire, after Tris, after Gus, after Nannie, and after Bee, it was Phee's turn to talk to her brother.

"Hi," she said, "I guess you're all talked out by now."

Jamie chuckled. "Kinda, but it's alright. I always have plenty of ear time left for you."

"So, great news about Dad and Helen, huh?"

"It is, but I don't want to talk about that. I want to know how you're doing."

"Great," she said, hoping her voice didn't betray her true feelings.

"Can you talk?" he asked.

She peeked around the corner. "Yeh, everyone's busy elsewhere."

"Good. How's Horst?"

"He's fine—great—I guess."

"You guess?"

Phee sighed. "Well, he'll most likely be gone in a month, or a month and a half. Obviously, I'm not happy about that."

"Do you still see him every week?"

"Almost. We meet most Sundays for an hour or two. We just play music, that's about it."

"Maybe I could meet him if he's still there when I get home."

That idea really perked Phee up. "Oh, I would love that! I'm so happy you'll be here for the wedding. You will be for sure, right?"

"I'll check tomorrow. I don't think it'll be a problem. Most of the boys who want off for Christmas will be back by the time I'd need to catch the train."

"We'll have a houseful, you know."

"Indeed, we will," he said. "Well, I should probably let you go."

"Guess so. See you in a few weeks."

"You sure will. Take care, Phee. Love you."

"Love you too, Jamie. 'Bye."

Before she got up, Phee replayed her conversation with her brother. *He wants to meet Horst! That would be so perfect!*

Tue. Dec. 4, 1945

—Dearest Daisy—

my friend—my confidant. It's for sure—I'm pregnant. I found out this morning when I called Doc Z to get the test result. (Dad was at church.) Of course, it wasn't a surprise. I've known for weeks that I was. I suppose, when I think long and hard about this, I'm going to be a wreck, especially when I have to tell Dad and Helen and the rest of the family (after the wedding). At this moment, I don't know how I'm going to do that. I'm scared, Daisy. Dad will be shocked and disappointed and worried. I hope he's not angry. I don't think I could handle that. And just when he's so happy, with a new wife and all. Doc Z said I should talk to Mrs. Z about this soon. I told him I'd already thought about that. So, between now and my next lesson, I need to figure out how I'm going to tell her. Oh, and of all things to worry about, I asked him about the bill. I want him to hold onto it until after Dad and Helen know, and he said he would. I'm so blessed to have such a good friend as my doctor. I can't imagine going through this with a stranger. In 7 months, I'll give birth to Horst's baby, and I'll love him or her forever. (I kind of hope it's a boy, but I don't really care.) Because of our child, I will always be connected to Horst, even if he's on the other side of the world and doesn't know. If I remember that connection, I'll be fine—I hope. I'm counting on you to help me get through all this.

And somehow, my life will go on. Good night, Daisy.

52

MONDAY 10 DEC. 1945

AMIDST THE SEASON'S HUSTLE and bustle, Phee appreciated her music more than ever. As her pregnancy progressed, the pianos in the parsonage living room and the church's sanctuary continued to bring her comfort and companionship.

This afternoon, as she drove to the Zetterholms' for her lesson, Phee was prepared to tell all, or almost all. She wondered if she'd change her mind at the last minute. But Doc Z was right; she needed to share her secret with someone. It really had to be Mrs. Z.

"Phee, come in," Edith said after Phee rang the doorbell and waited patiently for almost a minute. "Sorry it took me so long. I'm just about to put a roast in the oven."

"No problem, take your time. I'll get warmed up."

While Edith returned to the kitchen, Phee found the check in her pouch and dropped it in the box on the bookcase. After she finished her major scales, Edith arrived with two glasses of water and handed one to Phee. "So, do you have your dress for the wedding?"

"No, not yet," Phee said, taking a sip. "I was hoping to get down to Crystal's this week. I'm sure I'll find something there."

"I'd be happy to go along, if you'd like the company."

"I would, thanks. I'll give you a call."

"You might want to check with Helen if you haven't already to see what she'll be wearing. You wouldn't want to clash with the bride's dress."

"That's a good idea. We talked about it at Thanksgiving but didn't decide on anything specific."

"I think your dad's taking all this in stride, don't you?"

"Mostly. He's been through this before."

"He has, but he didn't have a family to think about, right off the bat. Six children now!"

Phee smiled, then sighed, and Edith could tell something was not quite right. She knew when Phee walked in the door she had something on her mind, so began the inevitable conversation with two questions: "Phee, is something wrong? Is it the wedding?"

"Are we alone?"

"We are for now. I expect Paul home soon, though."

"Can we close the doors?"

"Yes, of course." Edith closed the french doors and their sheer white curtains. "So, how can I help?"

Phee hesitated, then said, "Please don't hate me."

"Hate you? Oh, my heavens, child, I could never hate you, not in million years. I love you like a daughter. You know that."

"That's what Doc Z said when I saw him at his office."

"Phee, look at me. There's nothing you could do or say—"

"I'm pregnant."

Edith didn't react at once. Then, she reached for Phee's hands, helped her up, and held her close.

"Are you sure?" Edith finally asked while gently rubbing Phee's back.

"Yeh, Doc Z confirmed it last week." Phee returned to the bench. "I'm due in July."

Edith took a long drink from her glass, then asked, "Does your dad know?"

"No, and I'm not going to tell him, or Helen, until after the wedding. I won't ruin their day."

"But Phee, think how he'll feel when you finally tell him. I'm sure he'll be disappointed you didn't share this as soon as you found out."

"He will be, but I'm not changing my mind."

"Alright, that's fine. Goodness, where do we go now?"

"What do you mean, 'go now'?"

Edith put her water glass on the bookcase, then walked to the far end of the piano. "Well, what are your plans for the future? Will you marry the father, and, if not, will you keep the baby or place him with an adoption agency? Do you still intend to start college next fall? It'll be very difficult with a baby, especially if you're raising him alone."

"One thing's for sure," Phee said. "I won't be getting married, at least not to the baby's father."

"Are you sure about that?"

She sighed. "Yes, I am."

"Phee, I hope you don't think I'm prying by asking you these questions. I just . . . I want you to think about the ramifications."

"I've thought of nothing else for weeks. I haven't made any decisions except I want to keep the baby. Nothing is more important than that."

Edith smiled. "You and I can have a conversation about that later."

"I know, you think adoption is—."

"Another time, Phee. Now, let me ask you this. Is the father in a position to help you, financially, I mean?"

"No, he's not," she answered meekly.

"Have you told him you're pregnant?"

"No, and I won't. I can't."

"Are you sure? It might help."

"I can't explain everything. You'll just have to trust me. He can't know about the baby." Phee's lips quivered, and her eyes filled with tears.

"Alright, we'll let that go, for now. My concern is for your physical and emotional health."

Phee brushed away her tears and sniffed. "Doc Z did a physical, said I'm 'healthy as an ox.' He wants me to go in for regular check-ups, and I will, after Dad and Helen know."

"Have you thought about how you're going to tell them? What about Jamie and the kids?"

"They'll be stunned, and disappointed, Dad more than anybody."

Edith thought for a moment, then said, "What if Harold and I were with you when you told Frank and Helen? We could have you three over for dinner some night after the wedding."

"I'll think about it. It sure would help to have you and Doc Z in my corner. You are in my corner, aren't you?"

"Oh, Phee, of course, I am—we both are. Never ever doubt that."

"I'm so relieved. I wasn't sure you would be. I mean, I was, but—"

"Come here," Edith said, reaching to embrace her again. "We love you and only want the best for you and your baby."

"Thanks, Mrs. Z."

"Alright, then. Is there anything else you want to tell me before we're done here?"

"Don't think so. That's enough shock for one day, don't you think?"

"Heavens, yes! Enough for a year!"

There was still time for making music, so Phee opened J.S. Bach's *Well Tempered Clavier* to "Praeludium III." It looked simple enough on the page but was in fact quite challenging. Tackling it once again this afternoon was a much-appreciated diversion.

At the end of the hour, Phee packed up her music. Edith pushed back the curtains and opened the doors just as Harold and Paul came in the front door.

"Good, you're home," she said. "We're just finishing up."

"It's good to see you, Phee," Harold said. "Say, we drove out to see the nativity scene at the camp yesterday. Very impressive."

"Did you get to hear the *Männerchor*?" she asked.

"We sure did. Sergeant Ebinger had some very nice things to say about your piece."

"I heard them sing it a week ago," Phee said. "It was pretty exciting."

"I can only imagine," Edith said.

"Well, I'd better get going. Thanks for the lesson, Mrs. Z."

"You're welcome, dear. Do you want to meet again next week? I know you're busier than ever now."

"Yeh, let's meet one last time, before Christmas, I mean."

"Very good. And do call me if you'd like a second opinion about a dress for the wedding."

"Second opinion," Phee mused, "very good."

Harold, glancing through the stack of mail he'd brought in, looked up and said, "Huh?"

The ladies laughed, then hugged once again. Phee whispered in her teacher's ear, "Thank you."

Her teacher whispered back, "You're welcome."

On her way home, Phee imagined the conversation she was sure Harold and Edith were having right about then. She did feel a sense of relief, sharing everything—or almost everything—with her teacher today. It wasn't too hard, and Phee hoped her conversation with her dad and Helen would go as well.

"January," Phee said as she turned south on North Cleveland, "I'll tell them in January." Would Horst still be at the camp? She'd find out in thirteen days.

53

SUNDAY 23 DEC. 1945 - PART 1

"Yippee!" Gus shouted when he heard the latest weather forecast from the radio in the kitchen. There was no doubt they'd have a white Christmas this year. The kids couldn't be happier, but Frank's reaction was dread and despair. He'd insisted that Helen and Claire drive down yesterday because, starting tonight, the roads between Spirit Lake and Algona would most likely be impassable for at least a couple of days if not longer.

After a quick lunch, they all drove out to Camp Algona to hear the *Männerchor* perform Phee's song and to see the nativity scene that was on display in an empty warehouse near the motor pool. It was a perfect venue for public viewing, with just enough room for Horst's small group to gather off to the side.

They took two cars so Phee could stay behind to meet with Horst at the theater after the *Männerchor* finished their performance. In her music pouch was a Christmas gift for Horst, a slightly worn picture book about Iowa she'd found on the discard shelf at the library last week. There were two photos in the book she was especially pleased to see: "Sailboats on West Okoboji," and "Birds-Eye View of Arnolds Park" where she could almost but not quite see the edge of Bee's Bungalows off to the right.

When they turned south off the highway and drove up to the gatehouse, the predicted snow was just beginning to fall. A Private Bitterman was on duty, and when Phee asked about Private Mattingly, she was told he was transferred to a camp in Nebraska last week.

"Oh, poo!" she cried. "I didn't get a chance to say goodbye. I don't suppose he'll be coming back."

"Sorry, ma'am, I'm 'fraid I don't know anything about that."

"That's alright. Thank you, Private. Oh, I don't need a visitor pass, right?"

"That's right. If you're here for the nativity scene, you can park in the theater building lot and walk from there. It's less than a block. Just make a left turn—"

"I can find it, Private. Thank you."

The theater lot was almost half full, and Phee wondered if they'd have to wait in line to get inside the warehouse. She looked at her watch. The *Männerchor's* performance would begin in ten minutes. Frank pulled up in Helen's car, and everyone piled out. With Phee leading the way, they all walked quickly through the snow to the warehouse.

There wasn't a line of people waiting to get in, but those who were there to see the beautiful nativity scene and hear the music were packed inside like sardines. Phee made a point to stand as close as she could to the space reserved for Horst and his group who filed in just before two o'clock.

It took almost an entire year for six prisoners to create the sixty-five figures in the impressive tableau. The U.S. government was not allowed to fund the project, so the prisoners paid for all the materials with money they'd earned while working on nearby farms and from assigned jobs they had inside the camp. The artistry on display was quite remarkable, considering the limitations the prisoners faced as they designed and created each individual figure. Mary sat next to the blond, blue-eyed baby Jesus lying in the manger, and Joseph stood nearby, holding a lantern. There were shepherds, camels, and sheep, the three wise men, and a beautiful angel hanging from the ceiling near the stable. The half-size figures were made of wood, wire, and cement, and were painted with brilliant colors that were enhanced by the special lighting.

The *Männerchor's* thirty-minute set began and ended with "*Stille Nacht*," with Phee's song, "*Wiegenlied des Christkindes*," coming after "*O Tannenbaum*" and "*Es is ein Ros' entsprungen.*" Horst explained to the gathered crowd how Phee's song became part of their repertoire. "A special friend of our *Männerchor* has written a beautiful Christmas lullaby over the past summer months. She gave it to me so I could make a version for us to sing in our native language. Thank you for listening to "*Wiegenlied des Christkindes*," or "Christ Child's Lullaby," by Fräulein Phee Swensson."

Curious to see reactions to her song while the men sang, Phee turned to her right to look across the crowd of people. Almost everyone was smiling. And then, just as she began to turn back, she saw them on the far side of the room. *Christa! Adam! Oh, my God!*

At the end of the lullaby, there was a brief pause, then Horst began the next carol. As politely as possible, Phee pushed her way through the crowd until she got close to her best friend. Christa, brushing a tear from her cheek, smiled when she saw her. For a moment, they didn't speak. Then Phee took her hand and led her to the nearby exit and outside where it was snowing harder.

"My God, Christa... I can't believe you're here!" Phee exclaimed as she embraced her best friend.

"I know," Christa said, chuckling as she hugged her back. "I can't believe it either."

"When did you get home from school?"

"Last night. I stayed up late talking to Mom and Dad, and slept in this morning, so I missed church. Mom insisted we come out today to see this. I had no idea I'd hear your song. Oh, Phee . . ."

They hugged again, then Phee whispered, "I'm so glad you got to hear it."

"It was stunning. Those men, the choir, they're just wonderful. It was touching, hearing them sing it in German."

Phee was very surprised at Christa's comments. "Horst did a wonderful job," she said, "arranging and translating it, I mean. I'm truly blessed."

"I'd like to talk to you about that, about him, about everything. We have a lot of catching up to do."

"Yes, we do. Oh Christa, I've missed you so much. When can we get together?"

"Let's try Wednesday or Thursday? We're heading back to Ames for New Year's Eve."

"I'll call you. We'll make a date. We'll definitely want to go sledding."

"Absolutely. Looks like we'll have more than enough snow."

Just then, the nearby door opened, and people began filing out. Adam found the girls and they walked back to the parking lot together. When they reached the edge of the lot, Frank called from behind, "Phee, I'm not sure I want you driving back to town alone in this snow."

"I'll be careful," she said over her shoulder. "It'll still be light out when I leave."

"If you change your mind, I'll come get you."

"I won't. Don't worry."

When they got to Adam's car, Phee asked Christa, "Will you be at church tomorrow night?"

"Oh, yes," she replied, "wouldn't miss it for the world."

"Be careful driving back to town," Phee said as Adam rolled down his window and started the car.

"We'll be fine," he said. "It was great to see you, Phee."

She waved as they drove off. It certainly seemed the two young women were on track to be best friends again. How Phee hoped that was true, and what a wonderful Christmas present it would be!

54

SUNDAY 23 DEC. 1945 - PART 2

"YOUR CHOIR SOUNDED WONDERFUL again," Phee said as she and Horst walked into the theater hall together. "The acoustics in there make the group sound much larger, don't you think?"

"*Ja*, I would agree. I was happy to see your family. It was a pleasure to meet Frau Engstrom."

"Oh good. I'm glad you got to meet her."

"You were not there at the end."

"Yeh, I missed the last carols, but it was a good reason. My friend Christa was there with her boyfriend, Adam."

"Not the famous Christa who made you sad."

"Yes, that Christa. I was so shocked to see them."

"And is she . . . making friends again?"

"I hope so. We'll get together after Christmas, talk about a lot of stuff, I'm sure."

"*Gut!* And now, I have something for you in my bag."

"You do, huh? I have something for you, too."

"You should open it now," he said, handing her a large envelope.

Inside, she found several black and white photos. Someone with a nice camera had walked around the camp, snapping shots of places and people Phee would recognize. The photo on top showed the gatehouse with a smiling MP guard waving at the photographer. "Private Mattingly!" Phee cried. "But he's gone. I heard he was transferred to Nebraska. Boo hoo!"

"Continue," Horst ordered, "you will see more."

The second photo showed the front of the headquarters building with a portion of an army staff car in view on the right. "Yes," Phee said, "I've spent time there, and possibly in that very car." She chuckled when she saw the third photo. It was Ed Mattson and Julie O'Reilly in Ed's office. "Ed and Julie, such wonderful people. Oh, Horst, these are just terrific. How did you—?"

"Please continue."

The fourth photo, taken recently, showed a portion of the nativity scene and the *Männerchor* singing on the far-left side. "You can always see my comrades singing your song."

"Okay, now I'm gonna cry."

"No crying—there is more."

The fifth photo showed the theater building and the parking spaces near the lobby door. "My parking spot!"

"I am sorry we were not able to make a picture with your car in that place."

She moved on to the sixth photo and was surprised to see Corporal Bickford sitting in a chair in the theater lobby. "Sleepy Bickford!" Phee shouted. "But he doesn't look all that sleepy."

"We asked him to remain awake for the photo. He said he would, just for you."

She chuckled. "Very funny."

The seventh photo was taken outside the west stage door, showing the landing and the steps up to it. For a moment, Phee was puzzled, then she remembered. "Our first kiss was there."

Horst kissed her cheek, then insisted she continue.

The eighth picture was taken from the back of the hall when the chairs were stacked at the sides, the shiny hardwood floor gleaming in the sunlight from the west windows. The stage was empty except for the piano and bench where Horst sat with his hands on the keys. "There you are. I was beginning to wonder."

"You can imagine I am practicing my beloved Brahms, because I am."

"Are you? I wasn't sure."

The next photo showed a smiling Roy Phillips sitting on the steps outside the east stage door. "Roy, there you are. Look at those dimples!"

The last photo in the stack immediately became Phee's favorite. She and Horst were performing the Dvořák during the concert at Algona High School last July. The photographer managed to capture them both in a picture-perfect moment. They were both smiling, with Phee glancing at Horst who was focused on the music.

"I love these! Who took them?"

"They are from the camera belonging to Corporal Phillips. One day, he showed me some pictures he took in the camp. And then I made an idea."

"So, you took the one of Roy?"

"*Ja*, it is a good picture."

"It's wonderful. They're all wonderful, just perfect."

She gave him a hug and a kiss, then reached for the wrapped book in her pouch. "I hope you like it."

"Hmmm," he said, feeling around the edges, "I will be very surprised to find a gift that is not a book."

"I know. Sorry."

"*Beautiful Iowa*," he read as he stared at the cover after unwrapping the book. "I can agree with it."

"I found it at the library last week. I'm sorry it's not new."

"I believe old books are better than new books," he said. "They hold the thoughts of all the people who have turned the pages until now. There is more to learn from that."

"Do you really believe that?"

"I do. I will always feel your thoughts because I know you have touched each page."

She smiled. "I did. Oh, and there are two pictures I want to show you now. They're close to the end."

"'Sailboats on West O-ko-bo-ji'," he said, reading the caption under the picture on the right. "It is the lake where you have celebrated the birthday of your brothers."

"Yep, and . . ." She turned the page.

Horst read again, "'Birds-Eye View of Arnolds Park'."

"See this door? That's the shop where I found the little sailboat I gave you last summer."

"And there is the Roof Garden—I see the sign—where you can dance for many hours, sometimes with Corporal Phillips."

"Yes, I did. And over here, you can almost see Bee's Bungalows, where we stay with Bee and Nannie. There's a path from the park . . . there."

"It is beautiful. I would like very much to see it. We would spend many hours sailing on the water."

"I can just feel it . . . if I don't look out the windows and see all that snow. Oh dear, it's sure coming down! My dad said to call if I didn't want to drive home. I really don't want to bother him."

"Then we will ask Corporal Phillips. He will take you home."

"Oh, I don't think—"

"I will insist because it is . . . how you say . . . wicked weather."

"Yeh, it is kinda wicked." She looked at her watch. "Let's wait for a bit. Half an hour? I can decide then. We can call him from the headquarters building."

Horst walked to the piano bench and sat, then motioned for Phee to join him. "I have something I must tell you," he said.

"What is it?" she asked, hoping it wasn't bad news. But it was.

"I have seen the list for those who will leave the camp on the first day of the new year. My name is there."

Phee heard "I have seen the list" but no more, so she asked him to repeat what he said.

"I must leave our camp in one week and two days. I will be on the train to Nebraska, then to the east."

"Are you sure?"

"The United States Army will make the final decision. They can change the list, but we should prepare for it."

Phee laid her head on Horst's shoulder and wept. He took her hand and kissed it, then tenderly rubbed her back.

"But we'll still have next Sunday, won't we?" she asked, wiping her eyes.

"We should be on the calendar. I will speak with Corporal Phillips about it."

"Roy will make sure we can meet."

"He has been a good friend, for both of us. His name is on my list so he will also leave on the train. They say some of the guards will sail with us to England or France."

"Horst?"

"*Ja?*"

"Maybe it would help if we played something."

"It should be your Dvořák and then my Brahms."

"Yes, it should," she agreed.

They played as one once again. When they finished, Phee looked outside and discovered her car was buried under at least ten inches of snow, and it was still snowing heavily. She would not drive home alone this afternoon.

"We should call the Corporal now," he said.

As they walked to the headquarters building, they passed four soldiers making valiant efforts to clear the sidewalks as best they could. Once inside, Phee was able to reach Roy on the second ring. "Roy, hi, it's Phee Swensson. I'm so glad I caught you."

"Hello, Phee. What can I do for you?"

"Believe it or not, I'm stuck here at the camp. My car's buried in the theater lot, and I need to get back to town. I can call my dad, but I don't want him to get out in this storm."

"No, of course not. Uhm . . . let me see if I can figure something out. Give me five or ten minutes and I'll get back to you."

"I'm in no hurry. I'm in the lobby at the headquarters building with Sergeant Ebinger." She checked the clock on the wall; it was twenty minutes to five. "Do you need to be back to your barracks by five?" she whispered to Horst. He nodded. "Roy, Sergeant Ebinger needs to be in his barracks in twenty minutes."

"Tell him not to worry. I'll walk him back after we get you home. Just wait there. I'll call you as soon as I've got it worked out."

"Thanks, Roy, I sure appreciate it. Oh, and it's extension 713."

Phee knew her dad was worrying, so gave him a quick call. He was relieved to know Corporal Phillips was taking charge.

A few minutes later, the phone rang. "Phee, I've got you a ride into town," Roy said. "You two stay there. I'll be over in five minutes." And he was. Phee and Horst waited at the door, watching as a large truck with chains on its tires and a snowplow attached to the front end pulled into the parking lot and stopped. The passenger door swung open, Roy jumped out, and hurried to the door.

"Don't tell me I'm riding home on a snowplow," Phee said as Roy came in and stomped his feet on the rug.

"'Fraid so," he said, "it's the only way."

"*Das ist sehr gut,*" Horst said. "Is it possible for Sergeant Ebinger to ride along?"

"It's possible if you promise to behave yourself," Roy answered with a smile.

When they got to the truck, Roy helped Phee in first, then Horst, then he squeezed in and slammed the door. "Okay, Sergeant Stewart," Roy said to the driver, "let's go."

In good weather, the ride into town took just a few minutes, but in a blizzard, it took quite a bit longer. Horst found Phee's right hand, squeezed it, and she squeezed back. As he watched the truck's windshield wipers push the heavy wet snow from side to side, he began to sing "*Stille Nacht,*" and Phee, then Roy, then Sergeant Stewart joined in. As the army truck with its snowplow pushed slowly but confidently into Algona's city limits, the sounds of the beloved Christmas carol filled the cab, and Phee thought it was the most beautiful "Silent Night" she'd ever heard.

They arrived at the parsonage after a couple of bumps along the way.

"It's the first house past the parking lot," Phee said reluctantly, wishing the parsonage was on the south side of Algona instead of the north side so she could hold Horst's hand a few minutes longer. Sergeant Stewart pulled up to the end of the driveway. He kept the lights on and the engine running.

"We made it," Roy said. "Good job, Sergeant."

"Yes, thank you so much for getting me home in this blizzard," Phee said.

"My pleasure, ma'am."

"You be careful on the way back. If you go around the block—"

"Yes, ma'am, I'll find the way. You have yourself a Merry Christmas."

"I will—you, too."

Roy opened the door and jumped out. Horst hesitated, then turned to Phee and said, "Thank you for our meeting today, Fräulein. We will meet again on the next Sunday."

"I look forward to it," she said.

Horst slid over and climbed out of the cab, turning to help Phee out. When her right foot touched the running board, she slipped and fell into Horst's arms. Their embrace lasted a moment or two longer than it should have, but Roy was patient.

"Are you alright, Fräulein?" Horst asked.

"Yes, I'm fine."

"Phee, I'll walk you to the door," Roy offered.

She squeezed Horst's hands one last time. "See you next weekend. Merry Christmas, Sergeant Ebinger."

"*Frohe Weihnachten,* Fräulein Swensson."

Roy took her hand. When they reached the porch, the front door opened, and Frank appeared, his relief apparent.

"You made it! I can't thank you enough, Corporal. Please, come in for a minute. We've got hot cider on the stove."

"Thank you, sir, but I need to get the plow back to camp before someone misses it."

"Oh sure, I understand," Frank said. "I hope we'll see you at St. Pete's tomorrow night."

"I plan to be there," Roy said. "Eleven o'clock?"

"That's right—bring a friend. You be careful on the way back."

"Yes, sir, we will."

"Phee, are you coming in?" Frank asked.

"I need to talk to Roy for a minute. I'll be in shortly." Frank closed the door, then she turned to Roy. "Horst told me you're on the list for leaving the camp on January first."

He nodded. "Yeh, we found out a few days ago."

"I really hate that you're leaving, both of you. I can hardly believe it."

"Well, the war's over. Life goes on, I guess."

"I guess so. I'll miss you, a lot." She reached for his hand. "I mean it. You're a wonderful friend."

"You are too, Phee."

"I know you need to get back, but I have one more favor to ask."

"Sure, what is it?"

"Do you think you could write to me after you get back from . . . wherever it is you're going?"

"Looks like it'll be England, but that could change between now and when we board the ship."

"I suppose it'll take several weeks."

"At least."

"Do you know where you'll be stationed when you get back?"

"No. I'll have about another year, unless I decide to re-up." Just then, Sergeant Stewart hit the truck's horn and revved up the motor. Roy smiled. "Guess I'd better go."

Phee kissed his cheek. "Thanks again, for everything."

"I promise I'll write when I get back, let you know how it went." He walked back to the truck and turned to wave. After he slammed the door shut, the truck moved slowly south, continuing to push the heavy snow out of its way. Phee waited until they reached the corner and turned west, then went inside to greet her family.

55

SATURDAY 29 DEC. 1945

"Phee, wake up!" Frank whispered.

It was two thirty in the morning, and Phee was fast asleep. Her dad sat on the edge of her bed, nudging her shoulder. "Phee, you need to get up," he urged as she snuggled deeper into the warmth of her many covers on this bitterly cold, snowy morning.

"No, I don't," she moaned and rolled over.

Frank was insistent. "Roy Phillips just called. Sergeant Ebinger's at the station. He's waiting to board the train to Omaha."

Her body stiffened. She rolled back and rubbed her eyes. "What did you say?"

"Horst is at the station. Roy said you'll have to get there in the next thirty minutes if you want to say goodbye."

She looked at her dad in disbelief. "No, he's leaving Tuesday." She yawned.

"Sorry, babe, I only know what Roy said on the phone five minutes ago." He pulled back the covers and helped her sit up on the edge of the bed. "You'd better get dressed and get down there. I'll get the car warmed up."

Phee shuffled to her closet, wondering what she should wear the last time she saw Horst. *He won't care what you're wearing, Phee.* She dressed quickly, opened the drawer of her nightstand, grabbed the letter she wrote to Horst two nights ago, and stuffed it in her pocket. When she got to the bottom of the steps, she remembered the necklace, so she ran back up to get it and returned just as Frank came in the front door.

"I'm sorry, Phee, the dang car won't start. You'll have to walk, I'm 'fraid."

Phee sighed as she sat to pull on her boots. "Just my luck."

"I can come along," he offered.

"No, it's alright," she said as he helped her with her coat. "Go back to bed. I won't be long."

Fortunately, it was just four blocks to the train station. Fresh snow blanketed everything in sight, and the only sounds Phee heard were her footsteps crunching the snow beneath her boots. She walked quickly, thinking about what she'd say to Horst, and what she wouldn't say. And then, she realized she might not get to see him. *Oh God, please let me see him, please!* Picking up her pace, she ran as fast as she could on the snow-covered sidewalk.

Nearing the station, Phee saw a large group of prisoners, a hundred or more, huddled together near the front of the single-story red brick building, steam rising from their heads as they breathed the bitterly cold air. Or maybe it was smoke from the cigarettes dangling from their mouths while their gloveless hands sought warmth in pockets. At least a half dozen armed guards stood nearby, but she didn't see Roy. The train hadn't yet arrived which gave Phee hope she'd have some time with Horst if she could find him in the crowd.

Almost out of breath as she arrived at the station, she looked for a familiar face. Just then, the heavy white station door opened, and Roy walked out.

"Excuse me . . . sorry . . . I have to get through," Phee mumbled as she pushed her way through the crowd of prisoners. "So sorry . . . I need to speak with Corporal Phillips . . . sorry." When she was about ten feet away, she yelled, "Corporal Phillips! Roy!"

Roy looked up from the piece of paper in his hand, and when he saw Phee waving, he motioned for her to come up the steps. "You made it!" he said.

"Oh, Roy," she said, catching her breath, "we have to find Horst!"

"He's inside. The station manager said he could wait in the cloak room."

She gave him a quick hug and whispered, "Thank you so much."

"Follow me."

Once inside, she saw a few guards standing around the coal-fired stove in the corner of the dimly lit passenger waiting room. At first, she didn't see Horst, then he appeared from the small room just to the left.

"You don't have much time," Roy said. "I'll be back when the train arrives."

Phee ran to Horst. He took her hand and led her to the back of the cloak room. They held one another but didn't speak.

At last, she asked softly, "Why are you leaving now?"

Horst pulled away and explained. "There are three men on the list who are in the infirmary, so they found three others. They said it was Sergeant Ebinger's turn."

"But it's not fair!" she cried. "We're supposed to meet on Sunday. And Jamie's coming home today. I so wanted you to meet him."

"And there will be no *Männerchor* performing for the nativity scene on the last day."

"But couldn't Roy do something? He was supposed to leave Tuesday, too."

He touched her rosy cheek. "Do you think he has done enough, keeping our secrets, giving us this time together?"

She sighed. "Yes, I guess he has."

"So, perhaps I cannot make trouble for him. To be honest, I am grateful he will be with me on my journey."

"I'm grateful, too, Horst, really I am."

"So, we should not speak about Corporal Phillips. We can say the words in our hearts now."

"I don't want to talk. I just want to hold you and look at you. Oh, God, I love you so much!" She began to sob.

Horst smiled. "Shhh . . . I should have a long memory of your smiling face."

"How can I smile? You're leaving me, and I'm not ready. I thought I would be, but I'm not . . . I'm not!"

He kissed her tear-stained cheeks. "I would like to tell you something while we have time. Will you listen?"

She nodded and sniffed. "Of course."

As he held her mitten-covered hands, he said, "At the beginning, last year, it was difficult to be here, so far away from my home and my family."

"But you'll see them soon, won't you?" she asked.

Horst shook his head. "*Nein*. They say we must first go to England, to rebuild the damage from the *Luftwaffe*. It could take many months, and it must be done before we return to our homeland."

"I'm sorry, Horst."

He touched her lips and continued. "When I first came to our camp, I was . . . angry, in some ways. Everything I believed was not true. I knew it as soon as I arrived in America. I had been lied to by those who I trusted. And then, you came with your father to visit our piano, and I saw you and I thought you were a Fräulein with many things in her mind. But, somehow, my darling Phee found me and . . . how you say . . . saved me from myself. Do you understand what I have said?"

She squeezed his hands and nodded. "I think so."

"And then we shared our love for music for more than one year, and that also saved me. Now I would be a different man, a hard man, without it . . . without you. I must say thank you to my friend Phee."

She smiled through her tears. "You're welcome, dear friend Horst. It's beautiful, how you've said it. I believe you . . . I do."

"*Gut*. And now I will stop talking."

Phee touched his cheek and said, "Oh, gosh, there's so much I want to say. I'm afraid I'll say it wrong."

"Nothing you say can be wrong."

She took a deep breath and began. "It took some time for me to, I don't know, get used to you, or understand you, I guess. But I did, finally. I think it was during the first *Männerchor* concerts last year, while I watched you conduct your choir. You're so good with them, Horst. I imagined I was watching a professional conductor."

"Did you?"

"I did. You are so talented. I admire you so much, and I appreciate the way you talk about your family—your mother, your sister, the love and concern you have for them. We have that in common, too."

"*Ja*, we do."

"I'm so sure you'll do great things with your life, Horst, if you're given the chance. You might not be famous, but you could be. I'm just so sad I won't be there to watch you . . . what's a good word . . . shine!"

Horst chuckled. "*Scheinen* . . . I like it."

"We've shared so much over the past year. It was all so unexpected, wasn't it, and incredibly special. I am so blessed to have known you, Horst, and I will miss you, always."

Just then, a whistle blew in the distance as the train, arriving from the north, crossed the highway about a mile from the station. A distant train whistle could be a pleasant, reassuring sound on any given day or night. But now, it was the most dreadful sound, and Phee despised it. She covered her ears with her hands to block it out, but it didn't help. The wickedly shrill whistle continued to get louder as the train approached the station. The train that would steal Horst away from her had arrived. And at that moment, Phee knew the letter in the pocket of her slacks would remain there. She knew without a doubt it was the right thing to do. Something, or someone, guided her decision to keep Horst from reading the letter that would tell him everything. When she got home, she'd tear it up.

He smiled. "I cannot leave you, but I must."

"Send me your address. I'll write to you every day."

"I will, as soon as it is possible."

They shared one last tender kiss before Roy poked his head around the corner. "Sorry, it's time."

With tears in her eyes, Phee held onto Horst's hands a moment longer. He kissed her forehead, reached for his duffle bag, and followed Roy to the back door.

Remembering the necklace around her neck, Phee reached for it and called out, "Horst, wait! I meant to show you . . ."

He smiled, nodded, and said very softly, "*Ich liebe dich.*"

"*Ich liebe dich*, dear Horst."

The two men walked out to the platform. Watching from the nearby window, Phee saw them move through the sea of men shuffling slowly around the building from both sides. She hurried to the north window for another glance, but by now, they were out of sight. With a lingering hiss, the troop train pulled into the station and stopped. The doors at the center of each modified Pullman car were opened by white-jacketed porters, and the prisoners, most carrying duffle bags over their shoulders, began to step aboard. When the last guard boarded the last car, the doors were closed.

Phee stepped outside and found herself alone. After a long shrill blast from the engine's whistle, the train began to move away from the station. Hoping Horst and Roy would see her, she waved as the cars passed slowly by. She managed to hold back her tears until the last car passed, then the flood gates opened. She sat on a bench next to the back door and had a good long cry.

Finally, she looked at her watch; it was three thirty. It had been fifteen minutes since she last saw Horst. Soon it would be thirty minutes, an hour, two hours—a day, a week, a month.

Phee returned to the empty waiting room, but before she left the station, she stood alone in the cloak room. She could still feel him there.

The snow on the pavement in front of the station was packed hard by the prisoners who had waited there for almost an hour. While Phee walked across the street and turned north, she heard a train whistle blowing from the south. She wondered if she'd ever hear that sound again and not feel sad.

On the way back to the parsonage, Phee tried to count the number of times she and Horst had been together since August last year. There were a lot—rehearsals and concerts and meetings and even a couple of serendipitous encounters. And then, there was the night at the parsonage. She didn't expect to fall in love with a German prisoner of war, but she did. She especially didn't intend to have his baby. Heavens! Who could keep that secret forever? Phee could, and somehow, she would.

As she walked, she felt completely numb, but not from the bitterly cold air or the snow that was falling heavily once again. She'd feel numb for some time, now that he was gone. Eventually, she'd feel love's warmth again. Eventually, she'd marry and have a family. Eventually, she'd be happy again, truly happy. But on this sad, early morning in late December, Phee knew—just knew—she would love Horst forever.

56

THURSDAY 23 MAY 1991 - PART 1

THE MORNING WAS COOL and drizzly, and Mollie MacAlister and Jason Webb were on their way to Maestro Horst Ebinger's home in Wannsee in southwestern Berlin. Yesterday afternoon, as Mollie and Herr Ebinger wrapped up their interview session at his studio, she managed to finagle the invitation, thinking it would be a more comfortable venue for their final session today when they'd talk about Camp Algona. Plus, she wanted to meet his wife, Inge.

In her briefcase, laying on the back seat next to Jason's camera bag, was the envelope holding pieces of her mother's young life. Today, she intended to share most if not all of it with Maestro Ebinger. Hidden for now under her sweater was the necklace Horst had given to Phee for her graduation from Algona High School. Mollie's plan was to reveal the necklace at an opportune time—if there was one.

"Burt tells me you're divorced," Jason said as he swerved his ten-year-old BMW in and out of traffic.

"Yeh," Mollie said, not at all keen on sharing details of her private life with her new colleague. "I guess it's been, gosh, almost five years."

"Are you dating anyone?"

Oh, good grief! "No, I'm pretty busy."

"Would you like to have dinner tonight?"

Mollie smiled. "Jason . . ."

"No strings, just a couple Americans enjoying a nice evening in Berlin. I know a great Thai restaurant. Do you like Thai food?"

"Sorta, but I don't think we should make any plans. My session with the Maestro could go late. And they might invite me to stay for dinner."

"I hear ya. But if you get back to your hotel and want an after dark tour that only I can offer—"

"I'll call you," she said with a chuckle.

Jason grinned and changed the subject. "Did you know the Brandenburg Gate is two hundred years old this year?"

"I most certainly did," Mollie proudly proclaimed, "but only because I read about it in my hotel room." And then she remembered the Friedrich Schiller monument outside the Schauspielhaus. "You don't happen to know anything about Friedrich Schiller, do you?"

He did, quite a bit. So, during their journey to Wannsee, Mollie learned about the eighteenth-century German poet-historian-philosopher. She was impressed the Bureau's photographer had all that knowledge tucked inside his semi-attractive head. And she was glad she'd managed to steer the conversation away from her ex-husband.

Just before nine thirty, Jason pulled up to the front of the Ebinger home on Am Grossen Wannsee. "Nice digs!" he said. "I read somewhere they moved here from the Eastern part of the city earlier this year."

"That's right," Mollie said as she opened the car door. "He told me they wanted to be near the water so they could go sailing 'easily and often,' I think he said."

"We'd better get in. I need to be back at the office in an hour."

A tall white wrought-iron fence stretched across the front of the property. Mollie walked to the gate, found the intercom, and pressed the button. After a few seconds, she heard Herr Ebinger's voice. "Is it Mollie MacAlister?"

"Yes, it's me," she replied. "I've got Jason Webb with me."

"Splendid! I will unlock the gate from here. You can follow the path to the door." There was a click, and the gate opened a few inches. Mollie pushed it forward and they entered the yard.

The pale-yellow two-story house sat about forty feet from the fence. The yard was immaculate, with just the right combination of trees, grass, shrubs, and flowering plants. At the end of the driveway to the left was a detached three-car garage. As they approached the front door, it opened, and Frau Ebinger was there to greet them. She was a handsome woman, rather petite, with silver hair cut quite short. Mollie's first impression? *She's nothing like Mom.*

"Ms. MacAlister, welcome to our home!" Frau Ebinger said.

"Thanks for inviting us," Mollie said. "This is my colleague, Jason Webb."

"Ma'am," Jason said politely while shaking her hand.

"Mr. Webb, we thank you for coming. Please, do come in. Let me take your coats."

"Your home is lovely," Mollie said as they stepped into the foyer, "and look at this!"

A striking wooden statue sat on a marble-topped table next to the staircase that curved up to the second floor. The piece, about three feet tall, displayed a man holding a conductor's baton, his arms spread like a bird's wings in flight, his face tilted up, his eyes closed.

"How beautiful!" Mollie admired.

"It was a gift to my husband for his twentieth anniversary with the orchestra."

"It'll make a great background shot," Jason said. "The lighting here in the foyer is just about perfect."

"Was there anything else you had in mind for your photos?" Frau Ebinger asked.

"I just need a few shots of you and your husband, and then a few of him at his piano."

"I should have the Maestro join us here before you go to the music room. He's on the telephone. I'll see what might be keeping him."

As she walked away, Jason stuck his head into the room off the foyer where a nine-foot ebony Bösendorfer grand piano covered almost half the floor space. "Wowzer!" he whispered. "Don't think I've ever seen a full-sized grand in a private home."

While Jason found all the equipment he needed for the photo shoot, Maestro Ebinger hurried into the foyer. "So sorry!" he said. "I was speaking with my assistant about a reception to celebrate the end of our season. There is an issue about inviting a certain member of the press. I prefer to invite everyone."

"As a member of the press," Mollie said, "I wholeheartedly agree."

"So, we should pose now for our esteemed photographer," Herr Ebinger said. "Inge, come join us!"

For the next fifteen minutes, Jason snapped the requisite number of photographs in the foyer and the music room while Mollie stood back and waited anxiously for her final interview session to begin. Herr Ebinger insisted Mollie be included in the last few shots with both of them sitting on the piano bench. Mollie couldn't resist imagining her mother sitting next to her friend Horst all those years ago. Would he think about that later today, after he learned the truth?

After Jason left, Herr Ebinger led Mollie to the library where a wood burning fireplace warmed the room. Tall bookcases filled with books and LPs and CDs lined most of the walls, and where there weren't bookcases or windows, there were framed black and white and color photographs attractively displayed in several collages. At the back of the spacious but still cozy room, two tall windows overlooked the beautiful garden. French doors led out to a small patio, and the tall wooden fence surrounding the yard offered privacy.

Under one of the windows near the french doors was a large desk where framed photos of Frau Ebinger and their daughter Anika and her family were displayed. On the opposite corner was a stack of music scores, a dozen or more.

"Are these for next season?" Mollie asked as she touched the stack.

"*Nein*, next season is . . . how you say . . . in the can. Those are for the following season. I will make my final decisions in the next weeks."

"I'd better make a note," Mollie said as she laid her briefcase on the nearby round table.

"And we should begin our discussion now. Oh, and I want to unplug the telephone so we won't be disturbed."

As Herr Ebinger took care of the phone, Mollie found the small tape recorder in her briefcase and placed it on the table along with her note pad and pen. They would finish the conversation they'd started near the end of yesterday's session, another fascinating piece of Horst Ebinger's life as an orchestra conductor behind the Iron Curtain.

Just before noon, Frau Ebinger carried in a tray with cups of coffee and a plate of cookies. She was about to leave for the afternoon, with plans to visit their daughter and son-in-law who lived in nearby Potsdam. Mollie and the Maestro had been talking for almost two hours, so they welcomed the break.

"It is a good time to pause," Herr Ebinger said. "I will visit *die Toilette* while you sample Inge's delicious *Kekse*. When I return, we should speak about the time I was a prisoner of war in your country. I have much to say about it."

As soon as he left the room, Mollie pulled out the necklace from under her sweater. For months, she'd been thinking about and planning for today, and now, finally, it was time to tell him everything, or almost. As she walked across the room to look at a group of black and white photos on the wall, she realized they were copies of some of the photos in the envelope in her briefcase. And then, when she saw her mom, off to the side, sitting at the piano on the stage, she was overcome with emotion. *Oh dear, maybe I'm not ready for this.*

When Maestro Ebinger returned to the library, Mollie turned to him and smiled, discreetly brushing a tear from her cheek.

"Ah, yes, you have found the photos from the camp," he said as he joined her. "I can tell you . . . My dear Ms. MacAlister, is something wrong?"

Smiling through her tears, Mollie slowly reached to touch the necklace. And just before she intended to say, "I have something to show you," he saw it.

57

THURSDAY 23 MAY 1991 - PART 2

MAESTRO EBINGER WAS DUMBFOUNDED. He stared at the necklace he'd made for his friend Phee decades ago when he was a prisoner of war at Camp Algona. And now, Mollie MacAlister was standing in his library wearing that very necklace around her neck.

"Where did you find . . .?" he began to ask as he reached to touch it but didn't.

Her heart beating rapidly, Mollie answered very softly, almost a whisper, "It was my mother's."

Shaking his head slowly back and forth, he responded, "Your mother's?"

Mollie took a deep breath and brushed away another tear. "I found it in a box in her bedroom last year, after she died."

"Your mother . . .?"

"Phee Phillips—Swensson—from Algona."

He stood very still, then whispered, "Can it be? You are Phee's daughter?" Then more strongly, "I do not know what to say."

He walked to the french doors and looked out at the garden. The drizzle had ended, and sunlight now draped over the recently mowed grass and colorful flower beds bordering the yard near the fence. "For two days," he said, "I have shared so much of my life story with you, and you have not told me this until now."

"I'm sorry, Herr Ebinger. I wanted to wait until . . ." She sighed. "Today is our last day, and I knew it had to be today. We're about to talk about Algona. Please understand, it's not easy for me to tell you this."

"Phee's daughter," he whispered, still gazing out the window.

Mollie walked to the table, reached into her shoulder bag that was hanging on the back of the chair, and found her passport. "Here, you can see—my middle name is Phee."

He turned, took the passport from Mollie, and looked at the photo and the information next to it.

Surname MACALISTER
Given name MOLLIE PHEE
Nationality UNITED STATES OF AMERICA
Date of birth 24 SEP / SEP 54
Place of birth IDAHO, U.S.A.

"How long have you known about the necklace?" he asked while staring at the passport.

"Not long, just since last November. I was cleaning out Mom's things from their bedroom and I found—"

"Phee, she has died?"

And then, Mollie realized her earlier mention of her mother's death had not registered with him. "Yes, last September. She had cancer—leukemia."

Maestro Ebinger sighed, then walked around the table and sat in his chair. He folded his hands on the table and looked at Mollie with an intensity she'd not seen all week. "I should be angry with you for keeping the secret until now. Can you understand?"

Mollie didn't expect anger—sadness, most likely, but not anger.

"Herr Ebinger—"

"But I cannot be angry with the daughter of my friend Phee. I am quite sure she would not approve."

Oh, thank God!

"And enough of Herr Ebinger," he continued. "You are Phee's daughter. I have the proof. You will say Horst now. I will insist."

"Okay . . . Horst, and I'm Mollie." At last, there was a modest smile on his handsome face, and she was relieved, at least somewhat.

"And so, you were not aware of this when I was in Chicago last year?"

"No, none of it. Mom and I were at your final concert—"

"Phee was there?"

"She was. Center orchestra, eight rows back."

"Center orchestra . . ."

"I glanced at her several times during the concert. I could see she was watching you very intently the whole time. After the concert, I asked her if she'd go with me to meet you in the Green Room. I thought sure she'd jump at the chance, but she said no, she was tired and wanted to go back to my apartment, so we did. And then, of course, our interview the next day was cancelled because you needed to get back to Germany."

"*Ja*, my sister's husband was in a serious accident on the Autobahn. He died after two days. It was very difficult for my family . . ." His voice trailed off as he remembered. "But, please, tell me more about your mother. Was she ill last summer, at the concert?"

"Apparently, she was, but we didn't know. She was diagnosed in August and died about a month later. It was so fast, horrible, and sad."

"And your father, the Corporal. Is he still living?"

The Corporal? How does he know about Dad?!

"He is, still lives in Denver. I want him to move to Chicago, to be closer, but he's not interested."

"Ms. . . . Mollie, my mind is busy, hearing all of this. I must have many questions for you, but you are here to ask *me* questions."

She smiled. "Yes, I am, but I knew you'd want to know about Mom. I'll be happy to tell you anything."

"Then I will ask the most important question."

Here we go.

"How can you know the necklace you wear has a connection with me?"

Yep, there it is.

Mollie reached for her briefcase and set it on the table. "You mean, besides your initials on one side? I have more." Finding the large envelope, she pulled out the photos and music, telegram, letters and cards and programs. She kept the diaries hidden away.

Horst stared at the items and smiled. "So, you have already seen the photos on the wall."

"Yes, I have, some of them anyway."

Engulfed in a flood of memories, he reached over to touch the artifacts from his relationship with Mollie's mother. "I am not surprised Phee has kept all of it. Do you think she wanted you to find them?"

"I don't know, maybe. I know she didn't forget about them. She cut this article from *Time* magazine from 1984 when the Schauspielhaus was re-opened. It was in the box with the other things."

Horst took some time to look at each letter, the programs, and the piece for piano he wrote while he was a prisoner. "Ah yes, my meager attempt to follow my beloved Brahms." He hummed the melody for a few bars, then handed everything back to Mollie. "I would like very much to hear more about your mother. What can you tell me so I will rest tonight, knowing my friend Phee had a good life?"

"A good life? Hmm . . . I guess I've never thought about it. I think she had a good life. It certainly wasn't extraordinary like yours."

"We can argue about that at another time. Tell me about her life."

Mollie purposely skipped the first half of 1946. Horst would eventually learn the truth about those months, but not from this conversation. She began by telling him what she knew about Phee's college days in Sioux Falls, about her dad moving there after he was discharged from the army in 1947, about their wedding at St. Pete's in 1950 and their move to Boise, Idaho. There were three children—Roy Junior, "RJ"—Mollie—and Edward, "Eddie." She talked about the family moving to Denver in 1960 when Roy was transferred by his company. Phee had many piano students over the years, and in 1973 became the accompanist of the Denver Symphony Chorus, a position she held until just before her death.

The family vacationed on West Okoboji most every summer in the fifties and sixties. When Mollie mentioned it, Horst stood and walked to his desk. "I have something to show you." He found a small object in his desk drawer and brought it to the table. "Your mother gave this to me when she returned from the Lake O-ko-bo-ji. I have kept it for all this time."

Mollie knew about the little sailboat from her mom's diary but didn't let on. "How cute. It's still in good shape."

Horst chuckled. "*Ja*, I have not allowed it to crumble until now."

As Mollie held the souvenir from Okoboji in her hand, she proposed, "Can we take a break? I need to use the loo."

"Of course. You will find *die Toilette* through there, just off the kitchen. I see the rain has stopped. We can walk in the garden now."

"I'd like that."

"*Gut*! I will find our coats. We will need them."

While she washed her hands, Mollie wondered when she'd reveal her mom's diaries to Horst. And then she remembered two questions she needed to ask: do Inge and Anika know about Horst and Phee, and if they do, how much do they know?

"Are you hungry?" he asked as she joined him on the sun-drenched patio. "I can find something for us in the kitchen."

"No thanks. Inge's delicious cookies were very satisfying." As they began their stroll through the garden, Mollie asked, "So, what else would you like to know about Mom?"

Horst thought for a moment, then asked, "If it is not too much to ask, can you tell me about your relationship with your mother?"

The question surprised Mollie, but she answered it honestly. "Sure. I loved my mom, but we had a few moments over the years, didn't see eye to eye on things. It was mostly me being rebellious, I guess, and immature."

"It is not . . . unusual. We saw the same from Anika in her teenage years."

"I'm happy to hear it. I guess it's a rite of passage to argue with your mother."

"And with your father?"

"No, not really. Dad and I got along great, still do. I was his 'little princess.'" She smiled. "Gosh, that sounds horrid now, doesn't it?"

"Not at all. I can understand those words from a father for his daughter."

"I guess the last time Mom and I had a serious argument was about six years ago when my husband Ewan and I separated. For some reason, she just couldn't accept that we couldn't find a way to stay together."

"Perhaps she hoped for you to have what she had with your father."

"Well, in hindsight, maybe she wanted me to have what she didn't have—couldn't have—with you."

He stopped and turned to her. "What do you mean?"

"I know she loved you deeply, Horst."

"But how can you know that from the things you found in the box? Your mother and I were friends—"

"Because there were also diaries in that box."

"Diaries?"

"Mom kept diaries all through high school and for about a year after, so, all during the time you were at Camp Algona. She wrote something almost every night."

"And you have read them?"

She nodded. "Twice, so far."

Horst looked at his watch. "Our time together is growing short, and we still have much to talk about. I would like to make a proposition, and you cannot say *nein* when you hear it."

"And what is your proposition?"

"I will drive you to your hotel, you will go inside, gather your things, say goodbye to the nice person behind the desk, and return here with me. You will sleep in our guest room tonight. I insist, and Inge will also insist. We will enjoy a nice dinner together and talk more tonight."

See, Jason, I was right! "Well, I'm sure my mom would approve, so, thank you. I accept your kind invitation."

"*Wunderbar!* I will find my keys and we will go."

58

THURSDAY 23 MAY 1991 - PART 3

MOLLIE WAS A LITTLE anxious on the ride to the hotel. The cat was out of the bag, but she wasn't sure where the cat was headed. For now, Horst was more interested in hearing about Phee's family, so she told him about her Grandpa Frank—Poppee to his grandkids—and his wife Helen. Horst said he had met Helen at the nativity scene at the camp, not long before he left Algona. She talked about her Uncle Jamie who eventually left The Army Band, moved to New York City, and played professionally for many years. He married an actress, and both their sons were actors.

"Would I know them?" Horst asked.

"Oh, I doubt it. Marc and Kevin Swensson? They've mostly done off-Broadway, but Marc was in *42nd Street* for a while, and Kevin's doing *Cats* now."

"And the brothers with red hair," he said. "They were so much alike."

"Yeh, Uncle Gus and Uncle Tris. They were a hoot."

"A hoot?"

"Funny guys, always joking and poking fun. Mom adored them. It was so sad when Uncle Gus died, from AIDS, almost . . . ten years ago now, I guess. They said he was one of the first AIDS deaths in the U.S.

Uncle Tris moved to San Francisco to take care of him and he ended up staying out there."

"It must have been difficult for Phee. I know what it is like to live more years than a younger brother."

"That's right, you do."

"And the sister who shares your name?"

"Aunt Mollie? Actually, she's Aunt Serena now."

"Aunt Serena?"

"Apparently, when she got to college, she wanted to be called Serena. It's her middle name."

"A woman with a strong will."

"That's what I've heard. I don't know her at all. She joined the Peace Corps in the early sixties, met her husband Mateo, and moved to Spain. They breed horses . . . uhm . . . Andalusians?"

"*Ja*, they are very famous horses and would bring much wealth to them."

"Mom always said they're 'well off.' I'd love to get down to see where they live and interview them for an article. I think my readers would be fascinated by all that."

"As they will be fascinated to read about an old German man who once loved an American girl in Iowa?"

"I sure hope so," she said as they approached the front of the Zürich. "Do you want to find a parking spot?"

"I will leave you here and return in fifteen minutes. Parking is impossible, even for a famous orchestra conductor."

"Alright, I'll see you in fifteen."

As they headed west through the Brandenburg Gate, Horst confessed to Mollie. "I am very pleased to know about your family after so many years. But I should tell you something you might not know."

"And what is that?"

"You will know from our discussions about the conditions in Germany when I returned after my year in England rebuilding the damage from our bombs. My father was in prison and could not care for us. Everything we needed to exist was not easily available or available at all. It was very difficult to remain . . . optimistic."

"But you survived."

"We did. For some ways, it was because we had a friend who could help us. A man I knew, Heinz, who had also been a prisoner in America, told me he had written to the farmer who had hired him, asking the farmer to send whatever he could to Heinz. I believe he called them . . . care packages. The farmer did send it, more than one. So, I decided I would write to Pastor Swensson, at the church, to ask him to send food or clothes or anything at all that would help me, my mother, and my sister. He did as I asked. He was such a good man to help such desperate people. I wrote to him, 'do not tell Phee about it.' I was concerned that her life should be . . . not complicated, after the war."

"She might have known about your letter to Poppee."

"It was more than one. We wrote for several years, not often. He told me about his family, about Phee, her marriage to Corporal Phillips at St. Peter's—"

"So, *that's* how you knew about Dad."

"*Ja*, Pastor Swensson told me in his first letter that Corporal Phillips had moved to be near Phee after his time with the army had ended. I was very relieved, knowing he was a good man, and he loved your mother for many months and years, even while we were together at our camp."

"Yeh, he was crazy about Mom."

"And it was good for both of them to be together for such a long time, to have a fine family."

"Did Poppee know about your career starting up?"

"I believe I wrote the last time in the early fifties when I had finished at university in Leipzig. He did not reply, and our communication ended. I suppose we were satisfied that everyone had . . . how you say . . . moved on. It is a pity, though, is it not? It would have been nice to continue."

When they arrived at the house, Horst parked just outside the middle garage stall and grabbed Mollie's suitcase from the trunk. "We can take your bag up to the room, and then I will call Inge to tell her you will stay with us tonight. She will be very pleased."

"I hope you're right," Mollie said as they walked to the kitchen door. "If she's not, I can sleep on the street, I guess."

Horst laughed. "*Nein! Nein!* There will be no sleeping on the streets in Wannsee!"

THERE WERE TWO BEDS in the large guest room, so Mollie used one to lay open her suitcase. She walked around the room, admiring the blue and white Delft tile stove in the corner and the nicely framed BSO concert posters hanging on the wall over the beds. After freshening up in the WC next door, Mollie walked down the curved staircase to the foyer.

"Would you care for a glass of wine?" Horst asked as she got to the kitchen. "We can also enjoy some bread and cheese."

"That sounds lovely. Thank you."

"We will have dinner at eight o'clock. Inge will stop at the supermarket on her way home. She will make a typical German meal for us."

"Wonderful! I do love German food. One of my favorite restaurants in Chicago is The Berghoff. It's right downtown, been there almost a hundred years. I have a friend who's a bartender there."

"The fire has gone out in the library. I will start a new one and you can join me there. Bring the tray, *bitte*."

"Sure, be right there."

Mollie looked around the large, modern kitchen. It was bright and cheery with white cupboards, countertops, appliances, and red accent pieces—towels, canisters, oven mitts, and a chef's apron hanging from a hook on the wall. She walked over to look at the front. *Maestro's Menu—cute!*

The fire warmed the room as Mollie walked in with the tray. She set it on the glass-topped table between two leather easy chairs, took a seat, and poured the wine.

Horst stood next to an impressive stereo system. "We should have music. Do you have a preference?"

"Uhm, let's see. I've not heard Rachmaninoff for a while."

"Excellent choice! I have it, the Second Symphony. We performed it in 1988, I believe." When the music began, he sat in the chair opposite Mollie and lifted the wine glass to his lips. Then he asked about Phee's diaries. "You have learned much about your mother, things you did not know. A window into her soul, *ja*?"

"They are," Mollie agreed. "I started reading them that first night. I was so shocked to see your name! At first, I thought it couldn't be *the* Horst Ebinger. I mean, come on, really? The man I watched conduct the CSO last summer? The man I was supposed to interview? I was stunned! But then it made sense to me, why Mom asked me to get tickets for your concert. She wanted to see you, Horst."

"I have often thought about my time in Algona over the years. It was difficult for me, at first, a young German man in a prisoner of war camp in the middle of America. But they treated us well, and we had our music. At the beginning, I was not sure about it, but then I understood my life was saved at our camp. There was no question. Your mother *and* father had much to do with that."

All day, Mollie had wanted to ask Horst about Inge's knowledge of her mom. Now seemed a good time. "Horst, do Inge and Anika know about my mom?"

He smiled. "Inge, *ja*, Anika, *nein*."

"How much does Inge know?"

"It has been a long time since we had that conversation, perhaps thirty years or more. My memory is not . . . strong about it. It was a discussion about the people we had loved before we met, something like that. We were honest, at least it is what I believe and remember. Is it a concern for you?"

"No, not really. I was just curious."

"It is possible Inge has shared it with Anika without my knowledge. But I do not believe Anika knows of your mother. She has not asked me about the Fräulein in the photo on the wall."

"Will you tell Inge I'm Phee's daughter?"

"*Ja*, I will tell her, but not until tomorrow, after you are on the plane."

IT WAS HALF PAST five when they heard the kitchen door open. Inge was home from Potsdam and shopping.

"We should take a break now," Horst said. "You can rest in your room, and I will help Inge in the kitchen. Can you be down at . . . seven fifteen?"

"Sure. Can I take the tray to the kitchen?"

"*Nein*, I will do it. *Danke*."

Mollie decided to take a short nap before cleaning up for dinner. She kicked off her shoes, laid on the bed, and thought about the letter in her shoulder bag, the one Phee didn't give Horst at the station the morning he left Algona. She'd found it in the box with everything else last November. *I'll give it to him before I leave tomorrow . . . I think.*

WHILE THEY ENJOYED INGE'S schnitzel and *Kartoffelsalat* in the dining room, Mollie was mesmerized by the Ebingers' recounting of the events of November 9, 1989, the night the Berlin wall came down. During dessert, a delicious *Quarkspeise* with fresh strawberries, she heard about the concert at the Schauspielhaus the following month when Leonard Bernstein conducted Beethoven's Ninth Symphony.

"That must have been incredible," Mollie said. "Did many of your musicians get to play?"

"Twelve were chosen," Horst replied, "but everyone wanted it. It couldn't be, as there were others from the Berliner Philharmoniker and New York, London, Moscow, Paris. I was allowed ten minutes with the third movement to rehearse the orchestra. Everyone was smiling. I will never forget it."

Inge stood and began to clear the table. "I will clean up while you continue in the library. I know you have more to talk about."

"We do," Mollie admitted. "Thank you so much for the lovely dinner. Everything was wonderful."

"I am glad you enjoyed it," Inge said. "You two go on. I will try to be quiet for you."

When they returned to the library, Horst told Mollie, "I have remembered there is something I want you to hear." He opened a drawer in his desk, found two cassette tapes, and placed one of them in the player on the nearby shelf. "I wonder if you will recognize it."

As she sat in one of the leather chairs near the fireplace, Mollie heard a string group playing a familiar tune, and then she knew. "It's Mom's song!"

Horst smiled and nodded as they listened to Phee's Christmas song, "Christ Child's Lullaby." It was a short piece, and as it ended, he said, "Wait, there is more." He removed the tape, replaced it with the other, and pressed play. This time, there was a male chorus singing her mom's song in German.

"What a wonderful surprise!" Mollie said as the music ended. "Who's performing?"

"As you might know, your mother gave me a copy of her piece and I arranged it for the *Männerchor* at our camp. I did not see it for many years, and then one day I found it in a box. I gave it to the director of the men's choir in Potsdam in . . . I believe it was . . . 1980 or 1981. In a few months' time I received this tape in the mail. They have told me they perform it every year for their Christmas concert."

"And the string version?"

"I made the arrangement a few years later and recorded it with my orchestra."

"I'm so glad you remembered you had these."

"Here, you may keep them," he said. "I have copies. And now, before we are both falling asleep, we should finish what we began this morning."

They sat at the table where Mollie had left her tape recorder. She pressed the play button, and their conversation returned to Camp Algona. Horst described meeting Phee for the first time in the camp theater building. When he spoke about her mom, he smiled and laughed, and his eyes twinkled.

It wasn't a one-sided infatuation. That's very clear to me now.

As the evening's second tape clicked off, Horst said, "It is very late. We should end at a good place. What would you like to ask before we go up?"

Mollie thought for a moment, then said, "I'd like to know if you think it's appropriate for me to tell my readers about your relationship with my mom."

Considering her request, he smiled and said, "I would say, if it is good with your brothers and with your father, you should tell your readers about my friendship with your mother. I believe the nice people in Chicago would enjoy reading about a German prisoner and an American girl who fell in love during the war."

"What about Inge and Anika?"

"They will agree with us. I am sure of it."

When they reached the top of the stairs, Mollie thought of one more question. "When you left Algona that night, or morning, on the train, did you see Mom on the platform, waving as the cars passed by? She mentioned it in her diary."

"*Ja*, I did. I was very happy to see her, even for that brief moment."

"Good, I'm glad."

"*Gute Nacht*, Frau MacAlister."

"*Gute Nacht*, Herr Ebinger."

She closed the guest room door, leaned against it, and whispered, "I bet he'll dream about Mom tonight."

59

FRIDAY 24 MAY 1991

THERE WAS A KNOCK at the guest room door. "*Guten Morgen,* Mollie. Can you join us in the kitchen for our breakfast?"

Mollie's eyes popped open when Inge's words reached her ears. "Good morning! Yes, I'll be down shortly." She sat up, rubbed her eyes, and moaned. *Shit! I really need to get a new travel alarm.* She jumped out of bed and reached for the clothes she'd laid out mere hours before. There was no time for a shower. After dressing and stopping in the WC, Mollie ran down to the kitchen. Horst and Inge sat at the table in the corner near a large window. A lively conversation was underway, and Mollie was clueless. Music flowed from the large speakers in the library. This morning it was Bach.

"*Guten Morgen*, Frau MacAlister!" Horst said, wearing his "Maestro's Menu" apron. "Did you sleep well?"

"I did, thank you. The bed is very comfortable."

As Mollie sat, Horst offered, "Coffee?"

"Oh, yes, please. I sure need it this morning."

"So, your flight to Frankfurt leaves at eleven thirty," he remembered. "We should leave the driveway by ten o'clock at the latest. It will take only twenty minutes to arrive at Tegel."

"I can call a taxi; I don't mind," Mollie said, hoping he'd insist on taking her. Handing the letter to Horst at the airport fit her vision of their "farewell scene."

"Yes, you could do that, but we should have the most opportunity to talk."

"Of course, you're right. Thanks for offering."

While they ate, Mollie told Horst and Inge she expected her article would appear in two parts in the *CPD Sunday Magazine* section. She wasn't yet sure how she'd lay it out but would most likely end with the Algona experience.

"I am so happy it is you who will write about my husband's life," Inge said. "I have heard you say his 'remarkable life.' I can say it has been a joy to be part of it. My Horst is a good man, a wonderful husband and father and grandfather. I would say it is the most important thing."

"I'm sure I can fit that in," Mollie answered.

"It is very nice to hear about wonderful Horst," he said as he stood. "But we should prepare to leave for the airport. Mollie, do you need to pack your bag?"

"Yes, but it'll take just a minute. Oh, gosh, better not forget my tapes."

On her way upstairs, Mollie stopped in the library to grab the recorder and tapes, and as she left the room, she hummed along with the "Sanctus" from Bach's *Mass in B Minor*, one of her favorites.

After she packed, Mollie checked her shoulder bag to make sure her mom's letter was there. With it was a hand-written note for Horst from Mollie. It explained how her mother had intended to give him the letter that early morning at the train station but changed her mind at the last minute. There were also copies of diary pages where Phee wrote about the birth of their son in Brainerd, Minnesota on July 3, 1946, and how she cried for weeks after saying goodbye to her infant son that morning. Mollie thought Horst should know that, too.

As Mollie carried her suitcase down to the foyer, she saw Inge place a cloth bag next to the sculpture on the marble table.

"I have packed some food for your lunch," Inge said. "They will not give you anything on the flight to Frankfurt, and you will not have time to find something at the airport there."

"You are wonderful! Thank you so much, especially for inviting me to stay here last night. It really helped to have the extra time."

"I hope you can return after you finish the article. There is much we can show you in Berlin now."

"I'd love to," Mollie replied. She followed the sidewalk to the driveway where Horst waited near the open trunk of his black Mercedes. She turned to wave. "Goodbye, Inge! Auf Wiedersehen!"

On the way to the airport, Horst wanted to hear more about Phee's life. Mollie told him her mother loved to sing and would often sing solos at church. She wrote cards or notes or letters to friends and family almost every day and never failed to write to her kids once a week. Mollie saved a few of her mom's letters over the years but wished she'd saved more.

"Oh, and here's something you won't believe," she remembered. "Are you ready?"

"I am ready."

Mollie grinned. "Mom took belly dancing lessons."

"Belly dancing?"

"You know, like . . . Middle Eastern, the hips . . . thing."

"*Ja*, I know of it. But I cannot see my friend Phee with a dancing belly. I will have to think about it for some time."

"Dad thought she was nuts. There was a dance studio about a block from our house in Denver. The lady next door wanted to do it and talked Mom into it. I think she only did it for a month or two."

"And did you see the results of the lessons?"

"Oh, yes, I'm afraid so. She practiced at home in their bedroom when she thought no one was watching. Sorry Mom, we watched!"

Horst laughed like he'd not laughed all week, and Mollie was glad he did, here at the end.

"I do enjoy hearing these stories about Phee. She was a remarkable woman."

Mollie agreed. "She really was the best mom. I'm so glad I got to tell her that the day she died."

As they arrived at the airport, Horst found a spot in short-term parking, got Mollie's bag from the trunk, and they entered the terminal near the Lufthansa counters. The nearby departure board told them Mollie's flight was *Pünktlich*—On Time—and would depart from Gate A11. The check-in counter number was also listed and, as luck would have it, A11 was right in front of them. They both looked around, at the board, at the travelers waiting in line. Neither of them was quite ready to say goodbye.

Finally, Mollie said, "So, I guess this is it." She held out her hand, but Horst reached for her with both arms. She hugged him and said, "Thank you for everything, Horst, for being so open and honest with me, for giving me your blessing to write this article. And most of all . . . thank you for loving my mom."

Horst pulled away and smiled. "And I thank you for thanking me for loving your mother."

Mollie reached into her bag and pulled out the envelope. "I have something for you. I don't want you to open it till you get home. You should go to the library, alone, sit in your comfortable chair, have a glass of wine nearby, and open it."

"I will do as you say," Horst said, looking a bit puzzled. "I do like a mystery."

Mollie took the handle of her rolling bag. "Until we meet again."

"Auf Wiedersehen," he replied.

As he turned to walk away, Mollie noticed a few people watching him, pointing and smiling, their heads nodding in agreement. A smartly dressed older woman told her younger companion, "*Das ist Herr Ebinger, der berühmte Dirigent. Ich erkenne ihn an den Plakaten, die wir in der Innenstadt gesehen haben.*" Mollie didn't understand most of what she said, but clearly, she recognized the famous orchestra conductor, the man who once loved her mother. She joined the line of fellow travelers waiting to check in. *You'll have to read my article so you can learn all about him. You won't know the whole story if you don't. Well, almost the whole story.*

60

OCTOBER - NOVEMBER 1991

MOLLIE'S TWO-PART FEATURE LENGTH article covering Maestro Horst Ebinger's life, which she titled "My Mother's Friend," was published on the first two Sundays in October. Most of the feedback from her readers was very positive and complimentary. She was especially pleased with the letters from people in Algona. Some of them had seen Horst and Phee perform at the high school, and others had heard the *Männerchor* sing her mother's song at the nativity scene. Mollie's dad also liked the article because, as he put it, "you told the truth."

Mollie mailed two copies of the *CPD Sunday Magazine* section to the Ebingers the week after the second installment was published. Three weeks later, she received a letter from Horst and a note from Inge. Inge's review was short, very sweet, just right.

And Horst's reaction? He liked it, a lot. He said he appreciated Mollie's efforts to convey to her readers how his life's journey after the war had been focused on bringing joy to others through music. He thanked her for illuminating his desire to make amends for all the horribleness caused by his countrymen during the war. Over the years, he wanted to be proud to be German—not again, but finally. During their interview in May, he told Mollie he credited her mother for getting him started in the right direction, and she ended her article with that sentiment.

The first week's *CPD Sunday Magazine* cover photo, taken by Jason Webb in the Schauspielhaus concert hall, was Mollie's favorite. It showed a pensive Maestro Ebinger sitting on one of the orchestra-level chairs, facing away from the stage. His podium and the massive pipe organ could be seen over his shoulder. Near the end of the article's second installment was a photo of Horst and Mollie sitting at the piano in the Ebinger home in Wannsee. It uncannily mimicked the photo of Horst and Phee that was taken at the concert at Algona High School in 1945.

In her article, Mollie didn't mention the baby. She understood it wasn't her place to tell the world about Phee and Horst's son. Besides, she believed Horst's story was compelling enough.

Two days before Thanksgiving, Mollie drove from Chicago to Algona, intending to spend some time at her mother's grave. As she almost always did when she visited Algona, she drove around town to see if anything had changed. St. Pete's was still a neighborhood fixture and still without a bell in its belfry. The parsonage was no longer the parsonage. About ten years ago, the new pastor decided he wanted to purchase his own home, so the church council sold it to a real estate company. It's rental property now. Twenty-some years ago, the high school became a middle school, Polly's Ice Cream Shoppe closed around that time, and Rasmussen Hardware was bought by Sam Jacobs in 1968. He kept the name, though.

Before she went to Riverview Cemetery, Mollie drove out Highway 18 to the airport that occupied the land where Camp Algona was located. She parked the car and walked to a large clearing east of the small terminal building. There were no remnants of Camp Algona on the airport property, and Mollie lamented there was nothing—not a sign, a door, a step, a pipe, a foundation—that Horst, her mom, and her dad had at least seen if not touched. She'd have to use her vivid imagination to picture them here, in this space, forty-six years ago.

To the south and east of the clearing where she stood were cornfields with dried stalks pointing in all directions, and while it was a bright, sunny day, the wind was strong and cold, and Mollie realized she'd left her stocking cap back at the Super 8. She'd stop there on the way to the cemetery to get it.

After parking the car at the top of the hill on the east side of the cemetery, Mollie grabbed her shoulder bag and a small garden trowel. She brought them to Phee's gravestone which was just to the right of Mary's. When she got to the marble bench, she reached inside the bag for a small box wrapped tightly with duct tape. Inside the box was Phee's necklace from Horst. Today Mollie would return it to her mom.

But first, while she sat on the bench, she told her mom about her time in Berlin last May—the wonderful orchestra concert, meeting Horst in the Green Room, their interview sessions, and "the big reveal" in the library at their home in Wannsee. She spoke about Inge, the delicious dinner, and staying overnight in their lovely guest room. Lastly, she described how she handed Horst the envelope at the airport.

"I had to, Mom. You kept that letter all those years. I think you wanted him to know, somehow. I've still not heard from him, about the letter, I mean. I was sure he'd write or call right away, but nothing, so far. Maybe I'll never know."

Before Mollie left, she kneeled next to Phee's stone and dug a hole about ten inches deep, hoping it was deep enough. She dropped the box into the hole, covered it with dirt and dry leaves, and packed it down. "You should have this now," she said as she stood. "It belongs with you." And then, "Bye, Mom. I love you."

As she opened the car door, she heard a train whistle in the distance and thought about the early morning Phee and Horst said goodbye just a few blocks from where she stood. It was the end of a love affair, but it was also the beginning of a remarkable life—no, two remarkable lives.

WHEN MOLLIE GOT TO her office the Monday morning after her pilgrimage to Algona, she was surprised to find a letter from Horst in the stack of mail on the corner of her desk. Was it the letter she'd been waiting for since May? She quickly cut open the envelope and pulled out a single sheet of white paper. There was no date at the top, no "Dear Mollie" or "Dear Ms. MacAlister" or "Greetings from Wannsee!" She saw near the bottom, "Affectionately," and under that, the initials "H.E." There were just two words in the center of the page: "Find him." *Find him? Of course!* And at that moment, she knew she would—or at least she'd try.

The End

AUTHOR'S NOTE

I wrote *My Mother's Friend* after discovering a part of our country's World War II history that was completely unknown to me. In early 2015, my husband Joe told me there had been a prisoner of war camp outside of Algona, Iowa, about forty miles north of where he grew up. I was stunned! I'm from Iowa, too, but I didn't know anything about POW camps in the Hawkeye State or any other state. Most of the people I've talked to about this project also didn't know about prisoner of war camps in America during World War II. Did you?

At the height of the war, there were over 425,000 POWs imprisoned in over 500 camps across the country. Most of those POWs were German, but there were also Italian and Japanese soldiers behind barbed wire on American soil. Because most of our able-bodied men were off fighting the war, we needed their labor. The POWs worked on farms, in nurseries and orchards, in mills and forests, and in factories not directly related to the war effort. They earned eighty cents a day for their efforts.

The prisoners were well-treated. Unlike Germany and Japan, the United States followed the Geneva Convention protocols to the letter. Living conditions for prisoners mimicked the conditions for American soldiers in their own encampments—same barracks, food, and medical care. The prisoners were allowed ample opportunities to participate in music and theater groups, art, sports, and a variety of classes. At Camp Algona, beginning and advanced English were the most popular classes.

It is not entirely clear why Algona, Iowa, with a population of around 5,100 in 1944, was chosen as a POW camp location. There were many German immigrants living in Northern Iowa in the first half of the twentieth century, and many of those were farmers who could speak

German and would hire the prisoners. The Pioneer Seed Corn Company in Algona needed workers, and the city leaders must have concluded that prisoner labor and the economic impact from the 300 U.S. military personnel stationed at the camp would be an enormous benefit to the town and surrounding communities.

Construction on 272 acres of farmland west of town began in late summer 1943 and was essentially completed by the end of that year. The first group of German prisoners arrived by train in early April 1944, and eventually all 3,000 beds were filled. The final group of prisoners left Camp Algona in February 1946. The camp was completely dismantled, and eventually, the Algona Airport opened in that location.

SJB
September 2022

ACKNOWLEDGMENTS

Writing a novel, especially a first novel, can be a long and arduous journey. No matter what you pack for the trip, there are always bumps along the way. The following people helped smooth many of the bumps I encountered on my journey, and I offer my deepest appreciation and gratitude to all of them.

Without being asked, Charles Scott at the State Historical Society Research Center in Iowa City went to his office (on his day off!) to find information about Camp Algona. That afternoon I held the first tangible slice of my research pie. With that in hand, I knew for sure I would write *My Mother's Friend*.

I worked at Fintel Library at Roanoke College for almost twenty-four years. Before I retired in 2017, my colleagues threw me a lovely party. The lap desk from the library staff was the perfect retirement gift. I use it almost every day. (I'm using it now!) I offer special thanks to Piper Cumbo, Jeffrey Martin, Linda Miller, Elizabeth McClenney, and Patty Powell for their suggestions and resource recommendations.

Tom Johnson helped me see my story differently. He also shared what it's like to be a journalist.

Robert Huffman, historian of The United States Army Band "Pershing's Own," passed along two diaries and a memoir written by band members who were deployed to North Africa, the UK, and France during WWII. Those documents are fabulous resources and a joy to read.

In Algona, Keith Christie, Glenn Jones, Fritz Nielsen, Evelyn Ruhnke, and Jean and Jerry Shey graciously shared their WWII memories with a total stranger who wanted to write a book about their town. Susan Legore, who knows more about the history of Algona's First Lutheran Church than anyone else, most likely, shared her knowledge and provided access to a plethora of church documents and photos. Marvin Chickering, of Algona's First United Methodist Church Men's Club, drove me to the Kossuth County Fairgrounds so I could gaze at the beautiful nativity scene that was built by POWs at Camp Algona. Except for one year during the COVID-19 pandemic, the nativity scene has been on public display in Algona every December since 1945. And I especially thank Jerry Yocum, who liked my story idea even before he shared so much of his knowledge of Camp Algona. Jerry gave me the insider's tour of the wonderful Camp Algona POW Museum, sat with me for two interviews, allowed me access to the museum's archives, and encouraged me to use music as a vehicle to get Phee and Horst together. Brilliant!

One Sunday afternoon, the nice folks at Pick's Resort on West Lake Okoboji gave me access to one of their cabins so I could better imagine what the cabins at Bee's Bungalows would look like.

Jim Blaha reminisced about his years as a young boy on an Iowa farm during WWII.

Stefanie Fowler, daughter of Otto Scholand, a German POW who was captured in France in 1944, shared her father's inspiring story. (I think there might be a little Otto Scholand in Horst Ebinger.)

Many friends at Oak Grove Church of the Brethren in Roanoke, Virginia have shown genuine interest in my writing progress. I thank them for their patience and their prayers. Mike Tyler escorted me through two buildings in Salem, Virginia, where German POWs ate and slept during WWII. That was so cool! And Martha Gregory shared what it's like to raise twin boys.

I thank my "official" beta readers Carolina Bowen, Courtney Bowen, Norbert Dreifürst, Dan Dykema, Stefanie Fowler, and Jerry Yocum; and my "unofficial" beta readers Bob Benne, Joe Blaha, Dikkon Eberhart, Judy Gearing, and Mark Wadstrom. I really needed your undivided attention and your corrections, observations, recommendations, and words of encouragement. *My Mother's Friend* is a much (much!) better read because of your reactions and your input.

Michelle Gill, my web designer, created my beautiful page and encouraged me to consistently add stories to my blog page. Through those essays, I've learned and shared so much with my readers over the past eighteen months. It has been a blessing for me, and I hope it has been a blessing for my readers.

My editor, Jan Taylor, caught what needed to be caught and then caught much more. Jan went above and beyond what was required and expected. She read through *My Mother's Friend* not once, not twice, but thrice!

My author friends Mary Armstrong, Alan Bonsall, Dan Davidson, Dikkon Eberhart, Mary Crockett, Liza Jonathan, and Jocelyn Pedersen offered sage advice. I admire their work and their devotion to the craft.

I am more than grateful for my siblings Julie Buchanan, Peter Johnson, Nancy Johnson, and Chris Johnson for offering their constant love, patience, and unwavering support.

My husband Joe's enthusiasm for this project is surpassed only by my own. His creative genius has inspired me for more than fifty years. All those days when I closed the door to my writing room, I was not shutting him out—I was shutting me in. I thank him, and love him, for giving me my much-needed space.

And finally, I thank my mom, a beautiful, gracious, talented, loving woman who must surely know her second daughter has written a story—not about her—but about a time when life was both simple and complicated, when the citizens of Iowa's towns big and small lived for a while with a world war and its repercussions always close at hand. Mom was there. She would understand. I believe she would be very proud of this moment in my life. I hope so, anyway.

A
Senior Piano Recital
featuring
Phyllis A. Swensson
Sunday, November 19, 1944 at 4:00 p.m.
St. Peter's Lutheran Church
Algona, Iowa

Program

"Butterfly" from *Lyric Pieces*, Op. 43 no. 1 . . . . E. Grieg

   "Moto Perpetuo" from *Twelve Virtuoso Etudes*, Op. 46 no. 2
     Polonaise, Op. 46 no. 12 . . . . E. MacDowell

   Rondo Capriccioso, Op. 14 . . . . F. Mendelssohn

    Evening Reverie
    A Sunset Ride . . . . P. Swensson

~~ *Intermission* ~~

Sonata No. 15 in D Major, Op. 28 ("Pastoral"). . . . L. van Beethoven
            Allegro
            Andante
            Scherzo
            Rondo

*Please join us for a reception in the fellowship hall following this
afternoon's performance.*

My mom, Phee Pohlson, wrote this Christmas song in 1942 during her senior year of high school in Ottumwa, Iowa.

ABOUT THE AUTHOR

Born and raised in Iowa, Sally Jameson Bond holds a Bachelor of Music degree from the University of Iowa. She is the daughter of a World War II and Korean War veteran father and an artistic mother who loved to write. History was probably Sally's weakest subject in school, but after moving to Virginia in 1973, she soon learned to love it. History eventually became one of her passions which is probably why she chose historical fiction for her debut novel. Besides writing and history, other passions involve family, dogs, and traveling in Europe. After a thirty-year career in academic libraries, Sally retired in 2017. She lives in southwest Virginia with her husband Joe and Bart, Dog Number 8.

www.sallyjamesonbond.com
sally.jameson.bond@gmail.com

You can also find Sally on Facebook and Instagram.

Made in the USA
Columbia, SC
15 January 2025

51689802R00204